FLORIDA STATE
UNIVERSITY LIBRARIES

JUN 19 1995

TALLAHASSEE, FLORIDA

THE ORIGINS OF MIDDLE-CLASS CULTURE

THE ORIGINS OF MIDDLE-CLASS CULTURE

Halifax, Yorkshire, 1660–1780

JOHN SMAIL

Cornell University Press

ITHACA AND LONDON

Copyright © 1994 by Cornell University

All rights reserved. Except for brief quotations in a review, this book, or parts thereof, must not be reproduced in any form without permission in writing from the publisher. For information, address Cornell University Press, Sage House, 512 East State Street, Ithaca, New York 14850.

First published 1994 by Cornell University Press.

Library of Congress Cataloging-in-Publication Data

Smail, John.
   The origins of middle-class culture : Halifax, Yorkshire. 1660–1780 / John Smail.
      p. cm.
   Includes bibliographical references and index.
   ISBN 0-8014-2990-0 (alk. paper)
   1. Halifax (England)—Civilization. 2. Middle class—England—Halifax—History. I. Title
DA690.H17S63 1994
942.8'12—dc20   94-20852

Printed in the United States of America

⊗ The paper in this book meets the minimum requirements of the American National Standard for Information Sciences—Permanence of Paper for Printed Library Materials, ANSI Z39.48-1984.

To my parents

CONTENTS

Illustrations, Map, Figure ix
Tables xi
Preface xiii
Abbreviations and Conventions xvii

INTRODUCTION

1. Theory and Methods 3
2. The Middling Sort and Their World 19

PART I PROCESS: THE MAKING OF A MIDDLE-CLASS EXPERIENCE 45

3. Economic and Cultural Change in Halifax's Textile Industry 51
4. Loans and Luxuries: Setting the Textile Industry in Context 82

PART II CRYSTALLIZATION: THE MAKING OF A MIDDLE-CLASS CONSCIOUSNESS 115

5. Constructing the Public Sphere: Associations, Disputes, and Parliamentary Politics 121
6. Constructing the Private Sphere: The Family and Sociability 164

CONCLUSION

7. The Middle Class and Their World   191

8. Implications and Speculations   222

Index   237

ILLUSTRATIONS, MAP, FIGURE

Illustrations

1. Lower Snape, Sowerby, 1623   108
2. Hollinghey, Sowerby, 1577   109
3. Fieldhouse, Sowerby, 1749   111
4. Old Fieldhouse, Sowerby, seventeenth century   112
5. The Square Chapel, Halifax, 1772   135
6. A share certificate of the Calder Navigation, 1765   141
7. The Halifax Piece Hall, 1779   143
8. Whitewindows, Sowerby, 1768   177
9. Somerset House, Halifax, mid–eighteenth century   198

Map

The parish of Halifax   21

Figure

Number of broad and narrow cloths milled, West Riding of Yorkshire, 1728–1800   52

TABLES

1. Households subject to and exempt from hearth tax in townships of Halifax parish, 1664, by number of hearths taxed   25

2. Mentions of mortgages and of money loaned at interest in sample wills probated, Halifax, 1690–1785   88

3. Number of wills instructing sale of real estate, Halifax, 1690–1785   89

4. Exemptions from hearth and land taxes in selected Halifax townships, 1664 and 1782   102

5. Indicators of sociopolitical status of the principal inhabitants of Sowerby, 1749–1770   128

6. Widows' responsibilities in management of estates of their underage children under wills in a sample of all Halifax wills, 1690–1785   170

7. Widows' responsibilities in management of estates of their underage children under wills in a sample of wills of Halifax's elites, 1690–1785   171

PREFACE

There is no doubt that the publication of E. P. Thompson's *Making of the English Working Class* in 1964 revolutionized the history of class and class formation, and its importance for almost any aspect of social or economic history in the eighteenth and early nineteenth centuries is still enormous. Yet since the mid-1980s, the field created by his book has changed. Some historians, for instance, have finally begun to address the problem of middle-class formation, an issue on which Thompson is curiously silent. Doing so, however, requires significant alterations to the argument in his book, for there, and in much of the literature it spawned, the middle class is little more than a caricature, a class that behaved in such-and-such a way because of its relations to the means of production. Thompson, in short, perpetuated an older picture of the middle class at the same time that he transformed our thinking about the working class. I suspect that Thompson and others use a two-dimensional middle class because, as more recent work shows, the formation of the middle class has a complex and often confusing history. Consider one obvious point: the middle class's identity, unlike that of the working class, must emerge in relation not just to one group, but to two—the upper class and the working class. This double relationship suggests that anyone who set out to write a companion volume to *The Making of the English Working Class* would have no easy task.

Other changes in the field, however, suggest that it is unlikely that such a volume will ever appear, for historians inspired by poststructuralist theory have begun to challenge the conceptual heart of Thompson's book: class. They argue that the concept of class, not to speak of its historical reality, is no longer a proper object of the historian's attentions. Although this is a book about class, I am sympathetic to the questions posed by poststructuralist theory. This tension has posed some dilemmas but ultimately the evidence I am working with renders neither alternative intellectually satisfying. On one hand, to my mind, an abstractness creeps into even sophisticated Marxist analysis—an unwillingness or inability to see society and its discourses or cultures as multivalent. On the other hand, most poststructuralist accounts are theoretically ill equipped to deal with the fundamental social and economic changes that came about during the Industrial Revolution. As I will show, something happened in mid-eighteenth-century Halifax, and to explain that something, both Marxism and poststructuralism are necessary.

To accomplish this explanation, I have formulated a cultural theory of class formation. This is a theory about class, class in Thompson's sense of a social identity that emerges out of a common socioeconomic experience; but it incorporates many of the insights of cultural theory, fundamentally departing from even the relatively sophisticated approach to class found in Thompson's work. Maybe this attempt to fashion a truce in the ongoing theory wars will dissatisfy both the Marxist and the poststructuralist camps, but I urge readers to keep an open mind. Despite the apparent intensity of the theory wars, the two sides largely agree that both material reality and language/culture must enter into historical analysis. More often than not, the disputes are over emphasis and the conceptual terms in which this synthesis is packaged.

Ultimately, I believe, socioeconomic reality and a group's conception of that reality are in a semiautonomous relationship; neither by itself provides an adequate explanation of historical change. The task of the analyst is to provide a theoretical structure that can encompass this assumption. One could stretch either Marxist or poststructuralist theory toward the middle ground, but I propose to begin in the theoretical middle with a modified cultural analysis shaped by the theory of practice. This cultural theory of class formation makes us look for the ways in which experience shapes the world people make for themselves *and* for the ways in which this constructed world affects the actions of individuals—actions that in turn shape the reality they experience.

THE debts I incurred while I was writing this book are so numerous that the following list is bound to have omissions, and I apologize for them. That I have not accumulated tangible debts is due in part to the generosity of the agencies that helped to fund the research. They include Stanford University, the Fulbright Foundation, the Social Science Research Council, the Mabelle MacLeod Memorial Fund, the Whiting Foundation, and the University of North Carolina at Charlotte Foundation. I also thank John Hargreaves, honorary secretary of the Halifax Antiquarian Society, for allowing me to reproduce two slides from the society's collection. Parts of the argument have been published as "The Stansfields of Halifax: A Case Study in the Making of the Middle Class," *Albion* 24 (1992), and "Manufacturer or Artisan?" *Journal of Social History* 25 (1992), though those pieces bear only a slight resemblance to what appears here.

Much more personal but just as important was the assistance I received from the staffs of the Archives Department of the Calderdale Central Library in Halifax and the Borthwick Institute of Historical Research in York. I could hardly have asked for two more congenial or helpful environments in which to do research.

I owe a great deal in the way of intellectual debts to teachers and colleagues. Michael MacDonald first pointed me in the direction of Halifax and helped me to turn raw enthusiasm into some semblance of a real work of history. Paul Seaver continues to provide encouragement and advice. I also thank the community of scholars engaged in research on Halifax. Far from being defensive about their turf, they have been uniformly generous in sharing their ideas, comments, and information; I hope I have been able to contribute as much as I received. On numerous occasions, Alan Betteridge, a student of Halifax's history as well as its archivist, has helped me to interpret confusing documents and suggested others of interest. Ronan Bennett freely shared the results of his research on law enforcement in seventeenth-century Halifax. Finally, Pat Hudson, whose excellent work on the Industrial Revolution is cited throughout this book, has offered friendly criticism and advice all along the way.

While writing this book I received other help and stimulation. The humanities department at Kingston University provided me with office space and the time to do much of the writing, and they did their best to divert me with their offers of hospitality. Discussions during and after meetings of the "Long Eighteenth-Century Seminar" at the Institute of Historical Research in London were very helpful. Of this stimulating and very knowledgeable group I particularly thank Peter Mandler, Dror Wahrman, Amanda Vickery, Susan Brown, and John Seed. John Styles has given me the benefit of his knowledge of Halifax and the Yorkshire textile industry; citations of his published work do scant justice to my debt to his command of this material.

I also thank those colleagues and friends who read and commented on parts of this manuscript. Dror Wahrman, John Styles, and Pat Hudson deserve mention again here. Philip Ethington and Valerie Kivelson read substantial portions of the book, offering invaluable insights and equally invaluable support. Many colleagues at the University of North Carolina at Charlotte have helped with advice and criticism. Special thanks go to Anna Clark, who read the entire manuscript; I count myself very lucky to have a friend across the hall whose interests and expertise are so close to my own. Laura Smail saved me from innumerable syntactic and stylistic stumbles.

Finally, I thank those who have made so pleasurable the time I was not spending on this book in these past few years. Marj, Richard, Tom, Ben, and Amy have generously opened their home and their lives to me and my growing family. And if Christina Wright did not have much choice about putting up with me during these past years, she has not made me suffer for the many impositions; I could not have done it without her.

JOHN SMAIL

Charlotte, North Carolina

ABBREVIATIONS AND CONVENTIONS

BIY/CP   Borthwick Institute of Historical Research, York/Cause Papers.
BIY/OW   Borthwick Institute of Historical Research, York/Original Wills. Unless I note otherwise, all original wills cited were proved in the deanery of Pontefract. The citation gives the deceased's name, the place of residence, and the month and year of probate. Following the archive's practice, I use both the old and current years in citing wills probated in January, February, and March; for example, "March 1717/18."
BIY/PR   Borthwick Institute of Historical Research, York/Probate Registers. The citation gives the volume and folio of the will.
CDA   Calderdale District Archives, Halifax Central Library.
PRO   Public Record Office, London.
THAS   *Transactions of the Halifax Antiquarian Society*.
WYAS   West Yorkshire Archive Service. The citation gives the branch archive where the document is located.

All dates before the calendar change in 1752 have been cited in the old style, with the year taken to begin in January. Spelling and punctuation have been modernized.

INTRODUCTION

Chapter 1

Theory and Methods

TO THE INHABITANTS OF THE PARISH OF HALIFAX
GENTLEMEN,

You have, in the following pages, the most material observations relating to your neighborhood, which I made during several years residence amongst you; and it will give me pleasure to find that they contribute either to your advantage or amusement.

With these words the Reverend John Watson began his monumental *History and Antiquities of the Parish of Halifax in Yorkshire*, published in 1775; close to 800 pages filled with details of the parish's geography, Druidical and Roman remains, church and many chapelries, customs, townships and manors, charities, and, above all, distinguished families. As was typical, Watson published his history by subscription. Fifteen years before the book came out, in an advertisement addressed "To the Public," he had announced his intention to write the history and requested interested subscribers to notify him of their desire to obtain a copy of his work at the price of a guinea. While Watson's proposal attracted some attention from outside the parish, the bulk of the subscribers were active in Halifax's booming woolen textile industry.[1] Some, such as John Edwards, Jeremiah Holroyd, John Priestly, David Stansfield, and George Stansfield, were large-scale manufacturers of woolen goods who operated extensive putting-out schemes. Others,

---

1. T. W. Hanson, "The Subscribers to Watson's *Halifax*," *THAS*, 1950, 42, 44–46.

such as William Greame, William Pollard, Joshua Hudson, Samuel and John Waterhouse, and Nathaniel Holden, were merchants in the textile industry. Still others, such as Cyril Jackson, M.D. and the attorney James Carr, were members of a growing professional class that existed to serve the needs of this vibrant manufacturing community. Examination of the social reality behind Watson's address to the "gentlemen of Halifax," then, reveals a public made up of individuals with a commercial background who were sufficiently numerous, sufficiently interested, and sufficiently confident of their "ownership" of the parish to buy his antiquarian history. Yet the existence of this group raises some interesting questions. Where had they come from? And what does their subscription to the *History of Halifax* say about how they understood the social world they lived in?

If we jump back almost a century and a half, to the beginning of the Civil War, another episode involving a minister and his "public" gives a sense of the contrast between what Halifax was and what it had become by Watson's time. On 18 December 1642, a Sunday, the service at Coley Chapel was interrupted by a messenger bearing news of an attack by the king's forces on the neighboring town of Bradford. On hearing the news, the minister roused his congregation who then returned to their homes, collected what weapons they could muster, and went to join in the defense of Bradford.[2]

The contrast between these two episodes, the defense of Bradford and Watson's *History*, is quite dramatic. Instead of a minister exhorting his congregation to combat the immanent Antichrist, we have a curate buried in wills and deeds. Instead of a "public" willing to risk life, limb, and liberty in a good cause, we have a rather complacent mix of Anglicans and Dissenters whose interest in the book had as much to do with the prestige conferred on their parish by its publication as it did with the actual contents.[3] Of course, these two episodes are not strictly speaking comparable, but they do suggest how different those social worlds were. Halifax in the seventeenth century was not a town with a large merchant community; it was a rural parish dominated by the middling sort, the yeomen and clothiers who attended Coley Chapel. This middling sort did not constitute a public to whom a seventeenth-century Watson could have appealed for a subscription, not least because they did not have the sense of ownership that Watson's preface

2. T. W. Hanson, *The Story of Old Halifax* (1920; Otley, West Yorkshire, 1985), 142.
3. Hanson, "Subscribers," 46–47.

implies. A century later that public was emerging in the form of the group of merchants, manufacturers, and professionals who subscribed to Watson's history.[4]

This book explores the historical space that lies between the yeomen and clothiers at Coley Chapel and the merchants and manufacturers who subscribed to an antiquarian's history of their parish. It offers an explanation of the changes that get us, in the century that separates the Restoration from the Industrial Revolution, from the social world of the middling sort to that of the middle class. Obviously, the end point of this process of change is much more problematic than its beginning. Since the yeomen and clothiers who marched off to defend Bradford on a Sunday morning in 1642 clearly constituted a middling sort, this book's task is to prove that the public who subscribed to Watson's *Halifax* is best conceptualized as a middle class. I argue that as Watson was preparing his history in the third quarter of the eighteenth century, this group of men came to "own" the parish through their dominance of its economic, social, and political institutions. At the same time, they were adopting an increasingly distinct set of values and practices that had the dual effect of consolidating the sense that these manufacturers, merchants, and professionals had of their middle-class identity and of advertising their existence as a class to the world. Thus, by explaining how a community whose members rushed to the defense of Bradford came to produce the subscribers to Watson's Halifax, this book offers an analysis and explanation of the origins of middle-class culture.

TOWARD A CULTURAL THEORY
OF CLASS FORMATION

It must be stressed that this book is an account of the origins of middle-class *culture,* for cultural theory offers the greatest potential for resolving the host of theoretical and practical problems surrounding the history of the middle class. At first glance, it may appear inappropriate to use cultural theory as the basis for an analysis of class formation, for in the guise of the linguistic turn, it is largely responsible

---

4. Jürgen Habermas, *The Structural Transformation of the Public Sphere: An Inquiry into a Category of Bourgeois Society* (1962), trans. Thomas Burger (Cambridge, 1989).

for the current crisis that surrounds the concept of class.⁵ This crisis has come about as historians have adopted the insights that cultural theory gives into the ways that a group's culture—"discourse" and "language" are often used interchangeably with "culture" in this context—shapes and even constitutes the reality that its members experience. This insight is enormously powerful and it has enriched historical analysis immeasurably, but it has tended to undermine the traditional bases of class analysis. Historians who have explored the linguistic and political representations of class have argued that class discourse is a way of talking about the world that has no direct relation to socioeconomic reality, or that it is a kind of political rhetoric employed for its efficacy at a given historical juncture.⁶

Though this approach has raised important questions about the time-worn truisms of class formation, uncoupling socioeconomic reality and class identity in this way creates as many problems as it solves. Most important, it does not—because it cannot—explain why a particular construction of reality works when another one does not. Class is indeed a kind of political rhetoric, but a political rhetoric about class works only insofar as it resonates with people's experiences, experiences that are grounded in reality. Although it must be treated as an object of historical inquiry, something to be established and not assumed, the concept of class should not be discarded precisely because it implies that there *is* a connection between reality and consciousness.⁷ One can prove that economic relations have a particularly important role in structuring social consciousness and retain the insights of the

---

5. Patrick Joyce, *Visions of the People* (Cambridge, 1991), 1–23; William Reddy, *Money and Liberty in Modern Europe* (New York, 1987). For a defense of class against the onslaught of the linguistic turn, see David Mayfield and Susan Thorne, "Social History and Its Discontents: Gareth Steadman Jones and the Politics of Language," *Social History* 17 (1992): 165–88. On a very general level, these issues emerged in an exchange in *Past and Present*: Lawrence Stone, "History and Post-Modernism," *Past and Present* 131 (1991): 217–18, and Patrick Joyce and Catriona Kelly, "History and Post-Modernism," *Past and Present* 133 (1992): 204–13.

6. This argument is implicit in Ernesto Laclau and Chantal Mouffe, *Hegemony and Socialist Strategy: Towards a Radical Democratic Politics* (London, 1985); Gareth Steadman Jones, "Rethinking Chartism," in *Languages of Class* (Cambridge, 1983); Dror Wahrman, "Virtual Representation: Parliamentary Reporting and Languages of Class in the 1790s," *Past and Present* 136 (1992): 83–113; William Reddy, *The Rise of Market Culture: The Textile Trade and French Society, 1750–1900* (Cambridge, 1984).

7. Even critics of class agree that a class analysis is valid if class is conceived of as a social relationship that can be shown to exist in a particular historical context: William Reddy, "The Concept of Class," in *Social Orders and Social Classes in Europe since 1500: Studies in Social Stratification*, ed. M. L. Bush (London, 1992), 24.

linguistic turn, but doing so requires a theory that can connect in a coherent manner the apparently contradictory claims that class is a reflection of socioeconomic reality and that class is a social construct.

In order to resolve the tension between these two concepts of class—to construct a theory of class that accounts for but is not determined by socioeconomic reality—I have drawn on the concept of culture and cultural change articulated in the theoretical work of Pierre Bourdieu and Anthony Giddens and in the historical ethnography of Marshall Sahlins.[8] This approach, referred to here as the "theory of practice," is based on a Geertzian concept of culture, for these authors argue that culture is best understood as the way a group construes experience. They also modify Geertz, however, by insisting that the construction of culture is an ongoing process.[9] Culture exists in the customs, values, and very conceptions that shape and constrain human actions, but it also exists in the actions themselves. It is self-referential: while structures constrain agency, actions create the reality that is construed into structures.

In its various forms, then, the theory of practice historicizes cultural theory by emphasizing the interaction between social reality and human construct. Particularly valuable is the insight that change happens, in part, as a result of the unintended consequences of particular actions. By acknowledging that culture is always being remade, we can see that an action that is perfectly intelligible within one cultural frame of reference can also help shape, through its unintended consequences, a new cultural frame of reference. Though this theoretical

---

8. Pierre Bourdieu, *Outline of a Theory of Practice*, trans. Richard Nice (Cambridge, 1977); Anthony Giddens, *The Constitution of Society: Outline of a Theory of Structuration* (Berkeley, 1984); Marshall Sahlins, *Islands of History* (London, 1987), chap. 5; and the essays in Aletta Biersack, *Clio in Oceania: Toward a Historical Anthropology* (Washington, D.C., 1991). William Sewell's analysis of Thompson's theory of class formation also suggests that the theory of structuration is useful in this context: "How Classes Are Made: Critical Reflections on E. P. Thompson's Theory of Working-Class Formation," in *E. P. Thompson: Critical Perspectives*, ed. Harvey Kaye and Keith McClelland (Cambridge, 1990), 65–66. On a practical level, Stuart Blumin has used Giddens' theory of structuration to good effect in *The Emergence of the Middle Class: Social Experience in the American City* (New York, 1989), 8–10.

9. Clifford Geertz, *The Interpretation of Cultures* (New York, 1973). For critiques of Geertz's insufficiently historical approach, worth citing because his version of culture has been so influential among historians, see Ronald G. Walters, "Signs of the Times: Clifford Geertz and Historians," *Social Research* 47 (1980): 537–56; Paul Shankman, "The Thick and the Thin: On the Interpretive Theoretical Program of Clifford Geertz," *Current Anthropology* 25 (1984), 261–79: and William Roseberry, "Balinese Cockfights and the Seduction of Anthropology," *Social Research* 49 (1982): 1013–28.

approach has much to commend it to all historians, it is essential for historians of class precisely because it provides the analytic tools necessary to study the reciprocity between the world and the way a group construes that world.

This is a crucial issue, because understanding that reciprocity in its historical framework is central to the disagreements between Marxists and historians of the linguistic turn over class formation. Most historians working on class formation assume that the socioeconomic and the cultural-political aspects of class identity "happen" in different time frames: the long term and the short term. Consider, for instance, the contrast between "class experience" and "class consciousness" which E. P. Thompson so eloquently articulates in his preface to *The Making of the English Working Class:* "Class happens when some men, as a result of common experiences (inherited or shared), feel and articulate the identity of their interests as between themselves, and as against other men whose interests are different from (and usually opposed to) theirs."[10] In this two-phase model of class formation, the concept of class experience—what is inherited or shared—emphasizes class identity as a reflection of socioeconomic reality that arises through a group's day-to-day interactions with the world in the long term. In contrast, the concept of class consciousness—what is felt and articulated—emphasizes class identity as a social construct that develops as a result of a concrete historical process involving active human agents in the short term.

Though Marxists and their opponents agree here, they disagree about which of these two time frames is to be privileged in the analysis. On one hand, as William Sewell has shown, there is a lingering assumption, even in a relatively sophisticated Marxist analysis such as Thompson's, that (long-term) socioeconomic change operated independently of culture to create a class experience that then found expression in (short-term) political action. Thompson thus privileges the long term by implying that social and economic change was an autonomous force operating in a process of class formation. John Seed has made a very similar argument about the Marxist analysis that informs

---

10. E. P. Thompson, *The Making of the English Working Class* (Harmondsworth, 1968), 8. My use of the terms "class experience" and "class consciousness" in this way should make clear my theoretical debt to Thompson, particularly to *The Making of the English Working Class* and "Eighteenth Century English Society: Class Struggle without Class?" *Social History* 2 (1978): 133–65. Of all the accounts of class formation, his remains one of the most convincing.

Theodore Koditschek's history of Bradford.[11] On the other hand, while historians critical of the concept of class acknowledge the existence and even the importance of long-term socioeconomic change, they argue that most expressions of class identity were put together in the short term (albeit from existing discourses) to accomplish often specific political objectives. In short, they privilege the short term and see culture operating independently of experience.

The problem here is not that class experience and class consciousness do not have different time frames. They do. As I will argue, class experience becomes implicit in the social and economic practice of a group of individuals over the long term as the unintended consequences of their actions accumulate, and class consciousness happens in the short term as a group explicitly articulates their identity as a class vis-à-vis other groups in the social order. The problem lies rather in privileging one time frame over the other. The theory of practice solves this problem by suggesting that class experience and class consciousness result from the same kind of process, a process by which a group at once construes and constructs its socioeconomic reality. It suggests that class experience should be thought of as what emerges as a group *construes* their economic and social relations rather than as the relations themselves. Like class consciousness, then, class experience is also a cultural construct.[12] Similarly, the theory of practice suggests that class consciousness should be thought of in relation to the social experience of the individuals in question.

Class—encompassing both experience and consciousness—is thus best conceived of as a culture. It is a culture in the sense that it is the outcome of the process by which a group construes its world, creating, to use Geertz's phrase, the webs of significance through which its members conceive and understand their own and others' actions. It is a class culture, however, in the sense that fundamental to the particular construction that the group makes of its world is their consciousness of the political implications of socioeconomic relations; this recognition results in a worldview characterized by horizontally defined groups. A cultural theory of class formation, then, is useful because it directs our attention to the way culture emerges from the interplay between reality

---

11. John Seed, "Class Formation in Early Industrial England," *Social History* 18 (1993): 17–30.

12. Sewell, "How Classes Are Made," 63–66.

and construct and between structure and action. It suggests that class identity emerges as individuals and groups who are both shaping and shaped by their socioeconomic reality create structures that establish them, first through experience and ultimately through consciousness, in a distinct place in the social order.

THE PROBLEM OF ORIGINS

Although this cultural theory of class formation is valid for all class analyses, it is particularly useful for making sense of the origins of the middle class, for in addition to the theoretical problems confronting class analysis as a whole, historians of the middle class have to contend with a particularly intractable set of practical problems. As an indication of the extent of the problem, consider a trio of works on the origins of the middle class, each of which has a different perception of what the middle class was and which cover between them every decade from 1660 to 1850 except, rather curiously, the 1730s and 1740s.[13] This diversity of opinion arises out of a contradiction in the historiography on the middle class: on one hand, important aspects of the set of values, attitudes, practices, and worldview that together made up middle-class identity seem to have emerged at some point during the eighteenth century, yet on the other, it is difficult to identify a coherent social entity whose socioeconomic experience could have given rise to such a set of values and practices until the nineteenth century.[14]

The first of the two propositions that make up this contradiction can be demonstrated through an analysis of the history of the middle class in the period from 1780 to 1850. Traditionally, this has been seen as *the* era of middle-class formation in England, and a variety of works have revitalized the history of middle-class formation in this period by adopting innovative approaches to the problem.

13. Peter Earle, *The Making of the English Middle Class: Business, Society, and Family Life in London, 1660–1730* (London, 1990); Leonore Davidoff and Catherine Hall, *Family Fortunes: The Men and Women of the English Middle Class, 1780–1850* (London, 1987); and Theodore Koditschek, *Class Formation and Urban Industrial Society: Bradford, 1750–1850* (New York, 1990).

14. Some work would deny even this; given the concern here with culture, however, I am less concerned with the identity and experiences of a group than with the coherence of their culture. Moreover, though the coherence of the nineteenth-century middle class at the national level may be questioned, that coherence is much more obvious at the local level. Both of these issues will be discussed in due course.

These historians take two kinds of approaches. Some conceive of the middle class in an economic and political context, tracing how the struggle for economic and political power shaped an emerging middle-class consciousness. This, of course, is the traditional approach to the history of middle-class formation, but such historians as Anthony Howe, Theodore Koditschek, and Robert Morris avoid the rather sterile issue of the battle against aristocratic domination by examining the process of class formation in the local or regional context. This approach allows them to show that middle-class identity had as much to do with local political and economic struggles as it did with national ones.[15] Leonore Davidoff and Catherine Hall, in contrast, retain a national perspective, but they argue that middle-class consciousness emerged as a result of the articulation of common values and practices in which gender played a particularly important part.[16] This approach produces a different kind of story about middle-class formation in the nineteenth century, for they describe how an increasingly coherent middle-class identity was articulated in an England whose economy was transformed by the Industrial Revolution and whose politics were transformed by the French Revolution and the Reform Act.

However, crucial aspects of the middle-class identity that was articulated between 1780 and 1850 seem to have been "made" before these accounts take up the story. It is curious, for instance, to locate the entire history of the formation of the middle class in the period after the Industrial Revolution was well under way: if there was no middle class until after 1832, how did the Industrial Revolution happen in the first place? Work on the economic history of the eighteenth and early nineteenth centuries has stressed that the Industrial Revolution was a broadly based process of economic development.[17] This argument requires an explanation of the social and cultural changes that made this economic development possible. Such changes—the development of an ethic of competition, a profit motive, and a desire to remain in the commercial sector—have a distinctly middle-class ring to them, and they suggest that the origins of middle-class culture will be located in

---

15. Anthony Howe, *The Cotton Masters, 1830–50* (Oxford, 1984); Koditschek, *Class Formation*; R. J. Morris, *Class, Sect, and Party: The Making of the British Middle Class, Leeds, 1820–1850* (Manchester, 1990).

16. Davidoff and Hall, *Family Fortunes*.

17. Maxine Berg, *The Age of Manufactures: Industry, Innovation, and Work in Britain, 1700–1820* (London, 1985); Pat Hudson, *The Industrial Revolution* (London, 1992).

the eighteenth century, at a time when industrialization was just beginning.

In addition, a post–Industrial Revolution version of middle-class formation is difficult to square entirely with the history of working-class formation. Even if one does not accept Thompson's argument in its entirety, local evidence suggests that factory owners and other commercial people already had a well-articulated sense of the differences between themselves and the working class before the turn of the century. The existence of these differences implies a process of social differentiation in the eighteenth century that needs to be part of the story of the origins of middle-class culture. This aspect of the middle class's history is particularly important because historians have tended to neglect the factors that made these people a class in relation to their social inferiors.[18]

Such criticism should not be pushed too far. These historians—whether they take a political and economic perspective or a social one—tell an important story about the making of middle-class consciousness in the period they study. They are not so much wrong as incomplete, for the middle class they describe is a curiously rootless one. By concentrating on the ways in which a coherent middle-class identity was constructed in the nineteenth century, these works do not systematically examine the origins of the set of values, attitudes, practices, and worldview that made middle-class culture distinctive.

We come now to the second of the two propositions, for the current state of the historiography of the eighteenth century renders a simple account of the origins of middle-class culture problematic. Eighteenth-century historiography, once populated only with monarchs, ministers, MPs, and the occasional mob, is now the home of a teeming social middle.[19] Though the people who were in this social middle had property, and thus a degree of security and comfort unattainable by the laboring poor, they did not have the leisure or the social privileges that

---

18. In making this assertion I am agreeing with Stuart Blumin's point that a traditional Marxist two-class model of society is inadequate for dealing with the complexities of an industrializing society; see his *Emergence of the Middle Class*, 5.

19. Paul Langford, *A Polite and Commercial People: England, 1727–1783* (Oxford, 1992); Peter Borsay, *The English Urban Renaissance: Culture and Society in the Provincial Town, 1660–1770* (Oxford, 1989), 226–31. From a very different starting point, Dror Wahrman ends up making a very similar point: "National Society, Communal Culture: An Argument about the Recent Historiography of Eighteenth-Century Britain," *Social History* 17 (1992): 43–72.

came with a landed estate.[20] The emergence of this social middle in the eighteenth century was a significant development because it greatly increased the numbers of people who were not primarily dependent on owning or working the land for a livelihood. This social middle cannot be identified as a middle class, however, for it lacked coherence. Its members ranged from petty shopkeepers, tradesmen, and independent craftsmen up through provincial dealers and professionals to the great merchants and financiers involved in international trade. Industrialization merely complicates this mixture, adding factory owners, yet more merchants, and a whole range of new entrepreneurs to the already muddy social waters. Moreover, the social and cultural authority of the landed elite in eighteenth-century society exerted a tremendous pull on the identities and practices of this social middle, further complicating any story about the emergence of the middle class.

The historical complexity of the amorphous social middle of eighteenth-century society is reflected in the way the historians who have established its existence use or do not use the term "middle class." Some, such as Lorna Weatherill and Hoh-Cheung and Lorna Mui, avoid the word "class" altogether.[21] Others, such as Paul Langford and Peter Borsay, use the term "middle class" but only in a studiously vague way, interchanging it with the plural form, "middle classes," or with such constructions as "middling ranks."[22] The caution of these authors is appropriate. Even as late as mid-century, it is difficult to distinguish between a group one might want to call the middle class and what in the seventeenth century was known as the "middling sort," a term that contemporaries still used.[23] If the development of distinctly new forms of social and economic practice later in the century makes "middling sort" an unacceptable term, the diversity of the social middle does not seem to take to a class label.

---

20. John Seed, "From 'Middling Sort' to Middle Class in Late Eighteenth- and Early Nineteenth-Century England," in Bush, *Social Orders and Social Classes*, 115.

21. Lorna Weatherill, *Consumer Behavior and Material Culture in Britain, 1660–1760* (London, 1988); Hoh-Cheung Mui and Lorna Mui, *Shops and Shopkeeping in Eighteenth-Century England* (Montreal, 1989).

22. Langford, *Polite and Commercial People*, 61–68, where he defines what he means by "middle class." Also see Paul Langford, *Public Life and Propertied Englishmen, 1689–1798* (Oxford, 1991), and Borsay, *English Urban Renaissance*. Joanna Innes makes this point in her review of Langford: "Not So Strange: New Views of Eighteenth-Century England," *History Workshop* 29 (1990): 179–83.

23. P. J. Corfield, "Class by Name and Number in Eighteenth-Century Britain," *History* 72 (1987): 38–61.

To repeat, the problem that surrounds the origins of middle-class culture is that while crucial aspects of the set of values, attitudes, practices, and worldview that together made up middle-class identity must have emerged in the eighteenth century, it is difficult to identify a coherent social entity to whom those values and practices belonged. What is needed is an account of how this particular historical reality produced a middle-class identity. In these circumstances, a cultural analysis is vital because it focuses our attention on the relationship between a specific socioeconomic context and the class identity that was articulated in that context.

THE CASE FOR LOCAL HISTORY

If producing a convincing account of class formation requires an analysis of the connections between socioeconomic reality and class identity, then in addition to using cultural theory, we must pay more attention to the context in which the account is set. I argue that middle-class culture originated in the local rather than the national context. To argue for the importance of local history is to do more than simply offer the history of a particular community as an exemplar of a larger process. The argument suggests that local history ought to be fundamental to any analysis of class formation.[24] In the first place, it offers some assistance in efforts to sort out the complexities of eighteenth-century society and the place that class identity had in that social context. There is a sense in which class culture exists *only* in the local context, for only in such a setting is it possible to specify the nature of the reciprocal relationship that exists between socioeconomic reality and a group's construction of that reality. In Halifax, manufacturing—direct involvement in the production of woolen cloth on a large scale,

---

24. In quite a different historical context, that of the English Civil War, Ann Hughes makes a very convincing argument for the necessity of local history as a mode of analysis. Local history is necessary in an account of the causes of the English Civil War because it is impossible otherwise to explain how the conflict between king and Parliament ended up on the field of battle. Rather than treat each additional local history as another example of a single process, she argues that local history can identify the important factors that were operating in this historical process but might have been combined in different ways in other local contexts. Like mine, then, hers is an argument about local history not as exemplar but as a mode of analysis: "Local History and the Origins of the English Civil War," in *Conflict in Early Stuart England: Studies in Religion and Politics, 1603–1642*, ed. Richard Cust and Anne Hughes (London, 1989), 224–53.

as distinct from any mercantile or professional activity—was an important factor in shaping the middle-class culture that originated there, because it gave rise to a new set of social relations between manufacturers and their workers and helped to change the values and outlook of the manufacturers. Thus the class character of the culture that developed among this group in the mid–eighteenth century is relatively obvious from the local perspective.

This is not to say that "national" cultures do not exist. They do, and they have enormous influence on the ways in which a particular worldview is constructed in a specific socioeconomic context. It is useful, however, to distinguish between the way a group conforms to the "national" culture by adopting specific practices, values, and ideas and the way a group appropriates what it wants out of the larger culture. As Roger Chartier argues, the consumers of culture are not merely passive recipients; they actively shape what they take in from "outside," giving it new emphases and meanings that emerge out of their own experience.[25] Thus external influences become relevant for the story of class formation insofar as they get appropriated as part of the way a particular group articulates its middle-class identity. For example, the development of a regional and national money market (discussed in Chapter 4) and the pervasive eighteenth-century culture of gentility (discussed in Chapter 7) were important aspects of the middle-class culture that originated in mid-eighteenth-century Halifax, yet each of these influences was shaped in a particular way by the particular local context.

A mode of analysis that highlights local history also results in a different but much more workable account of the origins of middle-class culture in the eighteenth century and its articulation in the nineteenth century. It suggests that in the eighteenth century there was no single middle-class culture. Rather, a variety of local cultures developed, each a specific response to the local context, and in particular to the specific ways in which capitalist relations of production emerged in that locality. The situation in Halifax, characterized by large-scale but largely non-mechanized production, was different from that in Leeds or Wakefield, where large merchants and small to medium-sized producers were the norm; different again from the situation in the cotton industry in Lancashire, where mechanized production was more important; and finally

---

25. Roger Chartier, *The Cultural Origins of the French Revolution*, trans. Lydia Cochrane (Durham, N.C., 1991).

different again from a situation such as that of Birmingham or Sheffield, where the proletarianization of independent masters happened much later. This kind of analysis assumes the attention that is being paid to local and regional developments in the historiography of the Industrial Revolution and builds on it, providing an account of the cultural changes associated with industrialization.[26]

As middle-class culture originated in the eighteenth century, it took a variety of forms. These local middle-class cultures shared some features, and in the latter part of the eighteenth century and into the nineteenth the recognition and articulation of these common features resulted in the making of an English middle-class culture. Yet a cultural theory of class formation that pays attention to the local context sheds important light on the development and nature of the national class culture. Most important, it suggests that we should not expect the middle class of the nineteenth century to be any more coherent as a social entity than its eighteenth-century counterpart. Class is a culture, not a thing. In a sense, then, I agree with the critics of class analysis because in the nation as a whole it is *not* possible to identify a group that shared a single socioeconomic experience. However, class culture—other historians would call it "class discourse"—did exist in the nineteenth century. And "class" is the appropriate term to use, for local groups adopted this culture because it resonated with their socioeconomic experience. In this sense, those who question class analysis fail to appreciate the distinction between what William Sewell has called "class discourse" and "class institutions" or "movements."[27] Once the set of cultural concepts that created class consciousness emerged, once class became available as a way to perceive the world, it was difficult to turn the clock back even though the particular event or events that caused the cultural shift—agitation over war with America or France, over political and social reform—had faded away.

Some aspects of this nineteenth-century middle-class culture have already been described. Koditschek, for instance, provides a detailed analysis of a fully formed local middle-class culture in nineteenth-century Bradford. Davidoff and Hall argue for the articulation of a coherent national class culture on the basis of common values. The project of this book, however, is to tell the part of the story of middle-

26. Berg, *Age of Manufactures*, and Hudson, *Industrial Revolution*.
27. Sewell, "How Classes Are Made," 71.

Theory and Methods 17

class formation that has not yet been uncovered: the story of the local origins of this middle-class culture in the eighteenth century.

CHAPTER 2 completes the introductory section of the book by describing Halifax as it was in the later seventeenth century. After introducing the middling sort, it examines the political and religious independence of the middling sort in the Civil War and Restoration and shows how these values, combined with economic practice and social structure, formed a coherent culture.

The central thesis of the book is then argued in two sections whose content reflects the theoretical and historical concerns raised here. Part I, "Process," describes the long-term factors that contributed to the emergence of a middle-class culture in Halifax in the middle of the eighteenth century. Its two chapters deal with the relatively gradual economic, social, and cultural changes that occurred in the parish between the Restoration and the Industrial Revolution, and they argue that these changes, comprehensible within the terms of the middling sort's culture, eventually created a distinct middle-class experience. Chapter 3 examines developments in the parish's textile industry between the late seventeenth and mid–eighteenth centuries. It analyzes of the economic changes that gave rise to large-scale manufacturing and the cultural changes that stemmed from and contributed to this process of economic development. Chapter 4 considers two sets of economic and social changes that were related to but not derivative of the transformation in the parish's textile industry: the "money market" and patterns of consumption. An analysis of the interaction between practice and culture lies at the center of this chapter, too, but the particular nature of these issues shows the important connections between developments in Halifax and those elsewhere in the region and even the country.

Part II, "Crystallization," describes the events that led to the crystallization of a middle-class culture in the two decades after 1750. Its two chapters explore the making of middle-class consciousness in the public and private spheres and show how the potential for cultural change created by the long-term changes described in Part I was realized in the second half of the eighteenth century. Chapter 5 shows the transformation of "political" life in the parish in this period, both by the formation of voluntary associations and by a series of public disputes between factions of the parish's elite. Chapter 6 analyzes of the construction of a private sphere, for an equally important aspect of the emergence of a middle-class consciousness concerns the new social world that members of this class made for themselves. Central to the emergence of a middle-class identity in the private sphere was gender, for new sets of gender relations were crucial to the process of social differentiation necessary for middle-class formation.

The Conclusion also has two chapters. Chapter 7 examines the new set of social relations through which the members of Halifax's middle class understood their place in the world by exploring the ways in which members of Halifax's middle class saw themselves in relation to the other main social groups of the parish. Chapter 8 considers the implications that this study of the middle class in Halifax has for the wider problem of understanding the emergence of England's middle class, and it discusses how the argument of this book interacts with and enriches two other important debates in eighteenth- and nineteenth-century history: the Industrial Revolution and the formation of the working class.

Chapter 2

The Middling Sort and Their World

Located on the eastern flank of the Pennine mountains that separate Yorkshire from Lancashire, Halifax was typical of large upland parishes. Seventeen miles long and eleven miles across, it was huge by English standards, and its landscape was dominated by moorland tops (most of them too barren to cultivate), steep hillsides, and the small valley bottoms of the river Calder and its many tributaries. The landscape was rougher in the western part of the parish, becoming gentler, though hardly flat, toward the east. Predictably, population followed the same gradient: the larger settlements in the parish were located in the east. Chief among them was the town of Halifax. In 1664 the town was a community of about 2,500 souls, boasting the parish church, a weekly market, and a variety of shops and inns. Although the town was important as a commercial center, the bulk of the parish's population was dispersed in a host of smaller villages, hamlets, and isolated farmsteads. As Daniel Defoe described it on his tour in 1724, the houses and farms were scattered across this landscape, each farm having a few "small enclosures ... from two acres to six or seven acres each."[1] The town of Halifax could not even claim to be the administrative center of the parish. There were twelve chapels in the parish, and the administrative responsibilities of maintaining the poor and the highways, collecting

---

1. Daniel Defoe, *A Tour through the Whole Island of Great Britain* (1724; New York, 1968), 2: 600.

taxes, and seeing miscreants to justice were divided among twenty-three autonomous townships.[2]

Landholding was equally decentralized, for Halifax lacked a dominant landlord or group of landlords. Its manorial structure was highly fragmented, and the strong copyhold tenure customary in the parish, with fixed rents and entry fines, gave the many manorial lords very little control over their tenants.[3] Moreover, a significant proportion of the land was held in freehold by the occupiers of the houses and farms, further limiting the influence of manorial landlords.

The agricultural economy of this extensive parish was dominated by pastoral farming and geared towards the needs of the household instead of the market.[4] Large-scale arable farming was simply uneconomic, for the topography, the cold, wet Pennine climate, and the poor soil made growing even oats and hay difficult, let alone wheat or barley. An extensive analysis of probate inventories from the last decade of the seventeenth century reveals that the median value of the agricultural goods owned was £15.[5] This figure is near the center of a continuum that stretched from those individuals who owned only a milk cow, a pig, or a horse—hardly farmers in any sense of the word—to smallholders such as Edward Slater, a yeoman of Shelf. He had a herd of six cows, two heifers, and a calf valued at £22; a mare and "furnishings" worth £1; a few husbandry tools and oats, hay, and straw worth £8.[6] A small minority of Halifax's farmers, 7.5 percent, had farm goods worth more than £50, but even the most affluent were still pastoralists. James Oates of Warley, for instance, had agricultural goods worth £83, but this amount included only £18 worth of oats and wheat.[7]

Even for the largest farmers, then, there were limits to the income that farming could provide, and for many of the parish's residents, the

---

2. The administrative duties placed on the parishes in the Tudor/Stuart period had devolved to the more workable unit of the civil township, an arrangement made official in 1662: 13 and 14, Charles II, c. 12. The chapelries and townships did not necessarily have the same boundaries.

3. John Watson, *The History and Antiquities of the Parish of Halifax in Yorkshire* (1775; Manchester, 1973), 85–124; Martha Ellis, "A Study in the Manorial History of Halifax in the Sixteenth and Early Seventeenth Centuries," *Yorkshire Archaeological Journal* 40 (1960): 422–27.

4. Thomas Allen, *A New and Complete History of the County of York* (London, 1828), 5:5.

5. The date of this sample is determined by the fact that inventories in the diocese of York survive consistently only after 1689. Out of 292 inventories for the years from 1690 to 1699, 197 (67%) included some agricultural goods. The value of those agricultural goods varied widely, however, from an extreme of almost £350 down to a few shillings.

6. BIY/OW, Edward Slater, Shelf, March 1693/94.

7. Ibid., John Whittel, Elland, August 1697; James Oates, Warley, November 1695.

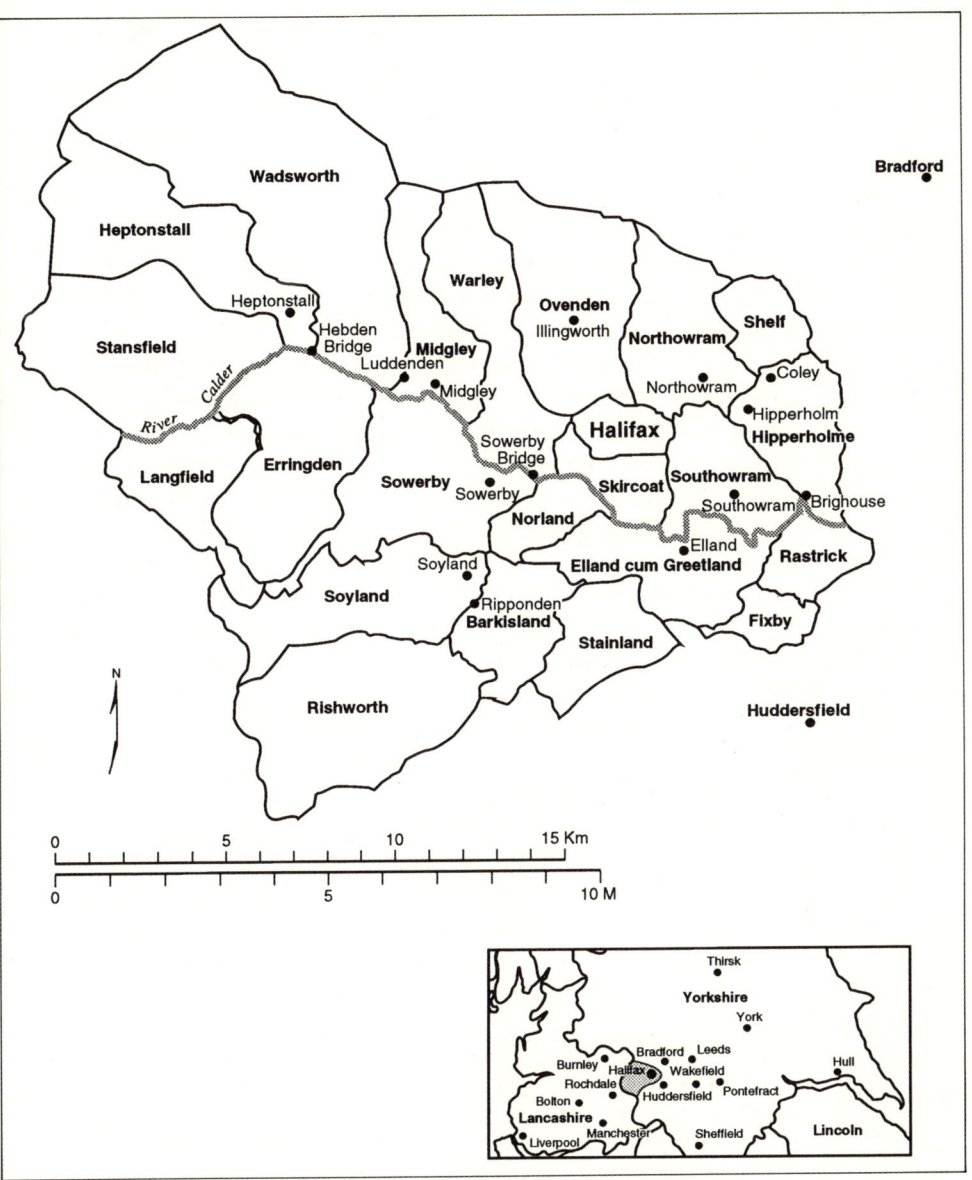

The parish of Halifax

livelihood represented by their small herds and even smaller fields had to be supplemented by other work. In Halifax that meant the wool textile industry.[8] There is evidence of a woolen industry in Halifax from as early as the fourteenth century, but it was not until the early modern period that textile production became a common way to make a living in the parish.[9] The development of the woolen industry in the parish was encouraged by some of the same factors that constrained its agricultural potential. The same steep valleys and abundant rainfall that made cultivation so difficult provided waterpower for the fulling mills where cloth was finished. Perhaps more important, the dispersed settlement pattern and the lax manorial system made it easy for the population to increase because land was readily available and no force was at work to prevent new settlements.[10] These factors made possible the rapid development of the parish's textile industry in the sixteenth and seventeenth centuries. We cannot measure this growth directly, but the dramatic rise in Halifax's population is suggestive: the number of residents doubled between the chantry survey of 1548 (9,000–10,000) and the hearth tax of 1664 (19,000), and the parish register from the Commonwealth shows that a substantial portion of this population worked in the textile industry.[11] By the later seventeenth century, then, the textile industry was a vital part of Halifax's economy.

From its beginning, Halifax's textile industry was dominated by small independent artisans who worked in their own homes along with members of their family and with their own materials, and inventory evidence shows that the domestic system was still dominant in the last decade of the seventeenth century. The most common product of Halifax clothiers, a cloth known as a kersey—a relatively coarse, narrow woolen cloth used for blankets and coats—was well suited to domestic production. Some families lived a hand-to-mouth existence, buying only

---

8. Most large landowners, including Oates, found it more profitable to lease their properties out than to farm them themselves. In 1707 the granddaughters of James Oates divided up an estate worth nearly £400 a year in rents alone: Mark Pearson, *History of Northowram* (Halifax, 1898), 229–30; CDA/MAC/119/17, 18, Oates family deeds.

9. Herbert Heaton, *The Yorkshire Woollen and Worsted Industries* (Oxford, 1920), 19, 75.

10. David Levine, *Family Formation in an Age of Nascent Capitalism* (New York, 1977).

11. For the chantry survey see Martha Ellis François, "The Social and Economic Development of Halifax," *Leeds Philosophical and Literary Society Proceedings*, Literature and History Section, 11 (1966): 225. For the hearth tax see PRO/E.179/210/393; a multiplier of 5 was used to get population from the number of households. An analysis of the Commonwealth registers is in Alan Betteridge, "Halifax before the Industrial Revolution: A Study of Local Administrative Records, 1585–1762," *THAS*, 1978, 27–28.

enough wool to weave one or two pieces of cloth and then selling them to buy more wool. Jonathan Crowther, for instance, owned only a loom and three spinning wheels, and his inventory suggests a family that lived on the edge of poverty, for he left only a sparse collection of household goods and a horse and some hay, which, with the loom and wheels, brought the total value of his inventory to £15.[12] Other clothiers had a larger cushion. John Fielden of Heptonstall lived in a house with nine rooms, and he had textile goods worth about £20, including just over £17 in wool and yarn and two looms. He was also a substantial farmer by Halifax standards, with almost £50 in agricultural goods, most of it, as one would expect, on the hoof. Similarly, Isaac Smith lived in a house with five chambers and three service rooms, and he had £22 in textile goods, again largely in the form of wool, yarn, and unsold cloth. He also had a herd of seven cows worth £17 and a small field of corn valued at £2/10.[13] Both Fielden and Smith styled themselves "yeoman," for that title was an apt indicator of their wealth and the social status that came with it.

Though the distinction between a poor clothier such as Crowther and yeomen such as Fielden and Smith was real, it should not be overemphasized. There were not two distinct types of clothier in Halifax, but rather a spectrum. Between these two end points were such men as William Pearson, with a pair of looms, four spinning wheels, a set of combs, and £3 in wool and yarn; Robert Omeroyd, with a loom and fifteen stones of wool worth £9; and Luke Greenwood with two looms, spinning wheels and other gear worth £3/5/-, as well as cloth, wool, and yarn worth £10/10/-.[14] More important, it is not possible to argue that the £20 to £30 worth of textile goods in a yeoman's inventory is indicative of a different mode of production. The wealthier clothiers were not obliged to go to the market each week to sell one cloth and buy materials for another, but they still produced cloth in their own homes with their own labor, and bought raw materials and sold their finished products at the local market. This last feature of the domestic system of manufacture is crucial because it guaranteed clothiers in Halifax a degree of economic independence from the merchants who bought their cloth for export or sale in London.

The parish's fragmented manorial structure, its relatively poor agri-

12. BIY/OW, Jonathan Crowther, Northowram, April 1694.
13. Ibid., John Fielden, Heptonstall, May 1695; Isaac Smith, Northowram, March 1694/95.
14. Ibid., William Pearson, Northowram, May 1691; Robert Omeroyd, Erringden, August 1695; Luke Greenwood, Erringden, June 1691.

cultural potential, and the economic independence made possible by its textile industry combined to give Halifax a very distinctive social structure, one dominated by a middling group of clothier/farmers. This social structure is revealed in the late-seventeenth-century hearth tax returns, particularly the Lady Day returns of 1664, which list exempted households as well as those that paid the tax.[15] As Table 1 shows, most households in the parish were poor. With just over a third of the population exempted from the tax and nearly another third paying for only one hearth, two-thirds of the population could be described as the laboring poor, living at or just below the subsistence level. Most of the remaining households in the parish paid tax on between two and five hearths; as a rule, they would have been above the poverty line in all but the most extreme circumstances. Finally a very small group, only 2.5 percent of the households, had more than six hearths. Even in this group, households were concentrated at the low end of the spectrum. In the township of Halifax, the wealthiest township in the parish, only seven households had more than ten hearths, and the largest number of hearths in the entire parish—appropriately enough, in the house of one of the parish's few resident gentlemen—was fourteen.

The hearth tax returns suggest that Halifax's social structure was relatively undifferentiated. There is a striking absence, in the parish as a whole and in individual townships, of a single "great household" or a cluster of very wealthy households separated from the rest of the population by a significant gap. The undifferentiated nature of Halifax's social structure is perhaps clearer if its hearth tax returns are compared with those of other communities. The Essex village of Terling, for instance, had about the same proportion of exempted households as Halifax, but it had more than three times as many households with more than six hearths, and that pattern was characteristic of the prosperous county of Essex as a whole. Terling was a predominantly agrarian community, but even in other "industrial" communities the proportion of

15. An exemption from the hearth tax was granted if the household was too poor to pay local church and poor rates, if the house was worth less than 20 shillings a year, or if the household occupied land worth less than 20 shillings or had goods worth less than £10: Roger Howell, "Hearth Tax Returns," *History*, n.s. 49 (1964): 45. The validity of the hearth tax as a tool for examining social structure has been established in detailed case studies: Margaret Spufford, *Contrasting Communities: English Villagers in the Sixteenth and Seventeenth Centuries* (Cambridge, 1974), 39, 41; Keith Wrightson and David Levine, *Poverty and Piety in an English Village: Terling, 1525–1700* (New York, 1979), 35; David Levine and Keith Wrightson, *The Making of an Industrial Society: Whickham, 1560–1765* (Oxford, 1991), 158–64.

TABLE 1. Households subject to and exempt from hearth tax in townships of Halifax parish, 1664, by number of hearths taxed

Township	All households	6+		3–6		2		1		Exempt	
		N	%	N	%	N	%	N	%	N	%
Halifax	502	36	7.2%	115	22.9%	75	14.9%	67	13.3%	209	41.7%
Southowram	148	4	2.7	31	21.0	32	21.6	27	18.2	54	36.5
Skircoat	85	1	1.2	23	27.0	25	29.4	8	9.4	28	33.0
Shelf	83	1	1.2	14	16.9	11	13.3	28	33.7	29	34.9
Hipperholme	199	5	2.5	48	24.1	36	18.1	43	21.6	67	33.7
Northowram	328	9	2.7	47	14.3	49	14.9	66	20.1	157	48.0
Ovenden	308	5	1.6	38	12.3	59	19.2	89	28.9	117	38.0
Midgley	95	2	2.1	14	14.7	15	15.8	39	41.1	25	26.3
Warley	256	3	1.2	28	10.9	40	15.6	102	39.8	83	32.5
Wadsworth	179	2	1.1	19	10.6	21	11.7	94	52.6	43	24.0
Heptonstall	160	2	1.2	9	5.6	19	11.9	70	43.7	60	37.6
Stansfield	211	3	1.4	10	4.7	23	10.9	112	53.1	63	29.9
Erringden	76	–	–	10	13.2	19	25.0	31	40.8	16	21.0
Langfield	61	1	1.6	4	6.5	12	19.7	33	54.1	11	18.1
Sowerby	468	5	1.1	66	14.1	72	15.4	185	39.5	140	29.9
Stainland	119	–	–	11	9.2	17	14.3	56	47.1	35	29.4
Barkisland	129	7	5.4	13	10.1	22	17.1	53	41.1	34	26.3
Rishworth	162	1	0.6	28	17.3	40	24.7	50	30.9	43	26.5
Elland	175	6	3.4	30	17.1	23	13.2	48	27.4	68	38.9
Rastrick	72	4	5.5	11	15.3	12	16.7	15	20.8	30	41.7
Fixby	28	1	3.6	1	3.6	8	28.5	11	39.3	7	25.0
All townships	3,844	98	2.5%	570	14.8%	630	16.4%	1,227	31.9%	1,319	34.3%

Note: The townships are grouped geographically, starting with the core around Halifax, and then moving out by relatively discrete geographical and economic units. The number of hearths in each category follows Keith Wrightson and David Levine, *Poverty and Piety in an English Village: Terling, 1525–1700* (New York, 1979), 35, except that I have separated exempted households from those that paid the tax for one hearth. I thank Ronan Bennett for allowing me to use his transcription of these returns.

Source: PRO/E.179/210/393.

households with more than six hearths was somewhat greater than in Halifax, and these parishes often had a much larger proportion of exempted households.[16] The value of such a comparison is limited, but it does emphasize the fact that the social structure of Halifax was dominated by an extensive social middle within which it is difficult to differentiate.

THE CULTURE OF THE MIDDLING SORT

When Lord Fairfax and his son Sir Thomas came to Halifax to enlist troops for the struggle against the king in 1643, one of the many volunteers who stepped forward was Samuel Priestly. The son of a moderately well-to-do clothier and a staunch Puritan, Samuel is reported to have answered his mother's pleas to stay at home with the following words: "Mother, pray be content; if I stay at home I can follow no employment, but be forced to hide myself in one hole or another which I cannot endure; I had rather venture my life in the field, and, if I die, it is in a good cause."[17] Samuel Priestly's brave words identify him as one of the "middling sort," part of the group of industrious craftsmen and yeomen that Christopher Hill has argued had such a vital place in the history of the English Revolution.[18] In explaining his position Samuel declared his political independence and his desire to work in a calling, both of which were underlain by his Puritan convictions.

Identifying Samuel as one of the "middling sort," however, does not actually tell us very much. In its most general sense, the term merely refers to that segment of preindustrial English society that was, as one seventeenth-century commentator put it, neither "the wealthy and powerful men" nor "the basest and lowest sort," but rather "the yeomen, farmers, clothiers and the whole middle rank of the

---

16. For Terling see Wrightson and Levine, *Poverty and Piety*, 35. For other areas for which hearth tax returns have been published, see T. Arkell, "The Problem of Establishing Regional Variations in England's Hearth Tax Household Structure during the Later Seventeenth Century," in *Regional and Spatial Demographic Patterns in the Past*, ed. R. Smith (Oxford, 1988), quoted in Levine and Wrightson, *Making of an Industrial Society*, 157.

17. "Some Memoirs Concerning the Family of the Priestlys, Written by Jonathan Priestly, 1696," *Surtees Society Publications* 77 (1883): 18, 26.

18. Christopher Hill, "A Bourgeois Revolution," in *Three British Revolutions*, ed. J. G. A. Pocock (Princeton, 1980), and his *Society and Puritanism in Pre-revolutionary England* (New York, 1964).

people."¹⁹ In this general sociological sense, the term reflects an important aspect of preindustrial society. The work of a generation of social historians has shown how the middling sort emerged out of the economic developments of the sixteenth and seventeenth centuries. They were the yeomen who bought the land their less fortunate neighbors were forced to sell as grain prices rose, and the craftsmen who benefited to a greater or lesser extent from the spread of a market economy.²⁰ Neither the existence of this middling sort nor an understanding of its socioeconomic origins, however, can explain the vehemence with which a Samuel Priestly announced his intention to fight against the king.

The most suggestive attempt to get beyond the general sociological sense of the term "middling sort" is David Underdown's *Revel, Riot, and Rebellion*; which argues that popular participation in the Civil War can be explained only with reference to the way that specific communities understood their world. Underdown identifies two distinct cultures, each associated with a particular social and economic environment. Supporters of the king often came from downland areas whose economies centered on arable farming; here the dominant culture was rather conservative, emphasizing traditional recreations and deferential social relations. Supporters of Parliament, in contrast, often came from upland areas with more diverse, commercially oriented economies; here the dominant culture might take on a Puritan flavor, emphasizing individualism and social control.²¹

As Ann Hughes suggests, Underdown has perhaps created a package that is too tidy, for the relations between Puritanism and market forces, between the middling sort and the gentry, may not have worked in the same way in every case.²² The real value of Underdown's work, however, lies in his emphasis on the necessity of a cultural analysis that explores the relationships between economy, society, values, and beliefs. Such a

---

19. John Corbet, "A True and Impartial History of the Military Government of the Citie of Gloucester," quoted in David Underdown, *Revel, Riot, and Rebellion: Popular Politics and Culture in England, 1603–1660* (Oxford, 1985), 169–70.

20. Spufford, *Contrasting Communities*; Wrightson and Levine, *Poverty and Piety*; Levine and Wrightson, *Making of an Industrial Society*. None of these works explicitly discusses the middling sort, but the social and economic processes they describe are quite clearly related to the development of this new social group.

21. Underdown, *Revel, Riot, and Rebellion*, 104–5, 165–82.

22. Ann Hughes, "Local History and the Origins of the Civil War," in *Conflict in Early Stuart England: Studies in Religion and Politics, 1603–1642*, ed. Richard Cust and Ann Hughes (London, 1989), 242.

cultural analysis need not be confined to the history of the Civil War. Samuel Priestly's declaration is recorded in the memoirs that his youngest brother, Jonathan, wrote some fifty years later. The pride with which Jonathan told the story suggests, as do many other passages in his memoirs, that the culture of the middling sort survived intact until the end of the seventeenth century.

Fundamental to this culture was the relationship between the values and concepts expressed in Samuel Priestly's steadfast declaration and many aspects of economic and social experience in seventeenth-century Halifax. We can discern the relationship between values and experiences most clearly in the set of social relations that defined this group's place in the social order, for they show how members of the middling sort conceived of and felt about their place in the world. Like most, perhaps all inhabitants of seventeenth-century England, the members of Halifax's middling sort saw their social world in hierarchical terms, and their social relations reflected assumptions about the fundamental correctness of social inequalities. From their point of view, the important features of the social hierarchy were the dominance of the gentry and aristocracy and the submission of the poor. The particular economic and social context of Halifax's middling sort, however, gave their conceptions of this social hierarchy two distinctive features.

The first was their relations with the landed gentry. On the whole, although individuals within this group might aspire to become gentlemen, the middling sort recognized the social superiority of the gentry and the profound cultural gulf that separated them from the landed elite. Parallel to this culture of rank and deference, however, was a well-developed sense of independence.[23] Deference, though natural, was contingent. Normally members of Halifax's middling sort were willing to follow the local gentry, giving deference where deference was due; but in the right circumstances they were capable of following their own path, ignoring their "natural" leaders and following instead someone of their own choosing.

The second important feature of the culture of Halifax's middling sort was its social inclusiveness. Theirs was a fairly broad social group, and social relations within it were relatively egalitarian. This is not to say that individuals did not recognize the existence of social and economic differences within their group. Rather, those distinctions, which

---

23. I owe the concept of parallel cultures to Stuart Blumin, *The Emergence of the Middle Class: Social Experience in the American City* (New York, 1989), 38.

were difficult to make in any case, were not a crucial part of their identity as individuals or as a group.

DEFERENCE AND INDEPENDENCE

The group against which Halifax's middling sort expressed this combination of deference and independence was the local gentry. As with most early-modern communities, it is difficult to identify Halifax's gentry with great precision.[24] Some families were undeniably members of England's landed elite. The influence of the most important gentry family associated with the parish, the Savilles, extended throughout the region and even the nation, and their landholdings included almost half of the parish's submanors. The Farrers of Midgley and the Thornhills of Fixby owned much smaller estates, only a submanor in each case, but members of these families served as justices of the peace, and since they were residents of the parish, their local influence may have rivaled that of the Savilles. Though the heads of two other families, the Hortons of Howroyd and the Sternes of Woodhouse, were not manorial lords, they can be identified as gentlemen by virtue of their appointments to the bench.[25] Finally, both the Listers of Shipden Hall and the Ramsdens of Greetland can be included in the ranks of the gentry on the basis of their behavior and connections.[26]

Some families, however, are more accurately described as marginal or pseudo gentry.[27] Indeed, the lack of a unified manorial structure, with the attendant fluidity of landownership, and the economic opportunities offered by the textile industry encouraged the development of such marginal gentry. This group included such men as John Hoyle and William Midgley, two lawyers who could describe themselves as

24. See Barry Coward, *The Stuart Age* (London, 1980), 40–41, or Keith Wrightson, *English Society* (London, 1982), 23–31.
25. J. W. Clay, ed., *Dugdale's Visitation of Yorkshire, 1666, with Additions* (Exeter, 1899); Watson, *History of Halifax*.
26. The Listers were a cadet branch of a more important family of Bradford, and they had been accounted as gentry for several generations, marrying into the families of other local gentry. Thomas Ramsden's will of 1698 suggests that he was a gentleman, for he left his landed estate to his eldest son and provided £2,000 as the portion for his other children, having sent one of his younger sons to university and the other to the inns of court: BIY/OW, Thomas Ramsden, Greetland, June 1698.
27. See Alan Everitt, *Change in the Provinces: The Seventeenth Century* (Leicester, 1969), 43–46, and his "Social Mobility in Early Modern England," *Past and Present*, no. 33 (1966), 70–72.

gentlemen by virtue of their occupations. It also included some substantial landowners who cannot be numbered among the "true" gentlemen because of their service as parish officers, confusion over their titles, or their practices in matters of inheritance.[28]

The middling sort's relations with the local gentry were strongly influenced by Puritanism. The parish had been a center of popular—even radical—Protestantism since the early Reformation, and in the seventeenth century that religious radicalism took on political overtones.[29] Puritanism provided, in Halifax as elsewhere in England, a focus for a constellation of social, economic, political, and religious forces that together helped to modify a traditional culture of deference by creating a parallel culture of independence so clearly expressed in Samuel Priestly's justification for going to fight against the king.[30] One example of the political independence of the middling sort is the role that freehold voters played in West Riding elections in the 1620s.[31] Another instance is the resistance of Halifax clothiers to plans to increase the duty charged on kersey cloth in 1613 and again in 1638. Although these challenges were propelled by a strong element of economic self-interest, important political issues were also at stake. On both occasions, the objection was against courtly interference in county affairs: "good government" in this case meant leaving things just as they were. In justifying their argument that the duties should not be increased, Halifax's clothiers made reference to wider political and religious issues: in 1613 and in 1638 they argued that there were no popish recusants in the parish because of the prosperity of the woolen

28. Stephen Ellis, Abraham Hall, and Joshua Dearden all had substantial landholdings and styled themselves gentlemen in their wills, but none of them can be considered true gentry. Ellis had served as a churchwarden and overseer of the poor for his township—offices that were not worthy of a gentleman: BIY/OW, Stephen Ellis, Hipperholme, May 1689; Oliver Heywood, *Autobiography, Diaries, Anecdotes and Event Books*, ed. J. Horsfall Turner (Brighouse, Yorkshire, 1882), 1:189. The status of officeholders in local government is discussed in Sidney Webb and Beatrice Webb, *English Local Government* (1906; Hamden, Conn., 1963), 1:15–19. Hall appears in other documents of the period as a yeoman: BIY/OW, Abraham Hall, Northowram, June 1694, and CDA/SH:6/LD/17/1, lease of charity lands. Finally, both Dearden and Ellis divided their estates by the partible inheritance customary in the region (BIY/OW, Joshua Dearden, Sowerby, November 1696), whereas all of the true gentlemen whose wills I have found practiced primogeniture. See, e.g., BIY/OW, William Farrer, Ewood, September 1695 and Thomas Ramsden, Greetland, June 1698.

29. Claire Cross, "Parochial Structure and the Dissemination of Protestantism in Sixteenth-Century England: A Tale of Two Cities," in *The Church in Town and Countryside*, ed. Derek Baker (Oxford, 1979), 269; A. G. Dickens, *The English Reformation* (London, 1964), 315.

30. Underdown, *Revel, Riot, and Rebellion*, 106–45.

31. Richard Cust, "Politics and the Electorate in the 1620s," in Cust and Hughes, *Conflict in Early Stuart England*, 143–51.

industry.³² The implication—that an increase in duties would let in popery—shows how closely economic self-interest and religious and political identity were intertwined.

The parish's support for Parliament during the Civil War also suggests that Puritanism contributed to the political independence of the middling sort. Clarendon records that "Leeds, Halifax, and Bradford, three very populous and rich towns (which depending wholly upon clothiers, too much maligned the gentry) were wholly at the disposition of the Parliament."³³ This popular support for Parliament went contrary to the royalism of the principal gentry families in the parish. Sir William Saville, the largest single landowner in the parish, was a commander in the Royalist army, and several Halifax gentlemen served under him.

Their willingness to take up arms against the king and the local gentry does not imply that Halifax's middling sort had completely abandoned deference. Men such as Priestly were not radical democrats or incipient Levellers. He did, after all, follow the lead given by Lord Fairfax, presumably because, as a gentleman, Fairfax had a kind of natural authority in Priestly's eyes. Priestly's deference, however, was contingent. He chose to give deference to Fairfax and to withhold it from Saville because he agreed with Fairfax's political and religious ideology.

Although this culture of independence was articulated in Puritan terms, it was structured by the socioeconomic context within which it developed. Men and women such as Samuel Priestly and his mother adopted Puritanism and the associated political and social attitudes because it resonated with their experiences. While the activities of a string of Puritan vicars no doubt contributed to the development of Puritanism in the parish, some weight must be given to the relative social independence and the thriving wool textile industry of this large upland parish. These factors gave members of the middling sort the exposure, opportunity, and means to take responsibility for their own salvation, a set of circumstances often associated with the spread of Puritan beliefs.³⁴

The connection between socioeconomic reality and the cultural iden-

---

32. Heaton, *Yorkshire Woollen and Worsted Industries*, 177–85, 197–203.
33. Quoted in H. P. Kendall, "Local Incidents in the Civil War," *THAS*, 1909, 7.
34. Cross, "Parochial Structure"; M. E. James, *Family, Lineage, and Civil Society* (Oxford, 1978), 130–35, 195–96. The success of Puritan beliefs in the parish is suggested by the outpouring of religious bequests in the late sixteenth and seventeenth centuries: Watson, *History of Halifax*, 549–728.

tity of the independent middling sort is equally relevant after the Restoration. Obviously, the specific cultural package that had prompted men such as Samuel Priestly to fight against the king lost some of its coherence with the failure of the Commonwealth and the return of King Charles II, for as Puritanism was forced into Dissent, it ceased to be part of the political mainstream. The socioeconomic structures that underlay this culture of independence, however, remained largely unchanged. Throughout the seventeenth century, before and after the Restoration, most of the parish's families were economically independent. As householders they were not subject to the whims of a single great landlord, and as domestic clothiers they were not tied to a single merchant or group of merchants who controlled access to markets. By continuing to limit the influence and authority that England's traditional rulers, the landed elite, could exert over the middling sort, these socioeconomic structures helped to maintain important aspects of this culture of independence even though the particularly Puritan articulation of it was no longer so important.

Of course, Puritanism did not disappear after 1660. Despite the changed circumstances, many features of the middling sort's Puritan culture survived in the form of a vigorous Dissenting tradition in the parish. Thanks to Oliver Heywood's prolific pen, his congregation at Coley Chapel is the best known of Halifax's Dissenting chapels, but there were others—Matthew Smith's congregation at Mixenden, Henry Root's at Sowerby, Eli Bentley's in Halifax town, and, representing the more radical side of religious developments during the Civil War, active Quaker meetings in Halifax and Brighouse.[35] Within this Dissenting culture, hierarchy continued to be as important as it had been before the Civil War. Heywood's diaries suggest that his worldview, like that of most of his contemporaries, was fundamentally hierarchical, for he makes constant reference to the social status of the people he mentions. They also suggest how heavily Dissent in Halifax depended on the good offices of some of the local gentlemen. Joshua Horton, for instance, built a meetinghouse at his own expense in the township of Sowerby, and Heywood and other Nonconformists preached there on a rotating basis.[36]

35. Heywood, *Autobiography*; H. Armitage, "Mixenden Chapel," *THAS*, 1964, 1–15; James Miall, *Congregationalism in Yorkshire* (London, 1868), 245–377; T. W. Hanson, "Henry Root and the Congregational Church of Sowerby," *Congregational History Society Transactions* 6 (1913–15): 327–32; University of Leeds, Brotherton Library, Friends Archives, EE/16/bis, Halifax Preparative Meeting, and Q4, Brighouse Monthly Meeting.
36. Heywood, *Autobiography*, 1:347; 2:260–61.

Heywood's respect for the gentry, however, was contingent on their beliefs and behavior. He reported with distaste and obvious disrespect that Thomas Thornhill, one of the local gentry, was heard to sing a bawdy song on his way to a horse race in the company of a justice of the peace and his brother. This JP, William Horton, appears again as the winner of a large wager at a cockfight; Thornhill was in attendance again, as were John Greenwood, James Oates, and Edmund Deane. Heywood's complaint about these gentlemen is clear. As he ruefully remarked on another occasion, "I have seldom heard of so many young women with child by fornication as lately...; in Halifax on Easter-day multitudes were playing at stoolball etc. in the streets. Oh what will be the end of these things, no restraint, no magistrate to put them to shame."[37] Far from suppressing such sinful activities, these gentlemen were encouraging them and were thus not worthy of deference.

Other passages in Heywood's diary suggest that aspects of this culture of independence were not confined to Dissenters. In May 1680 a great cockfight was to be held at the inn owned by Widow Mitchell in Halifax, and the event attracted gentlemen from the West Riding and even Lancashire. Heywood records that some trouble arose on the second day, when

> the poorer sort of Halifax brought their cocks which were to fight first, but Mr. Thomas Thornhill said what had beggars to do to fight their cocks among gentlemen, upon which Thomas Cockcroft's son tripped up his heels so they fell to blows, and they took sides and all fought desperately a long while, Abe Mitchell taking the poor men's part. At last John Mitchell drew his rapier and swore he would run him through that struck another stroke.

The cockfight then commenced, and, according to Heywood, not without a little pride showing through his disapproval, the Halifax cocks generally beat the gentlemen's.[38]

On the surface this appears to be another instance in which the local gentry were setting the poor a bad example, as they had done at a horse race on Swaithes Moor which attracted idlers from Halifax, Boothtown, Ovenden, and Holdsworth.[39] A closer reading,

---

37. Ibid., 2:274, 293–94, 279.
38. Ibid., 271–72.
39. Ibid., 279–80.

however, suggests that there was more to it than that. A crucial difference between a cockfight and a horse race is that while only a very few could afford to keep a racing horse, almost anyone could keep a cock. Though people of all social ranks might attend a horse race, the actual contests were between the gentleman's horses and thus reaffirmed hierarchy. The contests in a cockfight, in contrast, could cross social boundaries and thus could challenge hierarchy.

This was indeed what happened at Widow Mitchell's inn when Thornhill objected to the prospect of his cock's being tested against those of "beggars."[40] If the objection itself is not surprising, the reaction to it is. Thomas Cockcroft's son, who did the tripping, must have taken offense at the implication that his cock was not up to those of the gentlemen. Moreover, since his retaliation ended in a brawl and not a simple summons for assault, his feelings must have been shared by a good proportion of the men present. The whole episode reveals a contingent perception of the social superiority of the gentry in a group of men who were anything but Puritans.

A brief examination of one of the central characters of this episode confirms that the social relations of the middling sort were not confined to Puritans. Abe Mitchell, who took "the poor men's part," was anything but a poor man. The son of a wealthy draper, he was one of the parish's pseudogentlemen.[41] Yet his role in this little drama suggests that it might be better to think of him as one of the middling sort—albeit one who was untypically wealthy, for if he took the poor men's part in the brawl, he must have felt with Cockcroft the slight of Thornhill's objection to fights between gentle and plebian cocks.

Though the decline of Puritanism after the Restoration may have robbed the culture of the middling sort of one particularly coherent form of expression, their social relations with the local gentry continued to combine deference with independence, for carousers such as Abe Mitchell shared with Puritans such as Oliver Heywood and Jonathan Priestly a worldview that acknowledged the gentry's social superiority on a only contingent basis.

40. Heywood's straightforward account of this incident suggests that he, and perhaps others, did not consciously consider the highly relevant double meaning of the word "cock." Whether the colloquial meaning was explicit or implicit, it is clear that masculinity, and hence power, was an important issue in the subsequent contest.

41. Pearson, *History of Northowram*, 232.

INCLUSIVENESS AND EGALITARIANISM

The egalitarian character of the culture of Halifax's middling sort, like its independence, had its roots in the period leading up to the Civil War, and it too was conceived in Puritan terms.

Scholars have suggested that Puritanism adopted two distinct guises as it appeared in various communities in early-modern England.[42] One guise can be described as "social control" Puritanism.[43] Its significant feature was the message of social control implicit in Puritanism's distinctive doctrine and practice. Social-control Puritanism often appeared in communities that were experiencing rapid social polarization and consequent unrest, and its proponents, usually local gentlemen and yeomen, used Puritanism as part of a culture of discipline that they imposed upon an unruly element in the community. Puritanism also appeared in an egalitarian guise, whose significant feature was the inherent independence of Protestant theology and worship.[44] Egalitarian Puritanism appeared in communities, often upland or urban ones, that lacked a strong local gentleman and where economic and social conditions allowed immigration and economic independence.

Insofar as it is safe to distinguish between these two types of Puritanism in early modern England, Halifax certainly seems to fit in the latter category, for the middling sort's Puritanism was not socially exclusive. The autobiography of Oliver Heywood, for instance, reveals a social world where belief was more important than social status. When he first lived in the parish, this Puritan divine lodged in a household whose head he described as "the epitome of carnality" but where one of the servants was a "humble, gracious christian." Similarly, describing his decision to accept the ministry at Coley in 1650, Heywood gave some weight to the support of "the best people" in the chapelry, but he also took into account the "multitude that flocked up to show their free consent and call of me."[45]

The egalitarian nature of Halifax's Puritanism was not a cultural anomaly; the social and economic factors that made Puritanism attrac-

---

42. Hughes, "Local History," 242; Peter Clark, *English Provincial Society from the Reformation to the Revolution* (Hassocks, Sussex, 1977), 173–78.
43. William Hunt, *The Puritan Moment: The Coming of Revolution to an English County* (Cambridge, Mass., 1983); Wrightson and Levine, *Poverty and Piety*.
44. James, *Family, Lineage and Civil Society*; Brian Manning, *The English People and the English Revolution* (London, 1976).
45. Heywood, *Autobiography*, 1:163–65.

tive to yeomen and wealthy artisans also worked for their more humble neighbors. The presence of the textile industry spread the influence—positive and negative—of the developing market economy throughout the parish. Similarly, the social independence of an upland parish affected more than just the relatively well-to-do. If a poor family of domestic clothiers could not choose their own preacher by endowing a lectureship, they still had a choice of services to attend in the parish's numerous chapelries.

Though the egalitarian character of the middling sort's culture was expressed largely in the language of Puritanism, it, too, was shaped by socioeconomic reality. This relationship continued after the Restoration, despite the demise of the Puritan ideology within which it had been articulated. The central feature of the social and economic structures that persisted in Halifax throughout the seventeenth century was an economy that was fluid enough to allow individuals to increase or decrease the stock with which they had started out in life but at the same time set limits, especially at the upper end, to the mobility that was possible.[46] The society that arose in these circumstances was dominated by a large and relatively undifferentiated social middle. The argument is not that there were no social differences in Halifax but that the continuum within the social structure was more evident. People at the two extremes might appear to differ greatly—an affluent family that made and finished perhaps two or three pieces of cloth a week in their five- or six-hearth house could never be confused with a poor family that might just manage to make a piece of cloth a week in their one-hearth cottage. Between these two extremes, however, was a very solid social and economic continuum.

Egalitarianism, then, was a feature of the socioeconomic reality of the parish throughout the seventeenth century. Having found expression in the social inclusiveness of the middling sort's Puritanism before the war, it continued to be important in the parish's vigorous Dissent-

---

46. The history of the Priestly family illustrates this point very neatly, for the fortunes of individuals in the different generations of the family varied. Jonathan, his father, and his uncles did reasonably well out of the relatively small inheritances they received. Joseph Priestly, Samuel and Jonathan's father, was in the cloth trade and had done well enough to warrant maintaining a shop in the town of Halifax in addition to the work he did on the farm his father left him, valued at £25 a year. Two of Samuel's uncles pooled the portions they received from their father and, starting with a stock of £100, accumulated nearly £700 by the end of their lives. Jonathan reports that he had started life with only the inheritance of £20 he received from his father. Other family members, however, were less careful with their inheritances and died in penury: "Memoirs Concerning the Priestlys."

ing community. Indeed, the very survival of Dissent depended on the support that men such as Oliver Heywood received from the entire congregation when they were deprived of their livings in 1662.[47]

The egalitarian streak in the middling sort's culture was not confined to Dissenters; it is evident, for example, in the structure and workings of local government. In the townships of Sowerby and Halifax, where lists of the officers survive from the period of the hearth tax, participation was spread across the social spectrum. Although householders with between three and five hearths predominated in the ranks of the officeholders, those with one or two hearths could also serve their townships in an official capacity, and all of these officers carried out their duties with a large measure of independence.[48] The vestries that approved the officers' accounts and allowed them assessments were open to all rate payers, and there is no evidence that small groups of select individuals dominated local government in this period.[49]

Further evidence about the broad social basis of Halifax's middling sort comes from what probate inventories reveal about material culture. While the inventories show vast differences in the number of items owned by the various decedents and their total value, an examination of the value of specific kinds of goods and of the range of goods available to the residents of Halifax suggests a relatively undifferentiated material culture.[50] Items such as tables, chairs, stools, cooking utensils—the basic household furnishings—show some variation in value but the differences are not significant. Put simply, rich people did not own nicer chairs, they merely owned more of them. The only exception is the value of the bedding, which did reflect the family's overall wealth.

When we turn from basic household goods to luxuries, the pattern that emerges is of fairly widespread ownership of some of the items that could be considered luxury goods in the later seventeenth century. Out of a total of 292 inventories from the period between 1690 and

---

47. Armitage, "Mixenden Chapel," 3–4; Miall, *Congregationalism in Yorkshire*, 325; Heywood, *Autobiography*, 4:128.

48. CDA/MIC/8, Halifax churchwardens' accounts; CDA/SPL/143, 144, Sowerby constables' accounts. The names of officers were matched with the hearth tax returns: PRO/E.179/210/393.

49. Accounts survive from this period for the following townships in the parish: CDA/SPL/143, Sowerby constables' accounts, 1620–1805; CDA/HAS/69 (766), Northowram town book; CDA/HAS/65 (767), Hipperholme town book, 1665–1785; and CDA/MIC/8, Halifax churchwardens' accounts.

50. For a discussion of probate evidence in more detail, see Lorna Weatherill, *Consumer Behavior and Material Culture in Britain, 1660–1760* (London, 1988).

1699, almost a third (28 percent) owned clocks, a third (32 percent) owned at least some linen, a quarter (24 percent) owned glass cases, a quarter (23 percent) owned one or more mirrors, and, slightly more exclusively, a sixth (15 percent) owned dishes made of white plate. Yet the people who owned such items were not confined to the wealthiest stratum of the parish. Paupers, of course, did not own clocks, linen, or white plate, but above that lower bound such goods appear in households across the social spectrum, and they are not invariably found in the inventories of the well-to-do. Some items, of course, appeared in only a few inventories, and these were limited to the households of the wealthier members of the community. Only three households, for instance, owned chairs made of "russia leather," only nine had curtains on their windows, and only seven had maps decorating their walls. Yet the differential ownership of these very exclusive luxury goods was a matter of taste rather than a mark of social difference, for it was very rare for an inventory to list more than one of this type of goods.

The material belongings of the parishioners, then, are consistent with the general image of a largely egalitarian culture. Although there were lower bounds that were not often crossed, a relatively large group shared a common material culture. The significance of this material culture is hard to judge, but it must have been important that members of Halifax's middling sort, despite differences in their wealth and social standing, would have felt at home in each other's houses.

There is always the danger, of course, of reading too much into such evidence; it is therefore fortunate that a rare glimpse into the day-to-day lives of Halifax's middling sort in the period after the Restoration amply confirms the egalitarian character of their culture. This material comes from a Consistory court case over the disputed will of a wealthy yeoman clothier, Jonathan Baumforth, who left two wills when he died in 1720.[51] It was not uncommon for people to revise their wills as their circumstances changed, either through codicils or by making new ones, but trouble arose in Baumforth's case because he had suffered a "fit of palsie" (a stroke) between 1716, when he made his first will, and 1720 when he made his second. When his widow, who was the chief beneficiary of the second will, started the probate process, the executors named in the first will stepped in on behalf of the cousin who was named as the chief beneficiary of the first will. Their claim, which

---

51. BIY/CP, I/497, 498, 502, testamentary, Stead v. Baumforth. I/498 contains the depositions of the people named in the following paragraphs.

The Middling Sort and Their World

formed the whole basis of their case, was that as a result of the "fit of palsie" Baumforth had not been of sound mind when he made the second will. The testimony given by more than thirty witnesses was designed to establish the mental competency of Jonathan Baumforth in the weeks that passed between the day he suffered the stroke and the day he made his second will.

What is perhaps most striking about the social relations revealed in these depositions is the degree to which a relatively wealthy man such as Baumforth (the estate was valued at around £1,000) fraternized with his social inferiors. Indeed, the pejorative connotation of the word "fraternize" suggests a whole set of social distinctions that Baumforth did not perceive. Jonathan Hargreaves, a collier, described his visit to Baumforth just after the stroke. He had come to make one of his regular deliveries of coal and found the testator at home. Baumforth invited him in and asked if he would "club his two pence for ale"; Hargreaves did so, and they spent about an hour talking and drinking together. Two days later Hargreaves arrived with more coal and the two settled their account. Having paid his bill, Baumforth invoked the "old use and custom" that upon the settlement of an account, Hargreaves would put in four pence to Baumforth's two. Hargreaves testified that they duly sent for sixpence worth of ale and conversed for about two hours as they drank it.

Similar stories told by other deponents indicate that Hargreaves's relationship with Baumforth was typical of the way that this wealthy yeoman dealt with his neighbors, suppliers, and even workers. The overall impression of Baumforth's social relations is of an easy communality, and the sense of social equality is emphasized by the fact that most of his visitors "clubbed their two pence" with Baumforth, despite the fact that he must have been somewhat, if not considerably, wealthier than they were.

This is not to say that status distinctions were not there. People who were younger than Baumforth and other people's servants were often offered a bite to eat or even some beer without being asked to contribute to the common purse. John Hargreaves (age 25), the servant of a merchant who bought cloth from Baumforth, reported that when he finished his master's business with Baumforth, "the company having some liquor before them, . . . Jonathan Baumforth asked [him] to drink with them," and when he left, Baumforth gave him a penny. Similarly, Anthony Croyser (age 25) testified that he had come to see Baumforth to bring him the two pieces of cloth he had just finished weaving and to see about what kinds of cloth Baumforth wanted made next. Their business done, Baumforth "ordered his wife to set him some victuals." These instances suggest that Baumforth, because of his wealth, was expected to be a bit more generous than others might be, but even though these young men were not "equal" enough to pay their own way, they were invited to join the company instead of being excluded from it.

Gender was another important mark of social distinction within the culture of the middling sort. Baumforth was very civil with his "employee" Anthony Croyser, but he did not hesitate to "order" his wife to serve him some food. Baumforth seems to have been a little less dismissive of women outside of his immediate household. Several women were among Baumforth's visitors, and though his interactions with them were similar to his dealings with male visitors, we can note differences. When Sara Pollard called, for instance, they clubbed only one penny for ale instead of the more usual twopence. Yet if they drank less, women were still expected to go equal shares in purchasing the "joint stock." Judith Wood found this out one day when she asked for a pipe of tobacco. Baumforth refused, but when she asked if he would club his penny with hers, he agreed and they enjoyed a pipe together. Even more important, women, like younger men, were included in the socializing that went on around Baumforth's fireplace; they were not relegated to a separate sphere.

CONCLUSION

The distinct features of the culture of Halifax's middling sort are perhaps best expressed in a pair of images. The first is of Jonathan Baumforth sitting by his fireside, being visited by neighbors and "business" associates and sharing with them a mug of beer and some conversation. This image encapsulates the social inclusiveness of Halifax's middling sort in the latter seventeenth century. With the possible exception of people such as the "beggar boy" who anonymously received his penny and disappeared, Baumforth's world was not one of clearly demarcated social stations or even social roles.[52] Business—both with his economic equals and with his workmen—and pleasure, the old and the young, men and women were all mixed together. This was not some

---

52. Ibid. The reference to the beggar boy is from the deposition of Grace Hargreaves.

kind of artisanal golden age; the conversations reported in the depositions included worries about the state of the trade and almost plaintive requests for more work, as well as humorous stories and calls for more ale. The lives of Halifax's middling sort were not exempt from the problems and inequalities of the seventeenth century; but their lives unfolded within a cultural context characterized by assumptions of relative equality within the fairly large group identifiable as the middling sort.

The other image, one that illustrates the character of the middling sort's relations with the gentry, is of Abe Mitchell taking a swing at Thomas Thornhill, Esq., in a cockyard brawl in 1680. Mitchell's attack on the "poor men's part" is as suggestive of the middling sort's contingent deference to the landed elite as is Jonathan Priestly's proud description of his brother Samuel's decision to join Fairfax and fight the king. Both Priestly and Mitchell were part of a social group whose culture made such challenges to the generally acknowledged privileges of the gentry quite possible, and, if provoked, quite likely. Moreover, Abe Mitchell seems to have shared other aspects of the culture of Halifax's middling sort. The depositions in a defamation case of the same period depict a scene in which Abe Mitchell, one or two other pseudogentlemen (including the John Greenwood who lost £30 to Justice Horton in a cockfight), and a dyer were drinking in an alehouse or tavern one day when one of the company boasted that he had fathered a bastard by the alehouse keeper's wife. Mitchell himself did not give a deposition, but his drinking companions, both the "gentlemen" and the dyer, were involved enough in the dispute to know details of the relationship between the alehouse keeper and his wife.[53] Like Jonathan Baumforth, then, this wealthy draper did not keep very exclusive company.

Both of these aspects of the culture of Halifax's middling sort must be understood with reference to the socioeconomic reality that shaped them, for there was a relationship between the economy and social structure of late-seventeenth-century Halifax and the way in which the middling sort understood their place in the social order. The characteristics of Halifax's economy—fragmented landholding, poor agricultural potential, and a thriving rural textile industry—explain a great

---

53. BIY/CP, H/3489, defamation, Lister v. Barraclough, 1682. Another defamation case of the same period finds two other "gentlemen" drinking in an alehouse and involved in local scandal: BIY/CP, H/3659, defamation, Saville v. Ramsden, 1685.

deal about the culture of the middling sort. The independence provided by the woolen industry enabled members of the middling sort to question the authority of the local gentry. Similarly, the woolen industry made individual advancement a possibility; as a result, social distinctions were difficult to maintain, for a person who started out as a poor servant might die a wealthy yeoman. The effects of biological fortune coupled with the practice of partible inheritance thus made the creation of status groups difficult in the long term, for it was unlikely that wealth accumulated in one generation would be kept together for long.

The relationship between culture and reality, however, must be recognized as reflexive. While reality does determine culture in the sense that members of a group construct their understanding of their world on the basis of the reality in which they live, culture also determines how that reality works, for it shapes people's behavior. The middling sort's assumptions about the social order of Halifax, and particularly their egalitarianism, helped to preserve the structure of the socioeconomic reality.

Oliver Heywood's diaries suggest, for instance, that he harbored a profound distrust of people whose economic activities took them above their station. He described Thomas Whitley, for instance, as a "mighty usurer, exceeding rich." Similarly, in his reflections on instances of God's providence Heywood took a certain relish in describing the cases of men who had made themselves rich and had then come to grief. Even his description of his own family's history implies that worldly success was less important than godly living; he glosses his father's failure in business as God's punishment for his greed.[54] As a committed Dissenting minister, of course, Heywood is rather untypical; but when we find his cultural assumptions about wealth echoed in Jonathan Priestly's memoirs we may see in this cultural tradition the Puritan or even Protestant understanding that wealth was acceptable only so long as it was used in appropriate ways.[55]

This attitude toward inappropriate wealth was not confined to Puritans or Dissenters; rather, it was a feature of the middling sort's sense of an egalitarian social order. One of the depositions concerning Baumforth's two wills recorded a conversation in which Baumforth asked his visitor what news there was in the *Daily Courant*. Jonathan Hargreaves

---

54. Heywood, *Autobiography*, 2:263, 274; 3:207; 1:17, 19–22.
55. "Memoirs Concerning the Priestlys"; Paul Seaver, "The Puritan Work Ethic Revisited," *Journal of British Studies* 19 (1980): 35–53.

replied that there was something about "Stock Jobbing" (he was referring to the bursting of the South Sea Bubble) but that he did not really understand it, and he asked if Baumforth knew what it was all about. Baumforth replied that "he could not tell what it was, but he was afraid it would ruin a deal of rich men, for if they sent cloth away they could not get no money for it." Baumforth was just expressing a traditional, and in his case not very well-informed, distrust of stockjobbing; but we are struck by the fact that this wealthy yeoman clothier saw the South Sea Bubble from the perspective of a producer, and he expected his visitor, a collier, to share his view. Within a generation, his economic equals were happily investing in the funds when they reached the end of their productive lives. They no longer assumed, as Baumforth seems to have done, that their economic world was the same as that of honest artisans.

Another conversation gives much the same impression and suggests the extent to which these cultural assumptions about relative equality could determine the shape of economic reality. In this instance, Baumforth asked his visitor "how trading went, and wondered how poor folks got a living the trade was so bad." The visitor replied that none of his neighbors "got any thing but one John Mackerill whom he took to be a saving man."[56] What precisely he meant by "a saving man" is unclear, but the term was not a compliment. The implication was that one man ought not to do better than his neighbors. Although this cultural assumption was not universally shared—John Mackerill was making money somehow—it must have had a profound impact on the potential for economic change within the world of the middling sort.

56. BIY/CP, I/498, depositions of Jonathan Hargreaves and John Badget.

PART I

Process: The Making of a Middle-Class Experience

The relationship between the middling sort of late-seventeenth-century Halifax and any potential middle class appears to be problematic. The coherence of the middling sort's world can be overstated, but it did exist; there were important ways in which economic and social practice and cultural understandings of that practice agreed with each other. But given the coherence of the middling sort's world as it existed in seventeenth-century Halifax, there does not seem to have been much potential for the emergence of a class identity, for the middling sort did not have an identity of (economic) interests between themselves and against "other men." Not that this was a society without conflict; rather, identities based on conflict, such as that between Dissenters and the establish church, were overlain by other competing identities, such as neighborhood or "country" independence.

It could not even be argued that the socioeconomic experience of the middling sort would have supported a class identity. The social and economic practice of the middling sort was not differentiated in ways even remotely suggestive of class experience. Class experience is not the same as class identity, but it is necessary for the emergence of class identity. Thus the story about the origins of middle-class culture must begin with an analysis of how a "common experience" capable of giving rise to a middle-class identity came into being.[1]

---

1. E. P. Thompson, *The Making of the English Working Class* (Harmondsworth, 1968), 8.

The attempt to answer this question confronts one of the central problems of cultural theory—the explanation of how cultures change. The great strength of cultural theory as a tool for social analysis is its emphasis on the role that culture plays as an intermediary between socioeconomic reality and the individual. The individual subject meets the objective world through the screen of culture, for culture (which is a property of groups, not of individuals) shapes experience by structuring the meanings that individuals give to their world. For many historians, and increasingly for many anthropologists as well, the value of this insight is marred by its curiously static and ahistorical picture of culture.[2] The wonderful readings of events as varied as cockfights, riots, and carnivals do not deny the fact of historical change, but the fit that is shown to exist between actions, meanings, and the world seems to preclude the possibility of change from within. The instance that concerns us here is a case in point. Given the coherence of the middling sort's culture—the fit between their world and the meanings they gave to their world—how did change happen? Given that actions, perceptions, and thus reality were shaped by the culture of the middling sort, how did a new kind of experience, a middle-class experience, emerge?

To answer this question it is not necessary to abandon cultural theory. An analysis based on the theory of practice makes possible an account of cultural change that both inserts a historical perspective into cultural theory and avoids the problems that arise from locating the causes of change entirely in the realm of socioeconomic reality or, conversely, entirely in the realm of individual action.[3] It does so by emphasizing the reflexive nature of the relationship between culture, reality, and the individual, and by focusing on how these reflexive relationships are maintained or changed through the practices of individuals as they lead their lives. The theory acknowledges that cultural structures constrain the actions of individuals by shaping their perceptions of their world, but it also stresses that these structures are con-

---

2. For two discussions of this limitation of cultural theory, one by a historian and the other by an anthropologist, see William Sewell, *Work and Revolution in France: The Language of Labor from the Old Regime to 1848* (Cambridge, 1980), 10–13, and Renato Rosaldo, "From the Door of His Tent," in *Writing Culture: The Poetics and Politics of Ethnography*, ed. James Clifford and George E. Marcus (Berkeley, 1986).

3. For discussions of this issue see William Sewell, "How Classes Are Made: Critical Reflections on E. P. Thompson's Theory of Working-Class Formation," in *E. P. Thompson: Critical Perspectives*, ed. Harvey Kaye and Keith McClelland (Cambridge, 1990); William Reddy, *The Rise of Market Culture* (Cambridge, 1984), and his *Money and Liberty in Modern Europe: A Critique of Historical Understanding* (New York, 1987).

stantly being remade by the actions they inform. In short, the theory of practice recognizes that culture both structures and is structured by practice *in time*.[4]

This mode of analysis is particularly relevant here, for an account of the origins of middle-class culture cannot claim that the culture changed as a result of external influences. In contrast, consider the case of the working class. E. P. Thompson argues, in essence, that working-class experience emerged as individuals who shared an artisanal culture construed the new economic, political, and social relations that developed as a result of industrialization. Such an argument has the advantage of maintaining the relationship between culture and action while allowing for change, but the impetus for change is located wholly outside the culture in question. In the right context, such a point of view is perfectly valid. It has, for instance, been developed in the anthropological literature by scholars interested in producing a historicized account of the interactions between traditional cultures and Western influences.[5] This approach, however, will not help to explain the transition from middling sort to middle class, because the changes involved were largely internal to the culture in question. A middle-class experience may have emerged as individuals responded to industrialization, but it was the same group of people were making industrialization happen in the first place. The theory of practice is vital for this analysis because it suggests that change can occur slowly as a result of shifting structures of practice. Between the late seventeenth and mid-eighteenth centuries new cultural structures emerged in Halifax which encompassed both new economic and social practices

---

4. Pierre Bourdieu's work is particularly important in this regard, for he argues that the element of time is crucial for unraveling the structuralist's account of a changeless society: *Outline of a Theory of Practice*, trans. Richard Nice (Cambridge, 1977).

5. Marshall Sahlins's description of Captain James Cook's reception in the Hawaiian Islands and Renato Rosaldo's history of Ilongot headhunting both embrace the issue of change and incorporate it quite deftly in their cultural perspective. Yet in both cases, and in Thompson's English working class as well, the cultural changes were ultimately caused by external influences—Captain Cook, different phases of colonial rule, and the spread of capitalist market relations, respectively: Marshall Sahlins, *Islands of History* (Chicago, 1985); Renato Rosaldo, *Ilongot Headhunting* (Stanford, 1980). There are two caveats to my comments on these works. First, these cultural changes were a "reaction" only at the level of the system as a whole; all three of these works offer carefully nuanced discussions of the role that individual action plays in cultural change. Second, the model of cultural change used in these instances is quite appropriate for the questions that these authors address, for in each case there *were* significant external influences on the course of events. Such an approach is inadequate, however, for the particular historical problem posed by the origins of the middle class.

and a new cultural framework in which those practices were construed. This process happened as a dual result of the way individuals *reacted* to changing economic and social circumstances and the way they *acted* out the implications of changes in how they were construing their world, and its outcome was the common experience of a distinct group, a nascent middle class.

Process is thus the main theme of both of the chapters of Part I. Chapter 3 examines the economic and cultural changes in the wool textile industry. Because this industry was so important to the economy of the parish, the relatively significant changes that occurred between the late seventeenth and mid-eighteenth centuries are of singular importance to an understanding of the origins of Halifax's middle class. The effect of this economic development was twofold. First, it created a substantial group of wealthy families, a group much larger than the marginal gentry of the late seventeenth century and much wealthier than the middling sort. Second, it made this group much more dependent on capitalist market relations for their wealth than either the marginal gentry or the middling sort had been. The developments in the woolen industry in this period were not revolutionary. The wealth of the merchants and manufacturers and the new modes of production that brought them that wealth evolved gradually, but both helped to create the common social experience necessary for the emergence of a middle-class identity.

Chapter 4 examines changes in the money market and in patterns of consumption during the same period, developments that were corollaries of the changes occurring in the textile industry. These changes suggest that the implications of changes in the textile industry extended well beyond the workshop and cloth market. As in Chapter 3, the analysis shows that these changes were the results of simultaneous and related economic and cultural developments—shifting structures of practice.

Part I also explores some of the issues that arise when cultural theory is applied to complex societies. Halifax was not a cultural island. Therefore, the analysis of the making of a middle-class experience in Halifax must determine the extent to which cultural changes resulted from developments peculiar to the parish or from processes that were occurring in England as a whole. Existing articulations of cultural theory are not particularly helpful here because they tend to deal with relatively undifferentiated societies. It is possible, however, to adapt the theory in ways that make it relevant for more complex societies by stressing the process of appropriation, as Roger Chartier does.[6] The same kind of reflexivity that occurs between culture and reality also occurs between the purely local and the regional or national versions of culture as themes are appropriated and then reabsorbed. This issue, touched on in Chapter 3's discussion of how developments in the textile industry were influenced by the changing structure of the market, is at the center of the analysis of Chapter 4. The changes in Halifax's money market and its patterns of consumption were related to much broader processes of change occurring in the region and the country as a whole. Yet cultural change that occurred in Halifax was not merely a pale reflection of larger, more important changes elsewhere. Rather, a distinct middle-class experience evolved during this period as a result of the ways in which developments in the country as a whole were appropriated in the specific socioeconomic context of Halifax.

6. Roger Chartier, *The Cultural Origins of the French Revolution*, trans. Lydia Cochrane (Durham, N.C., 1991).

Chapter 3

Economic and Cultural Change in Halifax's Textile Industry

Between the late seventeenth and late eighteenth centuries the wool textile industry in the West Riding of Yorkshire grew at a dramatic rate, surpassing its regional rivals in the West Country and East Anglia.[1] The extent of this growth is suggested by the West Riding's increasing share of the export market for English cloth: 20 percent at the beginning of the century, nearly 50 percent by 1770.[2] A less impressionistic measure of the industry's growth in the region is given by the records of the Riding's cloth searchers, who recorded the numbers of broad and narrow cloths that were milled before sale (see the accompanying graph). These figures, moreover, exclude worsted cloth, which was one of the most dynamic sectors of the West Riding's textile industry. Practically unknown before 1700, the Riding's worsted industry had almost caught up with the woolen industry in the 1770s as measured by the value of the goods produced, and it had equaled East Anglia's worsted production, once the greatest in England.

Since there is no way of disaggregating these figures, it is impossible

---

1. R. G. Wilson, "The Supremacy of the Yorkshire Cloth Industry in the Eighteenth Century," in *Textile History and Economic History: Essays in Honour of Miss Julia de Lacy Mann*, ed. N. B. Harte and K. G. Ponting (Manchester, 1973); Derek Gregory, *Regional Transformation and Industrial Revolution: A Geography of the Yorkshire Woollen Industry* (Minneapolis, 1982).

2. Wilson, "Supremacy," 229; John James, *History of the Worsted Manufacture in England* (London, 1857), 280–82, the evidence of Thomas Wolrich of Leeds, merchant, before Parliament. Wolrich's report is also printed in James Bischoff, *A Comprehensive History of the Woollen and Worsted Manufactures* (London, 1852), 1:187.

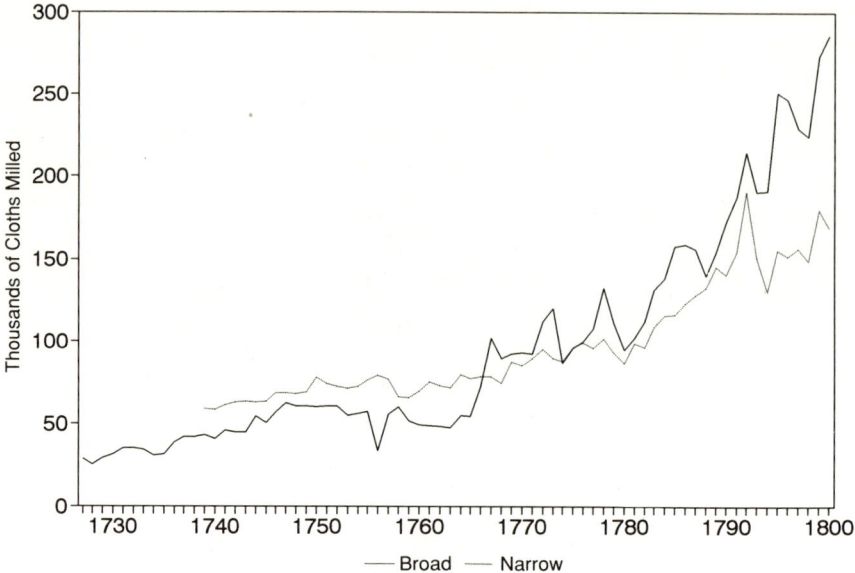

Number of broad and narrow cloths milled, West Riding of Yorkshire, 1728–1800. British Parliamentary Papers, 1806 (268), vol. 3, *Report on the Woollen Manufacture*, 25.

to give a precise indication of the place that Halifax had in the West Riding's textile industry. Certainly it was important, for Halifax was accounted one of the centers of the West Riding woolen region, along with Leeds and Wakefield. That the parish's economy grew significantly in the eighteenth century is suggested by the growth in its population and prosperity. In a period when the population of the nation as a whole was rising only slowly if at all, Halifax's population grew dramatically, from 3,844 households in 1664 to 8,263 in 1764. The population continued to increase in the latter part of the eighteenth century, reaching 12,031 households by 1801.[3] Given the parish's meager agricultural endowment, it is probable that these families made their living by producing textiles. Although wealth is more difficult to measure, developments in the textile industry made at least some of the parish's residents considerably richer during this period. After 1750 several large mansions were built in the parish and comforts suited to the pocketbooks of the well-to-do became much more common. The

---

3. PRO/E.179/210/393, hearth tax returns, Lady Day 1664; CDA/MISC:8/116/21, vicar's "census," 1764.

growth of the textile industry in the parish and the group of wealthy merchants and manufacturers it created brought about cultural changes central to the emergence of a distinctive middle-class experience.

THE EMERGENCE OF MANUFACTURING

The increase in the production of textiles in Halifax was achieved, in part, through an expansion of the domestic system. The small amount of credit necessary to start up as a clothier, the availability of land, and even the life-cycle expectations of domestic clothiers made it possible for independent artisans to multiply, as apparently they did, if we may judge by the growth of the parish's population and a continuing process of enclosing wasteland and building cottages. The more important change in Halifax's woolen industry during the eighteenth century, however, was structural, for growth was associated with the emergence of a more centralized mode of production. Whereas cloth-making in Halifax had relied on independent artisans who produced cloth for sale in the local market, it became increasingly dominated by individuals described as merchant-manufacturers or simply manufacturers. The manufacturers' relations of production were different from those of merchants and artisans in the domestic system. Like merchants, they sold large quantities of cloth on the national and international markets, but unlike them, they were directly involved in the production of the cloth, buying wool, getting it spun, and getting the yarn woven into cloth. Like domestic clothiers, manufacturers produced cloth, but unlike them, they paid other people to do the work. Manufacturers thus combined and transformed the roles of merchant and clothier, organizing the production of large quantities of cloth by wage laborers and then selling it themselves, often by-passing the local market entirely.

The earliest evidence for this kind of structural change in Halifax's textile industry comes from inventories of the later seventeenth century.[4] These records reveal that some individuals possessed far more textile goods than even wealthy domestic clothiers. The scale of these

---

4. John Smail, "Manufacturer or Artisan: The Relationship between Economic and Cultural Change in the Early Years of Eighteenth-Century Industrialization," *Journal of Social History* 25 (1992): 791–814.

manufacturers' activities varied considerably. Some of the early manufacturers confined their activities to finishing.[5] Thomas Longbotham had a well-equipped finishing shop in his house, with shears, shear boards, presses, and tenters valued at £34 and a large stock of kerseys valued at £200 when he died in 1693. Other manufacturers dyed the kerseys before finishing them: Thomas Kitson left behind dyestuffs and vats worth £85 and a large stock of colored and white kersey cloths valued at £220. Still other manufacturers were directly engaged in making large quantities of kerseys. Like Longbotham, Nathaniel Kershaw had a reasonable stock of finishing tools and £135 worth of kersey cloth, but he also owned £87 in wool and yarn. Since Kershaw left a bequest in his will to the "spinners of my wool or makers of my cloth," he was probably putting this large stock of raw materials out for spinning and weaving and then finishing the cloth in his own shop. The inventory of another manufacturer, Benjamin Holroyd, records "pieces in the makers hands" worth £49, while that of Daniel Walker records some cloth "out at making."[6]

Since no probate inventories before 1689 survive, it is impossible to be certain that Longbotham, Kitson, and Kershaw were among the first of Halifax's textile manufacturers, but that is the impression the evidence gives. Their limited numbers—only 32 out of a sample of 497 inventories from 1690 to 1716 belonged to manufacturers—and the limited scale on which many of them operated suggest that in the decades around 1700 the market was only just becoming suited to such businesses.[7] It is likely that the emergence of large-scale manufacturing in Halifax after the 1690s was associated with the general improvement in the fortunes of the English textile industry that occurred as a result of the wars undertaken by William III.[8]

Although manufacturing eventually undermined the domestic system in Halifax, initially the two were compatible. Both depended on the same infrastructure of trading links, fulling mills, and even labor. Man-

---

5. Finishing consisted of fulling, tentering, and, finally, cropping.

6. BIY/OW, Thomas Longbotham, Northowram, August 1693; Thomas Kitson, Northowram, August 1692; Nathaniel Kershaw, Soyland, April 1692; Benjamin Holroyd, Rishworth, April 1718; Daniel Walker, Hipperholme, September 1690.

7. This sample comprises all probate records for the years 1690–1701, 1705, 1706, 1710, 1711, 1715, and 1716. Of the 497 testators in this sample, 211 had some textile goods in their inventories.

8. D. W. Jones, *War and Economy in the Age of William III and Marlborough* (Oxford, 1988). Heaton also argues that the fortunes of the wool textile industry improved from the turn of the century: *Yorkshire Woollen and Worsted Industry* (Oxford, 1920), 255.

ufacturers such as Kershaw probably bought some of their cloth from independent clothiers in the market and relied on their own makers for either regular work or types of cloth that needed special attention. Thus the market was still the main conduit for the transfer of goods between producer and merchant, and the infrastructure that supported the domestic clothier remained largely intact.[9]

More important, manufacturing and individual manufacturers seem to have emerged quite naturally out of the domestic system.[10] A rare set of seventeenth-century account books shows that in the early 1650s John Lister was operating as cloth dresser and a factor; he bought pieces from domestic clothiers on behalf of a London merchant (his cousin), dressed them, and then shipped them to the buyer. John Lister's "profit" came from the wages he received for dressing the cloth and perhaps a commission on the sale. By 1658 Lister was becoming a manufacturer like Longbotham; although he was still paid for dressing cloths bought on his cousin's account, he was buying a larger volume of cloth on his own account, finishing it, and sending it to London for sale. By 1662 John Lister had died, and his son Samuel was in business as a manufacturer, buying cloths from several clothiers, finishing them in his own shop, and then sending them to the same cousin, who arranged their sale at Blackwell Hall.[11]

The Listers' history suggests how easily a manufacturer could emerge out of the ranks of the yeoman clothiers; even raising the necessary capital does not seem to have required a concerted effort on their part.[12] What can be discovered about the ancestors of other turn-of-the-century manufacturers suggests much the same conclusion. Nathaniel Kershaw's father, for instance, was a yeoman who paid taxes on three hearths and distributed a fortune of £330 to his grandchildren.[13]

---

9. Only two manufacturers in the sample—two of the largest—bypassed the local markets by trading directly with the Continent: BIY/OW, Benjamin Holroyd, Rishworth, August 1718, and Susanna Riley, Soyland, November 1707.

10. Smail, "Manufacturer or Artisan," discusses this issue in more detail.

11. CDA/SH:1/OB/1654, 1661, Lister account books. By the 1670s Samuel Lister had left manufacturing to become a wool stapler; his business consisted of buying packs of wool from a variety of suppliers around Coventry, paying carriers to bring them to Halifax, and then selling the wool in either whole or broken packs to manufacturers and clothiers: SH:1/OB/1668.

12. A fairly comprehensive collection of bonds relating to the family contains no evidence of large-scale borrowing associated with the change in the nature of the family's business: CDA/SH/AB:24, Lister family bonds, 1650s–1690s.

13. BIY/PR, 51/322; John Kershaw, Soyland.

Jeremiah Riley's background was somewhat less comfortable. His grandfather Henry possessed only a single messuage and does not seem to have had very much money, and his great-grandfather George's bequests came to only £12 in addition to the messuage.[14] Other evidence suggests that manufacturers could disappear back into the ranks of the yeoman clothiers equally easily. In the first decade of the eighteenth century a Halifax cloth factor tried to interest a correspondent in a bale of cloth in Holland that his brother had not been able to sell. His brother, he explained, had been caught out by a fall in the market and wanted to be rid of these goods even at a loss, and he went on to say that his brother had no intention of engaging in manufacturing in the future.[15]

Thus, while the manufacturer existed at the beginning of the eighteenth century, the effects of this new mode of production were as yet lost in the sea of the domestic system dominated by the yeoman clothiers of the middling sort. In the long run, though, the evolution of the wool textile industry did undermine the domestic system in Halifax. As manufacturers and their new mode of production became more prevalent, the ability of the independent domestic producer to survive gradually declined. This development should not be imagined as a wholesale shift toward "factory" production. Even at the end of the eighteenth century the domestic system of production was hardly moribund. The changes that occurred in the first half of the century, however, created a new group of wealthy manufacturers and merchants as well as the beginnings of a proletarianized workforce.

THE EIGHTEENTH-CENTURY TEXTILE MANUFACTURER

Two characteristics differentiate the manufacturers who came to dominate Halifax's textile industry by the mid-eighteenth century from the manufacturers who emerged around the turn of the century. First, within this group were some men who operated on a scale undreamed of in 1700. One of the largest and best known of these giant manufac-

---

14. BIY/OW, Jeremiah Riley, Sowerby, September 1697; BIY/PR, 46/615, Henry Riley, Sowerby, and 49/310; George Riley, Sowerby.

15. CDA/MISC:8/117/1, Holroyd letter book, Holroyd to Peter Michelez, 10 December 1706.

turers was Samuel Hill of Soyland whose annual turnover in 1745 was just over £30,000.[16] The Stansfields of Fieldhouse in Sowerby, both father and son, were also manufacturers on a grand scale, particularly George Jr. whose working capital was almost £8,000.[17] The partnership of Samuel Lees and John Edwards of Skircoat had a capital of £12,000, and the capitals of David Stansfield and Michael Wainhouse of Halifax may have approached £10,000.[18] These giants were merchants as well as manufacturers. In addition to putting out raw materials, they purchased goods from the market or had them made to order by smaller manufacturers, and they maintained a very sophisticated and extensive correspondence with houses in London and abroad.

Of course, not all of the manufacturers in the mid–eighteenth century were giants such as Hill, Stansfield, or Lees. Many had businesses similar in organization and scale to those at the turn of the century. Thomas Walton, for instance, was described as a shalloon maker, a label used to describe smaller manufacturers who employed combers, spinners, and weavers to do the work for them in their own houses.[19] Another manufacturer, John Sutcliffe, probably had an annual turnover of about £2,000, but he was not so far removed from the world of the domestic clothier that he had ceased to be an active farmer. In his memorandum book, alongside descriptions of how to set up a loom for a particular kind of figured cloth and how to dye a good shade of black, are recipes for "a cow that cannot clean" and "a beast that scoureth."[20]

Second, the group itself was much larger; many more manufacturers were active in mid-century, and their collective dominance over the parish's textile industry was much greater.[21] One reason for their dominance over production was the growth of a worsted industry alongside

16. CDA/FH/439/1, Hill invoice book.
17. CDA/FH/396, Stansfield ledger. In 1731 George Sr. wrote of his intention to make 2,000 pieces worth about £3,500; FH/409/2-3, Stansfield stocktaking, 1764.
18. CDA/MISC/2, draft articles of partnership, 1760; PRO/C.12/1856/38, Stansfield v. Martin; CDA/RP/209, Wainhouse bankruptcy, 1781.
19. Walton was the defendant in what he claimed was a malicious suit for theft; part of his defense was the argument that a "man of substance, being worth above £600," was unlikely to "steal two pounds of wool": CDA/RP/107c, defense brief, 1755.
20. CDA/HAS/449 (714), Sutcliffe memorandum book, 1768-77. In 1769, in a letter to his banker, Sutcliffe calculated that he had drawn £1077/15/6 in drafts since the last balance; this figure serves as a minimum for his annual turnover.
21. The absence of inventory evidence makes an accurate count impossible, but surviving wills and business records make this fact clear.

the traditional kersey. Unlike the kersey, a narrow, fairly coarse woolen cloth made from carded short-staple wool, worsted cloth was made from long-staple wool that was combed to align the long fibers in the same direction for spinning.[22] As a rule, worsted cloth was lighter than woolen cloth, and it did not require the same extensive finishing process. Worsted cloth also came in a huge variety of types—shalloons, tammies, camblets, calimancos, russets, everlastings, and grograms, just to name a few—and some varieties, such as bays, serges, and long ells, were made with a combination of carded and combed wool.[23]

Worsted cloth was introduced into Yorkshire in the last decade of the seventeenth century, often as an adjunct to the domestic production of woolen cloth.[24] From this small start worsted manufacturing in Halifax grew dramatically. In the early 1720s, when Daniel Defoe visited the parish on his tour through Great Britain, he commented that they make "one hundred thousand shalloons" each year in Halifax.[25] If Defoe's figures seem exaggerated, more weight can be given to the calculations of Thomas Wolrich, a Leeds merchant who gave evidence before Parliament on the state of the textile industry in the West Riding in 1772. According to Wolrich, the average annual value of the products of the West Riding's worsted industry (£1,404,000) almost equaled that of the woolen industry (£1,869,700).[26]

Although worsted cloth was first made in a domestic setting, it was not particularly suited to a home workshop, and its production came to be dominated by small and medium-sized manufacturers such as Thomas Walton and John Sutcliffe. Making a piece of worsted cloth required proportionally more spinning than other tasks, so the balance

22. Heaton, *Yorkshire Woollen and Worsted Industry*, 259–63.

23. These are just a few of the types that appear on a price sheet sent out by Samuel Hill in 1754: CDA/FH/447/1; James, *History of the Worsted Manufacture*, 226, gives a comprehensive list.

24. Heaton, *Yorkshire Woollen and Worsted Industry*, 267–68; John Watson, *The History and Antiquities of the Parish of Halifax in Yorkshire* (London, 1775), 67–69; M. J. Dickenson, "The West Riding Woollen and Worsted Industries, 1689–1770: An Analysis of Probate Inventories and Insurance Policies" (Ph.D. dissertation, University of Nottingham, 1974), 46–57. Probate inventories make the last point. Both Isaac Smith and Abraham Earnshaw had kersey pieces in their houses as well as combs and combstocks: BIY/OW, Isaac Smith, Northowram, September 1694, and Abraham Earnshaw, Ovenden, May 1695.

25. Daniel Defoe, *A Tour through the Whole Island of Great Britain* (1724; New York, 1968), 2: 605.

26. Bischoff, *Comprehensive History*, 1:187. It also equaled the production of the worsted industry of East Anglia, formerly the center of worsted production: Heaton, *Yorkshire Woollen and Worsted Manufacture*, 275.

between this and other relatively unskilled tasks carried out by women and children and the relatively skilled tasks carried out by men did not match the distribution of labor available in the typical household.[27] The manufacturer, of course, did not face this problem; since he was putting out material, he could employ a labor force of the appropriate size and skill. Making a piece of worsted cloth also required more capital.[28] The wool for worsted cloth had to be sorted very carefully, and after it was combed the worsted maker was left with the short fibers (noiles) that were of no use. Therefore, makers of worsted cloth were obliged to buy larger amounts of wool than they actually used. True, the unusable portions could be sold back to dealers and other manufacturers, but that required more capital reserves than the typical domestic clothier possessed.[29]

Domestic producers in the worsted industry were not forced to give up their independence. Becoming dependent on a putting-out manufacturer had its advantages. Consider, for instance, the importance of combing in the preparative processes associated with making worsted cloth. Unlike carding, which was a simple task that even a child could do, combing quickly became defined as a skilled and therefore male occupation that paid relatively high wages.[30] In these circumstances artisanal households emerged whose members never intended to carry out all of the processes associated with worsted manufacture, since they could rely on the high wages of the comber, supplemented, perhaps, by the wife's spinning. The introduction of drawlooms to weave figured cloths had a similar effect; drawlooms required skilled male weavers

---

27. Heaton, *Yorkshire Woollen and Worsted Manufacture*, 109, and James, *History of the Worsted Manufacture*, 218n, give estimates of the labor necessary to produce a kersey and a shalloon, respectively. One kersey weaver needed just under six other workers doing the sorting, carding, spinning, and other tasks exclusive of finishing to keep fully occupied; a worsted weaver needed just under twelve other workers.

28. Heaton, *Yorkshire Woollen and Worsted Manufacture*, 297; Pat Hudson, "Proto-industrialization: The Case of the West Riding Wool Textile Industry in the Eighteenth and Early Nineteenth Centuries," *History Workshop* 12 (1981): 38–40.

29. Sales of noiles were common: CDA/HAS/450 (713), Sutcliffe day book, 1791. Wool staplers did provide worsted manufacturers with sorted wool and they might often sell on credit. These two factors diminished but did not eliminate the capital that a worsted manufacturer required to maintain his stock of wool.

30. Heaton, *Yorkshire Woollen and Worsted Manufacture*, 310, 318. There was no physical reason why women could not comb wool, and much later in the history of the worsted industry, when artisanal control over combing had been broken, women did join their husbands and fathers at the comb pot: Theodore Koditschek, *Class Formation and Urban Industrial Society: Bradford, 1750–1850* (New York, 1990), 354.

whose time was too valuable to waste on the less remunerative parts of the production process. Domestic clothiers were thus giving up their independence in favor of higher wages, and the result was the subdivided production process organized by the manufacturer.[31]

The imperatives imposed by the production process necessary for worsted cloth, however, do not explain the spread of manufacturing in Halifax's textile industry as a whole, for Halifax's traditional cloth, the humble kersey, was also increasingly produced by manufacturers instead of domestic clothiers. Indeed, the dominance of the manufacturer in the kersey industry was even more spectacular, for kersey production was an important part of the operations of the parish's giant manufacturers. Samuel Hill and George Stansfield, for instance, made about twice as many kerseys as worsteds.[32] Moreover, while most of the giant manufacturers dealt in both kinds of cloth, they typically bought some of their worsted cloth from smaller manufacturers, but produced their own kerseys in extensive putting-out operations.[33]

Thus a second, crucial reason for the increasing dominance of the manufacturer was change in the markets and systems of marketing for both woolen and worsted goods. At the simplest level, the growth in the market for these goods gave manufacturers the potential to earn greater profits. Even the earliest manufacturers were in a position to make more profit because as their operations expanded, they were able to avoid the middlemen—both wool suppliers and cloth buyers—that the domestic clothiers had to deal with. More significant were the profits that became available to manufacturers once they began to export cloth on their own account. In 1706, for instance, Joseph Holroyd remarked that some manufacturers were beginning to send goods to Holland to be sold on commission because they were getting "more for

31. Heaton, *Yorkshire Woollen and Worsted Manufacture*, 313.
32. CDA/FH/439/1, Hill invoice book; FH/409/2-3, Stansfield stocktaking, 1764. These figures should serve as a reminder that, contrary to the parish's reputation in the historical literature as part of the West Riding worsted zone, the production of woolen cloth continued to figure prominently in its economy throughout the eighteenth century.
33. An analysis of Samuel Hill's dispatch book (CDA/FH/440) shows that Hill obtained all of his kerseys and some of his shalloons from workers whom he had provided with wool or yarn. A comparison of his invoice, dispatch, and letter books, however, reveals that he also got large batches of shalloons from independent worsted manufacturers: FH/439/1, invoice of 27 February 1748/49 to Messrs. Van Eck and Willink of Rotterdam; FH/440, dispatch of bale no. 21 to Van Eck and Willink, Rotterdam, 18 April 1749; FH/442, Van Eck and Willink to Hill, 12 August 1749. Luke Greenwood, the worker involved in these transactions, was a substantial householder in the township of Sowerby and therefore was probably a worsted manufacturer in his own right.

their goods that they send to be sold than by selling here."[34] Evidence from later in the century suggests that the profits in the export trade continued to attract manufacturers, despite the greater difficulties of trading on the continent. George Stansfield Sr. and Samuel Hill continued to sell goods abroad when fluctuations in the market reduced or even eliminated their profit in order to maintain their foreign contacts against the time when the export market would work in their favor.[35]

Samuel Hill's entry into the worsted trade in the 1730s was also motivated by profit he expected to make in the export trade. By the 1730s the worsted trade was fairly well established in Halifax; so Hill was not introducing a new product but changing the way in which it was marketed by using his extensive contacts to sell his worsted cloth abroad, bypassing merchants in Leeds and London. Hill had some work to do in selling this idea to his Dutch trading partners. In the early years of his trade in worsted cloth he had to beg them to take pieces of it on trial, and he was willing to sell them "for a small profit . . . till they be known."[36]

All manufacturers, whether shalloonmakers such as Walton or giants such as Stansfield, had another advantage in the developing markets for wool textiles in the eighteenth century. Because they were both producers and sellers, manufacturers created a close link between the production of a piece of cloth and its ultimate market. As producers, manufacturers had much more accurate information about what the market wanted than domestic clothiers could gather, so they were in a better position to shape their activities to suit the market. Merchants who bought domestically produced cloth had the same information, of course, but only manufacturers were able to incorporate that knowledge in decisions about the type and quantity of cloth to make, since they controlled its production.

---

34. CDA/MISC:8/117/1, Holroyd letter book, Holroyd to John D'Orville, 8 and 19 November 1706. Holroyd's comments are supported by probate records from this period, for there are occasional references to manufacturers who had sent cloth to Holland for sale. Susanna Riley (BIY/OW, Soyland, November 1707) had £448/15/– worth of "goods in Holland, safe arrived," and Benjamin Holroyd (BIY/OW, Rishworth, August 1718) had 416 pieces in Holland worth £738/8/–.

35. CDA/FH/396, Stansfield letter book, Stansfield to Abraham Visser and to Henry Hermans, 16 February 1730/31; FH/441, Hill letter book, John Lozer to Hill, 6 June 1749. Lozer wondered that Hill would "pay a commission in Holland, run the risk yourself, and be a good deal longer out of your money" by exporting instead of selling at home.

36. CDA/MISC:8/117/2, Hill letter book, Hill to Abraham van Broyel, 1 February 1737/38.

The accounts of Joseph Milner from the 1680s show how tenuous the connection between domestic clothiers and the market for their cloth in fact was. Milner, either on his own account or acting as an agent, bought cloth in the Halifax market and shipped it to a London merchant, who then exported it to a wholesaler in Holland.[37] Even the cloth traded by Joseph Holroyd, whose business as a factor in the early eighteenth century represents a relatively advanced version of the domestic system's market, still had to go through two or three hands. When Holroyd bought a piece of cloth on behalf of a Dutch merchant, he was buying it from an independent clothier who had produced it with no direct knowledge of the state of its final market.[38]

In contrast, the manufacturers who began exporting cloth to Holland in the early eighteenth century were much more closely in contact with the final market for their goods, for the only intermediary involved in the transaction was the Dutch factor who handled the sale of their pieces. This system of exporting goods on consignment had two significant drawbacks, however. First, manufacturers took all of the risks involved in the trade. George Stansfield Sr., for instance, contemplated giving up the trade entirely during a slump in 1729, for the price he was offered on two bales of goods in his Dutch factor's warehouse "makes me groan, being much to my loss." All the factor stood to lose was part of his commission. Second, manufacturers were dependent on their factor—usually they dealt with only one—for information about the market. At the beginning of a slump in 1728 Stansfield had little choice but to curtail production, as his factor advised, despite the evidence of a "flourishing trade" in Halifax.[39] In the consignment system, therefore, manufacturers were not much more than puppets, for entrepreneurial decisions about the market were made by their correspondents.

37. University of Leeds, Brotherton Library, Business Records, Joseph Lee ledger. This set of accounts, which covers the latter part of the seventeenth century, was kept by a merchant who owned the book before Joseph Lee did; internal evidence suggests that he was Joseph Milner of Leeds.

38. For Holroyd's reliance on independent producers see CDA/MISC:8/117/1, Holroyd letter book, Holroyd to Henry Carter, 9 September 1706, and the details of the order that was filled. For his reliance on the market see Holroyd to D'Orville, 7 January 1706/7, where he explains that he is unable to fill an order because the Leeds merchants have bought up all the cloth for sale.

39. CDA/FH/396, Stansfield letter book, Stansfield to Hermans, 15 March 1727/28, 24 May 1728, and 12 September 1729.

When the market for kerseys began to rebound in 1730, Stansfield took the opportunity to change the basis on which he exported cloth to Holland. In August, after a summer in which kerseys had been in short supply, Stansfield wrote to the Dutch firm of John and Peter Dorville offering to sell them a parcel of goods that had remained in Holland unsold throughout the depression. To clarify his intentions Stansfield concluded this offer: "As to a commission, trade, without, is much better. If what I propose is with your interest, shall be glad to serve you, otherways, let us live and love still."[40] Subsequent letters show that Stansfield was establishing a new marketing system, in which he sold cloth to Dutch merchants on the basis of orders they placed in advance. This system, which became standard in the industry during the next two decades, was less risky for the manufacturers and gave them greater control over the market. Risk was reduced because once the manufacturer had delivered the bales to Hull, the customer had to bear losses at sea and fluctuations in the market. More important, instead of being dependent on a single factor for dealings in the Dutch market, manufacturers could deal with as many merchants as they could satisfy. After the summer of 1730, Stansfield made contact with other merchants in Holland, and he was not above informing his regular customers of the fact that they were not the only potential buyers of his goods. Samuel Hill's letters from 1737 and 1738 also provide evidence of a new independence on the part of manufacturers: Hill told one firm that he would not "deal with those who will not accept my goods at the market price when ready," and he was also beginning to solicit orders from new firms. By the 1740s, Hill was supplying thirty or forty merchants with cloth. As a consequence of filling the orders of several merchants, manufacturers could develop a much better sense of the state of the market than clothiers in the domestic system.[41]

Indeed, once established on the basis of advance orders, the larger manufacturers' trading networks continued to grow, increasing their control over the markets for their goods. From the late 1740s Samuel Hill was trading directly with merchants outside of Holland—a signif-

---

40. Ibid., Stansfield to John and Peter Dorville, 11 August 1730. John and Peter Dorville are almost certainly related to the John D'Orville who appears in Holroyd's letter book. I have, however, retained the variant spellings of the originals.

41. CDA/MISC:8/117/2, Hill letter book, Hill to Hendrick and to Peter Kops, 31 January 1737/38; to William Preston, 3 February 1737/38; and to Mr. Vander Veit, 10 February 1737/38; CDA/FH/439/1, Hill invoice book.

icant development in view of the fact that most of the cloth sold to Holland was destined for reexport elsewhere in Europe.[42] George Stansfield Jr. also explored the possibility of export to places other than Holland. In the 1770s he employed Richard Hill, Samuel's son, as his agent to look into the possibility of establishing trading links in Boulogne, Leghorn, Bilbao, and San Sebastián, and to establish correspondences in inland cities with "houses of established fortune and repute who are themselves the retailers of goods."[43] Hill and Stansfield continued to send the bulk of their goods to Holland, but their access to other outlets for their goods and their knowledge about those markets were advantages they gained only by combining the functions of producer and merchant.

The advantages created by manufacturers' better knowledge of the market were especially strong in the worsted industry because of the huge and constantly changing variety of worsted cloths. Although it was surpassed by cotton in the latter part of the century, worsted was the "fashion" cloth for people in the middling and lower ranks of society in the eighteenth century, and the demand created by fashion helps explain the growth of the worsted industry in Yorkshire.[44] By definition, fashions change; and manufacturers, with their direct knowledge of the market, were in a position to find out what was in fashion. More important, the worsted industry could not have responded to the whims of fashion had it not been for the manufacturers, for only manufacturers could channel demand for such products to the makers. Both points are demonstrated by John Sutcliffe's attempt to persuade a London firm to take some of his patterned "drafts" instead of the figured worsteds it had ordered. As a producer Sutcliffe was in a position to explain that altering the looms with the "new gears" necessary to weave their order would be very expensive and time-consuming, but his pitch for his patterned drafts was made on the basis of intimate knowledge of what would sell.[45]

As important as the manufacturers' growing knowledge of the mar-

42. CDA/FH/441, Hill letter book, Lozer to Hill, 20 July 1749 and after, re the Spanish trade; Abel Fonnereau to Hill, 15 April 1749 and after, re the Russia trade; and FH/442, van Broyel to Hill, 29 August 1749, re the Portugal trade.

43. CDA/FH/461a, Hill to Stansfield, 20 February 1775, from Boulogne.

44. Hudson, "Proto-industrialization," 40; Beverly Lemire, *Fashion's Favourite: The Cotton Trade and the Consumer in Britain, 1660–1800* (Oxford, 1991).

45. CDA/HAS/449 (714), Sutcliffe memorandum book, Sutcliffe to Fox and Smith, 17 October 1769.

kets for their cloth was their increasing ability to control its production. Pressures for cloth of uniform quality can be discerned even in the market for kerseys in the domestic system. When Joseph Milner and Joseph Holroyd purchased their kerseys in Halifax market, they showed a distinct preference for makers who could sell them cloth in batches of between ten and twenty pieces at a time, and Holroyd apologized when he was forced to make up an order with the cloths of several makers.[46] The advantages of manufacturers on this score are obvious, for they could produce whole bales of cloth made from the same batch of wool and to the same standard. One customer, on ordering 300 shalloons from Samuel Hill, requested: "I should be glad if they were all of your manufacture."[47]

The pressures for uniformity were particularly evident in the worsted industry, for the range of goods and their complexity required a manufacturer's control over the process of production. Responding to a London firm's order for some figured shalloons, John Sutcliffe explained: "We cannot get the sort you had last from the same or any other good makers, at less money than sent you before.... It would not suit you to have *odd pieces, I mean six or eight makers for twenty pieces,* they must be all good clean wool, fine and good colored or will not dye for you."[48] The disadvantage of "odd pieces" was that with complex, figured cloths such as Sutcliffe produced, variations between weavers would spoil the effect, as would variations in the base color of the wool. Customers wanted to get a batch of cloth from the same weaver, or perhaps two weavers, and it was the manufacturer who organized such a system: obtaining the orders, supplying the weavers with the appropriate wool, paying them as they went along, and finally sending the completed order off to the customer.

The control over the production process which allowed them to make goods of a uniformly high standard was essential to the success of all manufacturers, small or large, and its importance can be gauged from their jealous protection of their trademarks. In the late 1730s,

---

46. University of Leeds, Brotherton Library, Business Records, Joseph Lee ledger; CDA/MISC:8/117/1, Holroyd letter book. For the size of his purchases compare Holroyd to L. de Dorpere, 27 August 1706, and to Dominicus Cramer, 30 August 1706; see also Holroyd to Henry Carter, 9 September 1706, and the details of the order that was filled. For apologies see Holroyd to James Baden, 4 November 1706, and to Peter Deynote, 2 August 1706.

47. CDA/FH/441, Hill letter book, Peter Gaussens to Hill, 2 March 1748/49.

48. CDA/HAS/449 (714), Sutcliffe memorandum book, Sutcliffe to Stevenson and Gentile, 1766 (my emphasis).

when Samuel Hill was just getting into the worsted trade, he wrote to one of his larger customers about his new line of goods: "Me thinks I like to make them [shalloons] and fancy I shall in time do it well, will you please, after I think I have got them up to a tolerable good pitch, permit me to put 'SAM:HILL' in the headend?"[49] Hill was aware that he would not want to put "SAM:HILL" on any old piece of cloth, and he wanted advice on whether he should risk the reputation of his kerseys on this new venture. The value of this reputation is suggested by the inquiry that Samuel Lees, another large manufacturer of kerseys, made in 1760 about the legal ownership of Samuel Hill's trademarks. Since Hill was now dead and his son was bankrupt, Lees wanted to use the trademarks himself, for, as he put it, they guaranteed good sale. Hill was not the only manufacturer to use and value his trademarks. When Samuel Lees's sons dissolved their partnership with John Edwards in 1785, Edwards (the senior partner) specified that he was to have the "right and title to marks or names inserted in kerseys and bays as thentofore made for the term of twenty years."[50]

The combination of knowledge of the market and control over production gave manufacturers one further advantage over the domestic system: unlike either the domestic clothier or the merchant, the manufacturer could innovate. Under the domestic system, innovation was difficult. For example, although Joseph Holroyd was a successful cloth factor with a large turnover, he was unable to supply a Dutch merchant's order for thirty long kerseys a "full yard broad" because "we have no such thing as yard broad of best sorts." Holroyd rattled off a list of possible alternatives: there was one maker who produced cloths that might do if they were specially milled, but that type of cloth was always sent undressed; still other cloths might "hold a yard broad or within one inch," but they were too expensive for his customer's specifications.[51]

As a merchant, Holroyd was constrained by what the independent clothiers produced, but they were unlikely to risk making new goods for an uncertain market. A manufacturer, in contrast, could have innovated to meet such an order. John Sutcliffe complained that making the particular pattern his customer requested was going to cost money,

---

49. CDA/MISC:8/117/2, Hill letter book, Hill to William Handley, 3 February 1737/38.
50. CDA/RP/148, 1760, 2201, 1785.
51. CDA/MISC:8/117/1, Holroyd letter book, Holroyd to L. de Dorpere, 30 [August] 1706.

but he could have produced the goods if the firm had insisted. More important, the new types of worsted cloth and the almost endless varieties of figures, colors, and colored patterns in both woolen and worsted cloth were crucial for the growth of the industry. Only manufacturers could fulfill the demands of fashion and create new fashions by innovating. John Sutcliffe's memorandum book is peppered with designs and directions for making new patterns of worsted cloth, and though we have no way of knowing if he invented them himself or copied them from someone else, it is obvious that this manufacturer paid a great deal of attention to changes in fashion.[52]

The ability to innovate also played a large role in manufacturers' efforts to escape the confines of the Dutch export market. In the Dutch trade, the expectations of makers, manufacturers, and merchants on both sides of the North Sea were much the same, but purchasers in the new markets had their own ideas. Samuel Hill was advised that if he wanted to trade with Russia, he would be wasting his time to send the types and sizes of cloth he made for the European market; rather he must produce cloth of the exact length, breadth, and quality specified. The same strictures held for trade with the East India Company; here Hill was competing with the broader, heavier, and much finer cloths produced in the west of England. Hill persisted for some time, sending the company's purchasing committee samples of his long ells and his shalloons. In the end, they rejected the ells because they were "not made properly: the spinning is not fine enough and it is not well covered," and they were narrower and lighter than the Exeter goods to which the company was accustomed. The company took a trial order of Hill's broad shalloons, however, admonishing him to produce the pieces to specifications.[53] Thus a manufacturer who wanted to compete in a new market had to have access to knowledge about that market and had to be in control of production in order to satisfy its demands.

While these developments were progressing, many aspects of the textile industry continued to operate much as they had done fifty, sixty, or seventy years before. A Quarter Sessions case of 1765, for instance, reveals relations of production typical of the domestic system; it involved cloth stolen from the shop of an independent cloth dresser who

52. CDA/HAS/449 (714), Sutcliffe memorandum book.
53. CDA/FH/441, Hill letter book, Fonnereau to Hill, 15 April and 9, 14, and 21 September 1749.

was finishing the pieces that a firm of Leeds merchants had bought, presumably in the local market.[54] Though older forms of production did not disappear, however, economic developments between the late seventeenth and mid–eighteenth centuries had transformed Halifax's textile industry. The manufacturers succeeded in their challenge to the domestic system because they were more closely connected to the ultimate markets for their cloth and had more control over its production. What these manufacturers achieved was a vertical integration of the business of textile production, encompassing all stages from the raw wool to the disposal of the finished product. Thus they were able to transmit knowledge about the state of the market directly to the weavers at their looms.[55] In a preindustrial age, when the economies of scale of mass production were not yet a reality, it was this kind of vertical integration that offered the most opportunities for growth and profit in the world of manufacturing.[56]

In the history of the Industrial Revolution, then, Halifax exemplifies one particular path of economic development. Here an increasingly centralized mode of production developed as the result of a very gradual process whose roots stretch back to a century before the first factories—of any description—appeared in the parish. Yet the mode of production characteristic of the midcentury manufacturers represents a point of transition in the process. Factory production was unthinkable in the economic world inhabited by Joseph Holroyd, Jonathan Baumforth, and even George Stansfield Sr., but the operations of men such as Samuel Hill, George Stansfield Jr., and Samuel Lees differed from those of the earliest "factory" owners only in the absence of a water-powered slubbing mill, some spinning jennies, and a weaving shed.

54. WYAS/Wakefield, QS1/104/2, West Riding Quarter Sessions, Indictments, Wakefield Sessions, January 1765; the case concerned the firm of Fountain and Wormald of Leeds.

55. Both R. G. Wilson and Derek Gregory offer similar arguments to explain the success of the West Riding's textile industry in the eighteenth century: Wilson, "Supremacy," 236–41; Gregory, *Regional Transformation*, 47–55. This argument does not necessarily apply to all sectors of the textile industry; exports to the American colonies, for example, were dominated by large London merchant firms that could afford the very long wait for payment.

56. John Styles, "Manufacturing, Consumption, and Design in Eighteenth-Century England," in *Consumption and the World of Goods*, ed. John Brewer and Roy Porter (London, 1993), 527–54. Styles argues that the term "mass-production" is quite inappropriate to describe manufacturing in the eighteenth century. I confine my comments to manufacturing because in more purely commercial concerns, economies of scale were an important factor and always had been.

MERCHANTS

The structural changes that gave rise to large-scale manufacturing were not the only important changes in Halifax's textile industry in this period. One did not have to be a Samuel Hill to reap benefits from the development of large-scale trade in wool textiles. Concerns that were more purely mercantile also thrived in the first part of the eighteenth century, producing a substantial number of wealthy merchants, who, with the manufacturers, formed a new commercial elite in the parish. Despite the obvious differences between manufacturers and merchants, the distinction is somewhat artificial. Most of the giant manufacturers behaved like merchants in that they bought worsted cloth from smaller manufacturers as well as making it themselves. Thus the line between merchant and manufacturer was fluid, and it must have been so from the very emergence of manufacturing around the turn of the century. An apprenticeship indenture of 1719 records the agreement between Abraham Walker, son of Richard Walker of Waterclough, wool stapler, and John Batley of Halifax: Batley agreed to teach young Walker the trade of "buying dressing, and pressing woollen cloth and buying and selling wool"; in short, everything a manufacturer did except put out wool to the makers.[57]

Mid-eighteenth-century Halifax was also home to an increasing number of merchants who confined themselves to buying and selling. The fortunes that these merchants could accumulate were spectacular, certainly on a par with the money made by Halifax's manufacturers. To give but one example, when William Walker of Crownest, merchant, married Elizabeth, daughter of John Caygill of Halifax, merchant, in 1746, the marriage settlement specified that Elizabeth was to come with a portion of £2,500, and the Walker family was to match this amount in her jointure; Elizabeth had at least two brothers and two sisters, so this was not the portion of an heiress.[58]

When it is possible to figure out what Halifax merchants were doing, the picture that emerges is of a multiplicity of activities. The Edwards family of Northowram (no relation to Samuel Lees's partner) were merchants in the Portugal trade, sending Halifax cloth to Lisbon and im-

---

57. CDA/MAC/101/7.
58. CDA/CN/96, marriage settlement, 1746; BIY/OW, John Caygill, Prerogative Court, March 1757. The marriage settlement of Elizabeth's sister Anne in 1761 shows that she had £4,500 in bonds and mortgages as well as a substantial amount of land: CDA/CN/95, 1761.

porting dyestuffs and wine in return.[59] Chris Wetherherd, another Halifax merchant, engaged in a similar range of activities. When he went bankrupt in the late 1760s, his debtors claimed his "stock in trade of wool, shalloons, and other woollen goods, wine, rum, brandy," and all of his household possessions and the money owed to him to settle debts amounting to £7,377.[60] The cases of Edwards and Wetherherd suggest that though wool textiles probably remained the most important commodity for most Halifax merchants, they also traded in other goods.

The emergence of large-scale manufacturing in the worsted and woollen industry and the development of the mercantile infrastructure made the Halifax of 1750 different from what it had been at the beginning of the century. Probate records, deeds, and the records of voluntary associations suggest that Halifax had a core group of 60 or 70 very substantial merchants and manufacturers and another group of between 50 and 150 medium-sized ones. These wealthy merchants and manufacturers had no equivalents in the world of the middling sort. They were as wealthy as the local gentry, probably wealthier than the pseudogentry, and more numerous and more influential in the community than such large landowners had been in the late seventeenth century. They were, of course, much wealthier than any members of the middling sort had been, and the social boundary separating them from the lower orders must have been easily identifiable. These were the people who would construct Halifax's middle-class culture.

THE NEW CULTURE OF COMMERCE

Parallel to the economic transformation that created this group of wealthy merchants and manufacturers was a cultural transformation that changed this group's understanding of their economic practice. During the first half of the eighteenth century, Halifax's commercial elite developed a more entrepreneurial approach to their businesses and a more distanced, objective relationship with the workers they employed. Obviously such cultural changes were linked to the process of economic development in a reciprocal relationship. On one hand,

---

59. W. B. Trigg, "Northowram Hall," *THAS*, 1932, 129–52.
60. CDA/RP/1978, 999, Wetherherd bankruptcy, 1769 and 1771.

these economic changes could not have occurred without changes in attitudes toward work; on the other hand, attitudes were forced to change as economic practice evolved. The development of this new culture of work, which was different from that of the middling sort, played a large role in the origins of a middle-class culture in Halifax, for the way a group construes its economic practice is as much a part of its socioeconomic experience as the economic practice itself.

Cultural change is also crucial to the history of the Industrial Revolution. Although there are signs of changes in historians' approach to the problem of industrialization, the economic history of the Industrial Revolution has concentrated too long on the fact of economic practice—how much was made by whom and for what price—ignoring the equally relevant cultural context that informed economic practice.[61] If mid–eighteenth-century manufacturers such as Samuel Hill, George Stansfield Jr., and Samuel Lees achieved a mode of production recognizably on the way to factory production, they did so in part because their attitudes toward their economic practice changed. These changing attitudes, encompassing entrepreneurship and social relations within the industry, amount to a new culture, and they provide a context within which the factory's relations of production would make sense. Thus the history of these cultural changes is also part of a parallel account of the origins of industrial culture.

To understand how these attitudinal changes came about, it is useful to remember that the initial emergence of manufacturing in the parish in the decades around 1700 was accomplished largely within the terms of the culture of the middling sort.[62] Recall Jonathan Baumforth, the wealthy manufacturer with the two wills whom we met in Chapter 2. Baumforth's economic practice was similar to that of mid-eighteenth-century manufacturers—he put out raw materials to workmen—but his worldview was closer to that of the middling sort. He did not approve of the more ruthless attitudes towards business that could allow an individual to succeed at a time when his neighbors were suffering, and

---

61. As Pat Hudson points out, historians attentive to the role that gender relations play in historical development have been at the forefront of the challenge to a purely economic interpretation of the Industrial Revolution: *The Industrial Revolution* (London, 1992), chap. 7. Martin Wiener explores the relationship between culture and economic change at the other end of the Industrial Revolution: *English Culture and the Decline of the Industrial Spirit, 1850–1980* (Cambridge, 1981).

62. Smail, "Manufacturer or Artisan?"

he recognized the economic independence of his workers and poorer neighbors.[63] In terms of the theory of practice, the implications of this example are twofold. First, new kinds of economic practice were possible within the artisanal culture of the middling sort. Baumforth had become a manufacturer of "half-thicks" while still thinking of himself as a yeoman. Second, while individuals might engage in new forms of economic practice within one cultural frame of reference, these actions helped to change their expectations and values. Simply by doing what they did, Baumforth and other early manufacturers were creating a new culture of commerce.

The entrepreneurship of eighteenth-century manufacturers is evident in their sense that business was an investment that ought to yield a profit. Profit, of course, was not unknown in the domestic system. Joseph Holroyd's letter books show that merchants were keenly aware of the profitability of their transactions, and so were independent clothiers. During a period when prices were high, for example, Holroyd reported that little was for sale because the makers were withholding their pieces in the anticipation of still higher prices.[64] However, profit took on new connotations in the manufacturers' world. They adopted more and more sophisticated accounting methods to keep track of their money. The ledger that George Stansfield Sr. kept in the 1720s, an early example, alternates between an "advanced" system in which debts and credits were entered on opposites sides of the page and a simpler system in which a customer's debits were listed and then crossed out when payment was received.[65] Such backsliding would not have been conceivable to Samuel Hill, and he was not alone in his diligence.[66] Many merchants and manufacturers hired a bookkeeper to look after their account books: the partnership Lees and Edwards, for instance, paid a bookkeeper £60 a year, plus room and board. Good

---

63. BIY/CP, I/498.

64. CDA/MISC:8/117/1, Holroyd letter book, Holroyd to D'Orville, 31 December 1706 and 7 January 1706/7.

65. CDA/FH/396, Stansfield ledger. The simpler of the two methods is typical of all earlier accounts surviving from Halifax: for example, CDA/SH:1/OB/1654, 1661, 1668, Lister account books.

66. CDA/FH/437, Hill ledger, 1737–38; FH/439/1, Hill invoice book, 1743–52; FH/440, Hill dispatch book, 1749–51; FH/441, 442; Hill letter books. Presumably Hill's accounting system also included a cashbook or daybook, but none has survived. George Stansfield Jr. must have had reasonably good accounts to be able to calculate his balance in 1764: FH/409/2–3, Stansfield stocktaking. Smaller concerns often kept less rigorous accounts;, for example, John Sutcliffe: CDA/HAS/449 (714).

accounts were particularly important in partnerships to ensure continued trust, and most partnership deeds contained a clause specifying an annual reckoning of accounts and the free access of all partners to the books.[67]

Implicit in the attention paid to profit is the assumption that clothmaking was an investment; it was one of a number of ways that manufacturers could turn their capital into income. When Samuel Lees made his will in 1760, he instructed his trustees to employ his assets "in the way of trade or business which I now follow" until his children came of age, but if the trade ceased to yield a return of 4 percent for two out of three years, the money was to be withdrawn and put out at interest.[68]

Further evidence that manufacturers of the mid–eighteenth century thought of their concerns as an investment comes from the dramatic growth in partnerships in this period. Rare before the 1730s, partnerships for merchants and manufacturers were increasingly common after midcentury. The very concept of a partnership required that the participants pool their capital in a common fund, the expectation being that they could earn greater profits together than they could individually. These partnerships established substantial concerns. The partnership between Samuel Lees and John Edwards in 1760 had £12,000 as its starting capital, and by 1777 Edwards and Lees's two sons established a partnership with £18,000 in capital. And partnerships were not confined to the giant manufacturers who dominated Halifax's textile industry. In 1774 Benjamin Irvin, James Stead, Joshua Holmes, and Thomas Irvin established a partnership to dye and finish cloth with an initial capital of £1,750, sharing all profits and losses. Even smaller was the partnership established between Jonathan Brook and Joseph Drake of Elland in 1768; Brook agreed to put up a capital of £110 for a shalloonmaking business that Drake was to operate, and the profits were to be shared equally.[69] These businesses suggest that throughout the commercial community in Halifax, investment for the purpose of mak-

67. CDA/RP/2032, draft appointment of a bookkeeper, 1763; RP/2111, draft partnership agreement, Edwards and Lees, 1773.
68. BIY/OW, Samuel Lees, Skircoat, Prerogative Court, July 1761. At current interest rates in Halifax, capital lent on mortgages could be expected to yield between 4.5 and 5 percent a year. This rate was higher than the national average for this period, which was 3.5 percent. See John Brewer, "Commercialization and Politics," in Neil McKendrick, John Brewer, and J. H. Plumb, *The Birth of a Consumer Society* (London, 1983), 208.
69. CDA/RP/2084, partnership agreement, 1760; RP/2118, draft partnership agreement, 1777; RP/2113, draft partnership agreement, 1777; RP/2107, partnership agreement, 1768.

ing a profit was increasingly the way these individuals conceived of their activities.

Merchants and manufacturers differed from yeoman clothiers in their approach to making a profit. The clothier who played the cloth market by withholding pieces when prices were high was engaging in a tactical ploy, an attempt to make a windfall by gambling that the market would rise still further. The manufacturer's attention to his enterprise's profitability was part of a long-term strategy. Strategy was necessary because merchants and manufacturers exposed a greater proportion of their total assets to the risks of trade in the expectation of greater profits. Success depended on their ability to make the correct entrepreneurial decisions, which was based in part on their ability to calculate the profit or loss that a particular transaction entailed.[70] In contrast, the yeoman clothier who made a bad choice and withheld his cloths just before the market began to fall never risked more than a fraction of his total assets.

The point about profit, then, is not that yeoman clothiers were happy to remain "poor" whereas manufacturers were greedy money grubbers. The cultural differences between clothiers and manufacturers did not exist beforehand; they developed along with the differences in economic practice and influenced the development of those practices. The large scale and relative complexity of the business of even a medium-sized manufacturer made profit calculation a necessary part of his business life in a way it was not for clothiers.

Yet the successful pursuit of profit made manufacturers' economic practice develop in specific ways. As manufacturers became more entrepreneurial in their attitudes toward profits, for example, they also became more competitive, for once the aim of the business was profit instead of simply survival, the manufacturer had to compete with his neighbors. Competition, of course, was not unknown in the domestic system. Joseph Holroyd's comments suggest the competition going on in early-eighteenth-century markets, but we find no sign that it affected the way he ran his business.[71] For manufacturers of the mid–eighteenth century, in contrast, competition was integral to the trade. In the late

70. Samuel Hill wrote Thomas Lee, 13 February 1737/38, that the price wanted would have allowed him a profit of only 4 pence and 3 farthings on each piece, which he thought was too little: CDA/MISC:8/117/2, Hill letter book.
71. CDA/MISC:8/117/1, Holroyd letter book, Holroyd to D'Orville, 19 November 1706 and 7 January 1706/7; Holroyd to Ludwig Wulfe, 24 September 1706.

1730s, when Samuel Hill was getting into the business of exporting worsted cloth, he wrote to one of his correspondents in Holland: "I think such goods, as I may say, are not to be out done in England, by any man, let him be who he will." Hill's dramatic challenge was the product of an entrepreneurial mind-set based on the competitive pursuit of profits. As he explained in another letter, he was willing to sell his shalloons "for a small profit . . . till they be known."[72] Hill was competing in a market where price mattered a great deal, and his correspondence is full of references to his ability to meet or beat the prices of other manufacturers. "I hope I shall never be such a fool as charging in making higher than the same quality can be made by others," he wrote in 1737. "I very well know what all the makers can do, and when I cannot serve my friends as well or better, I will leave off business."[73]

The correspondence of other manufacturers signals the same set of attitudes. Writing to the Dorvilles in 1730, George Stansfield Sr. complained: "As to comparing mine with James Hill's [kerseys], I cannot say anything to it for it is the proof that makes the penniworth," and he concluded by offering to send them some of his best cloth. Similarly, the worsted manufacturer John Sutcliffe, in his memorandum book, reminded himself "that a man should live with his enemy in such a manner as might leave him room to become his friend; and with his friend in such a manner that if he became his enemy it should not be in his power to hurt him." A further comment, "Discretion: in the first part very good, latter not so good, commendable," suggests that Sutcliffe may not have been entirely happy with the implications of the competitive world he lived in.[74] Far from troubling his conscience, such an attitude would not even have entered Jonathan Baumforth's or Jonathan Priestly's mind.

The reality of the competitive world that caused Sutcliffe some heartache is suggested by the concern that manufacturers expressed about their business secrets. George Stansfield Sr. and Samuel Hill com-

---

72. CDA/MISC:8/117/2, Hill letter book, Hill to van Broyel, 17 and 1 February 1737/38.

73. CDA/FH/441, Hill to Hendrick and Peter Kops, February 1737/38. On a letter from Abel Fonnereau, 29 June 1749 (ibid), which told him that he would have to price his long ells at 46s each to sell them to the East India Company, Hill calculated that he could make the pieces for 36s/6d. Other letters refer to the competition his cloths received from makers in Halifax, Norwich, and Holland: ibid., Lozer to Hill, 19 September 1749; FH/442, van Broyel to Hill, 25 April 1749.

74. CDA/FH/396, Stansfield letter book, May 1730; CDA/HAS/449 (714), Sutcliffe memorandum book.

plained to their wool suppliers about confidentiality, for if information about their orders for wool got out, other manufacturers would know what kinds of cloths they planned to make.[75]

The manufacturers' competitiveness, like their attention to profit, emerged alongside their new economic practices. Partly it was a question of scale. The domestic clothiers did not need to compete with one another because, producing at a rate of at most two or three pieces of cloth a week in a market where the differences between types of cloth were minimal, an individual clothier could do nothing to affect the sale of another clothier's goods. Thus clothiers were better served by a cooperative attitude, since that might help to protect them against the worst effects of the international market on which they depended. Merchants and manufacturers, in contrast, could affect each others' businesses, for, given the scale of their transactions and the volatility of the markets they traded in, it was possible to leave a competitor with a large stock of unsaleable goods on his hands. These new cultural attitudes emerged in part as manufacturers responded to the unintended consequences of the new forms their economic practice was taking. As entrepreneurial attitudes developed and manufacturers became better businessmen, economic and cultural change accelerated.

CLOSELY related to the emergence of the entrepreneurial attitudes of profit and competition was the development of a new set of social relations within the textile industry. The manufacturers' desire for a profit and the competitive pressures under which they operated required them to develop new kinds of relations with their makers. In place of the preindustrial relationship between merchant and domestic clothier or between yeoman clothier and independent journeyman, they had to create the relationship between capitalist and laborer. The difference between these two sets of relations is complex. Partly it was a transition from a personal to an impersonal economic relationship, for the maker ceased to be an individual and became merely one of many factors of production that had to be juggled in the quest for a profit. This change, of course, was never absolute. As Patrick Joyce has argued, the relationship between capitalist and laborer could retain a strong personal component even in the era of the factory.[76] Insofar as

---

75. CDA/FH/396, Stansfield letter book, Stansfield to John Patterson, 22 November 1730; CDA/MISC:8/117/2, Hill letter book, Hill to Ely Batterill, 17 February 1737/38.

76. Patrick Joyce, *Work, Society, and Politics: The Culture of the Factory in Later Victorian England* (Brighton, 1980).

Economic and Cultural Change   77

personal relations continued, however, their basis changed, for the independence of the domestic clothier and the journeyman was lost in the more paternalistic relationship between master and workman.

Yet the artisan's independence took some time to die. In the 1730s George Stansfield Sr. had to find a balance between market pressures and his makers' independence. In September 1731, replying to a letter that rebuked him for selling goods to Abraham Visser, another Dutch merchant, Stansfield reminded the Dorvilles that he had offered them the first refusal of the cloth at a lower price. Ten days later Stansfield wrote to urge them to order some of his better sorts of cloth, the type he had sold to Visser. Stansfield told them that if they did not, he would lose his best makers, "for they won't make a lower sort, and therefore he hoped they would not begrudge his selling these goods to other merchants."[77] Stansfield's predicament suggests how the unintended consequences of a manufacturer's economic practice helped to change attitudes. This episode occurred just as Stansfield was abandoning the consignment trade in favor of sales agreed to in advance, a development that encouraged the manufacturers' independence in the Dutch market. The implication of this transaction is that Stansfield was not eager to destroy his cozy relationship with the Dorvilles and enter the Dutch market as an independent operator, competing for orders from a number of merchants. His need to maintain some control over his makers, however, forced him to sell to other merchants; this move angered his regular partners and increased the competitive pressures on his business. Similarly, a few years later Samuel Hill explained to a Dutch merchant that he began making bays and long ells "to serve some of my workmen who would need desert to go to these manufactories."[78] Like Stansfield, he could not afford to ignore his makers' demands, but acquiescence in their demands forced him to enter a new phase in his business, the manufacturing of worsted cloth.

These signs of the makers' continuing independence, despite the fact that they were wage workers, appear alongside evidence of increasing tension between expectations of a personal relationship between master and servant and a new, more distant relationship between manufacturer and workman. In 1738 Hill commented that he could make a good quality of broad shalloon "provided I make constantly, but going

77. CDA/FH/396, Stansfield letter book, 28 September 1731; 8 October 1731.
78. CDA/MISC:8/117/2, Hill letter book, Hill to van Broyel, 17 February 1737/38.

from one sort to another spoils all the weavers."[79] In 1749, he received a sharp rebuke from a customer for the "very strange and pernicious circumstance" of allowing his makers to increase their prices when demand was high.[80] In both cases, the makers were made into anonymous factors of production by the pressures of the market, suppliers of labor who had to be controlled and managed. The imperatives of his business made Hill's relations with his makers less personal, for to keep them on one kind of cloth was to restrict their independence to choose what they made and perhaps even to choose the customer for whom they made it.

Manufacturers resolved this tension by adopting a more paternalistic stance toward their workers. Paternalism denied the workers' independence but maintained the customary personal relationship. In 1731, writing to a Dutch merchant to request orders for his cloth, George Stansfield Sr. acknowledged that the merchant already had lots of his cloth on hand, and he explained: "When I made them, poor people was very scarce of work and I employed them out of pity to my great loss, but trade continuing bad so long, the makers was obliged to turn to other work, and now we find it very hard to recall them." Five years later, in the midst of another depression, Stansfield was faced with the same problem again. In this case he did not keep his makers on, at least not for so long. I have "turn'd off a great many of my makers and keep turning off more weekly," he wrote in 1736, for as he explained, he preferred to do nothing rather than make goods at a loss.[81] These two letters must be interpreted with care, for Stansfield was pleading for orders, and perhaps his references to his makers were merely meant to arouse sympathy. There are probably both truth and guile in these comments. Stansfield was trying to manipulate his correspondent, but he also felt the legitimacy of his makers' claims on his protection. By thinking of them as "poor people" deserving of such protection, however, and indeed by giving them work for as long as he could during a slump, Stansfield was making these independent artisans into dependent workmen.

There are signs that such tensions were closer to being resolved by the middle of the century. One important reason was the sheer size of these manufacturers' operations. George Stansfield Sr. probably em-

79. Ibid.
80. CDA/FH/441, Hill letter book, Charles and Edmund Boehm to Hill, 6 April 1749.
81. CDA/FH/396, Stansfield letter book, Stansfield to Visser, 16 February 1730/31, and to John and Peter Dorville, 19 November 1736.

Economic and Cultural Change 79

ployed about fifty families as makers. George Jr. probably employed five times as many just to make his kerseys. Samuel Hill's payroll in this period, again just for kerseys, also probably approached 250.[82] These mid-eighteenth-century manufacturers were also separated from their makers by an increasingly large physical distance. George Stansfield Jr., Samuel Lees, and David Stansfield all put out a substantial portion of their work to makers living in Lancashire.[83] Since it was common to make use of a local innkeeper or shopkeeper to oversee the distribution of wool and collection of cloth, it is probable that these manufacturers only rarely met the makers who worked for them.

Even smaller manufacturers saw themselves as different from their workers. Thomas Walton, a shalloonmaker prosecuted for stealing two pounds of wool, was put in this embarrassing position because John Greenwood, his wool comber, informed on him. To explain how Greenwood might have been in a position to fabricate his story, Walton told the court that he was "*obliged* to keep woolcombers in his house at bed and board being distant from any town."[84] Wool combers were the artisanal elite of the worsted industry, yet in 1775 even a relatively small manufacturer could expect a jury to believe that such a degree of social proximity between master and workman was an extraordinary circumstance occasioned by his remote location.

By the mid–eighteenth century, paternalism was much more central to the way manufacturers regarded their workmen. Consider, for instance, the letters that Richard Hill sent to George Stansfield Jr. while he was acting as his agent in Europe. Commenting on Stansfield's intention to begin to trade in thin worsted goods such as "amiens," Hill recommended that he hire a former workman of his, one Peter Bancroft. According to Hill, Bancroft "knows well all our thin manufac-

---

82. The figure for George Stansfield Jr. is reasonably accurate, for his balance papers of 1764 list the names of the 57 makers who had 186 parcels of wool on hand, and indicates that other makers, not named, had 659 more parcels of wool on hand. Assuming the number of parcels per maker was the same, one comes up with an estimated 250 makers, remembering, of course, that each was probably the head of a household whose members assisted in the making of a piece of cloth: CDA/FH/409/2–3, Stansfield stocktaking. No list of names survives for George Stansfield Sr.'s nor Samuel Hill's makers. These rough estimates are based on the number of cloths each expected to make in a year (2,000 and 10,000, respectively) and the assumption that it would take a family a week to make a kersey.

83. Ibid.; CDA/RP/107c, defense brief, 1755; WYAS/Wakefield, QS/10/26, West Riding Quarter Sessions, order books, Pontefract sessions, 8 April 1771. Samuel Hill probably also put wool out to makers in Lancashire but no record of this activity has survived.

84. CDA/RP/107c, defense brief, 1755; my emphasis.

tures, when in the raw—in rolling up and papering pieces and in baling them afterwards, nobody can exceed him in neatness and judgement, . . . in singeing pieces carefully and well, and in finishing Amiens from first to last I think he has no equal." Yet the voice in which Hill spoke of this highly skilled artisan conveyed the distance between the social worlds of manufacturer and workman. "With me," Hill wrote, "he was forced to observe such exactness as has made him a real judge when goods are perfect"; "I have always found him honest and of modest behavior"; "I think I allowed him 12s per week and was kind to him besides."[85] We have entered a cultural world that Jonathan Baumforth could not have comprehended. The substantial manufacturer treated the workers he employed as abstract parts of the machine, objects who, if they were particularly useful, might be deserving of a little pity now and then.

CONCLUSION

Between the late seventeenth and mid–eighteenth centuries, the economic backbone of the parish's society was transformed. A rural textile industry dominated by the production of independent clothiers who sold their goods in the local market became an industry that was increasingly dominated by the concerns of large-scale merchants and manufacturers. The economic change was accompanied by a cultural transformation that brought into being entrepreneurial attitudes and new social relations. Both aspects of these changes in the textile industry were crucial to the emergence of a middle-class culture in Halifax. The wealth that economic development brought created a group of people who were capable of making a middle-class culture; the attitudinal changes associated with that economic development created the basis for that culture.

The relationship between these processes of economic and cultural change was reciprocal. The contributions of changes in practice to changes in attitudes have been emphasized here because they tend to be overlooked in accounts of how economic change occurs—images of the farsighted, risk-taking entrepreneur can be conjured up all too easily. Such images, however, are not wrong; the new attitudes these manufacturers and merchants developed encouraged further changes in

---

85. CDA/FH/461a, Hill to Stansfield, 31 January 1775, from Boulogne.

Economic and Cultural Change 81

practice and thus further changes in attitudes. No chicken-or-egg conundrum is involved in this process of change, for the situation seems illogical or contradictory only if the analysis artificially stops the reciprocal reinforcement of cultural structures and individual actions. The developments in the parish's textile industry were more than just economic changes; they represented a fundamental cultural transformation that helped to create the kind of distinct experience that was necessary for the origins of middle-class culture.

Chapter 4

Loans and Luxuries: Setting the Textile Industry in Context

Although the emergence of new economic practices among Halifax's merchants and manufacturers and the emergence of a culture that made those new practices possible was crucial to the long-term process of middle-class formation in Halifax, neither of these developments happened in isolation. Two other long-term changes—in the money market and in patterns of consumption—occurred in the parish between the late seventeenth and mid–eighteenth centuries. Both, of course, were closely related to the transformation of practice and culture in the textile industry. The money market changed in response to the financial complexity of merchants' and manufacturers' businesses and their requirements for capital. Similarly, the increasing availability of luxury goods and professional services in the parish was a reflection of the wealth of this new commercial elite. Yet neither of these developments was simply a derivative of changes in the textile industry.

In the first place, the increasing sophistication of the markets for money and goods in eighteenth-century Halifax was closley related to the world beyond the parish's boundaries, for both were features of the general economic and social developments of eighteenth-century society associated with the growth of a significant social middle. The impact of these external influences on the emergence of a middle-class experience thus involved the interplay between the locality and the nation. As Roger Chartier shows, groups are not necessarily passive recipients of new practices created elsewhere; rather, they appropriate those new practices and attach their own meanings to them.[1] To understand the origins of a middle-class culture in Halifax we have to recognize that developments associated with the emergence of the amorphous social middle in England as a whole were construed by the parish's commercial elite in a context increasingly dominated by the capitalist market relations of the textile industry.

In the second place, the new markets for loans and luxuries in eighteenth-century Halifax involved a much broader social group. The mere fact that George Stansfield Jr. employed some 250 "makers" in his kersey manufacturing operation does not make a middle class. Class identity involves the articulation of a common culture. We call it a "class" culture because its defining characteristic is the way that a group makes sense of its economic relations, but the culture itself determines and is determined by much more than simply the relations between a manufacturer and his workers. Hence it includes groups other than those who were directly involved in that economic relationship. The developments in Halifax's money market and patterns of consumption show that other groups, bystanders to the developments in the textile industry, shared a common culture. A new, larger group of wealthy professionals emerged alongside the merchants and manufacturers in the first half of the eighteenth century, and these families moved in the same social circles.[2] Gender is also important, for in contrast to the patterns of production in artisanal and laboring households, women were almost never active participants in the businesses of eighteenth-century merchants and manufacturers. Yet even though they were not directly engaged in the new economic practices of the textile industry, elite women joined men in making their new culture. To say

1. Roger Chartier, *The Cultural Origins of the French Revolution*, trans. Lydia Cochrane (Durham, N.C., 1991). T. H. Breen has used Chartier's insight to explore how consumer goods empowered a process of political resistance in the American colonies in the second half of the eighteenth century: "The Meanings of Things: Interpreting the Consumer Economy in the Eighteenth Century," in *Consumption and the World of Goods*, ed. John Brewer and Roy Porter (London, 1993), 249–60.

2. The legal profession has been extensively studied by C. D. Webster, "Halifax Attorneys" (in three parts), *THAS*, 1968, 69–87; 1969, 117–32; and 1971, 1–25. The other professions—medicine, the church, and such occupations as bookkeeping and schoolteaching—have not benefited from systematic studies of this sort. The close association between the professions and trade was typical throughout eighteenth-century England: John Seed, "From 'Middling Sort' to Middle Class in Late Eighteenth- and Early Nineteenth Century England," in *Social Orders and Social Classes in Europe since 1500: Studies in Social Stratification*, ed. M. L. Bush (London, 1992), 114–35.

that the families of the commercial and professional elites moved in the same social circles, for instance, is to imply that the relationship between those groups was mediated by women as well as men. These changes, like the developments associated with the textile industry, occurred as a result of a reciprocal relationship between practice and culture. Nobody set out to create a new market for capital or new patterns of consumption. Nor, for that matter, did existing cultural structures confine behavior in the money market or in buying household goods to the "traditional" patterns. Rather, change in what people actually did and in how they construed what they did occurred as a result of shifting structures of practice. This insight suggests the necessity of multicausal explanations for change; change happens because of unintended consequences, outside influences, *and* intentional actions. The cumulative effect of these forces in Halifax was the emergence of a common social experience and the elements of a common cultural conception of that experience among a new commercial and professional elite in the parish.

THE MONEY MARKET

While the economic success of Halifax's merchants and manufacturers was a significant achievement in its own right, it was dependent on other, more general developments. Among them was a network of financial services to meet the needs of manufacturers and merchants for long-distance financial transactions and investment capital. The evolution of these services was independent of the economic development in the parish itself, for the financial network that emerged in the eighteenth century was national and even international in scope. As R. S. Neale has argued, the network of short-term commercial credit became increasingly sophisticated in the eighteenth century, and it transformed eighteenth-century society by creating a complex and all-embracing web of economic relations that drew greater numbers and types of people into its ambit.[3] Pat Hudson and Francois Crouzet have shown that this developing network of bills of exchange was an important source of credit for merchants and manufacturers.[4] The market for capital was

---

3. R. S. Neale, *Bath, 1680–1850: A Social History* (London, 1981), chap. 5, and his *Writing Marxist History: Society, Economy, and Culture since 1700* (Oxford, 1985), chap. 1.

4. Pat Hudson, *The Genesis of Industrial Capital: A Study of the West Riding Wool Textile Industry*,

also transformed in the eighteenth century by the institution of the national debt, the host of new statutory authorities that could borrow on the security of projected income, and changes in the law concerning mortgages.[5] These national developments were introduced to Halifax by people active in the textile industry, but they came to be characteristic of a broader social group.

In late-seventeenth-century Halifax, as in England as a whole, credit was necessary for the day-to-day working of the economy. With cash in relatively short supply, a wide variety of transactions depended on the extensive network of short-term personal debt and credit in the community.[6] Although bills of exchange were known, they were not yet common. Only the occasional bill appears in the account books of Samuel Lister, a late-seventeenth-century manufacturer. All of these bills were payments from Edward Hill, a London cloth factor whom Lister frequently supplied, but even this account was often settled in cash. Lister did not use bills at all in his local dealings, even for relatively large transactions.[7]

As the scale and distance of their trade increased over the course of the eighteenth century, the dependence of Halifax's merchants and manufacturers on bills of exchange increased. By Samuel Hill's time the penetration of commercial credit into Halifax's economy was largely complete, for with one significant exception, Hill did not use cash in his business. Hill's domestic trade was carried out by a relatively straightforward exchange of bills drawn on the merchants whom he supplied with cloth and paid to those who supplied him with wool, but some exchanges were channeled through such merchants as Jeremiah Roydes of Halifax who facilitated exchanges by acting as a bank. Hill's trade with Dutch merchants required a more complicated credit network; their payments to him were sent to a banker in London, Peter Gaussens, who negotiated these foreign credits for a commission. But the ethereal exchange of bills that bound Hill up in a web of credit

---

1750–1850 (Cambridge, 1986); François Crouzet, ed., *Capital Formation in the Industrial Revolution* (London, 1972).

5. Paul Langford, *Public Life and Propertied Englishmen, 1689–1798* (Oxford, 1991).

6. B. L. Anderson, "Provincial Aspects of the Financial Revolution of the Eighteenth Century," *Business History* 11 (1969): 11–22. For direct evidence on Halifax see John Styles, "Our Traitorous Money Makers: The Yorkshire Coiners and the Law," in *An Ungovernable People*, ed. John Brewer and John Styles (London, 1980), 246–47.

7. CDA/SH:1/LB/1661–63, SH:1/OB/1668, Lister account books. Lister's wool sales, even of several bales at a time, were always settled with cash or pieces of cloth.

and debt stretching from London to Amsterdam to Halifax was no good for paying the workers who made the cloth he sold; Hill obtained the necessary coin by paying bills over to a William Elmsall of Wakefield in exchange for cash.[8] While the scale of his business may have been exceptional, Hill was not alone in his use of bills of exchange. From the 1730s, the use of bills spread to encompass transactions between manufacturers and merchants in the parish.[9] Their use also spread to people not directly concerned with the textile industry. Some shopkeepers, for instance, were willing to take bills in settlement of their accounts, and the household accounts of the attorney John Howarth show that, in some of his larger transactions, bills exchanged hands instead of cash.[10] Thus the national and even international web of credit involved not only the merchants and manufacturers of Halifax but also many others in the increasingly sophisticated economy of the eighteenth century.

The cultural implications of this web of credit were as great as the economic ones, for the spread of bills of exchange introduced new attitudes into the parish and reinforced existing developments. Perhaps most important were the more sophisticated accounts necessary to keep track of a business that depended on bills of exchange. As John Sutcliffe's operations suggest, involvement in a national web of credit imposed new accounting practices that required manufacturers to adopt a more rational approach to business finance. In 1769 Sutcliffe wrote a plaintive letter to his London banker apologizing for having "over drawn" his account; he also promised to remit bills to cover those he had drawn and to keep better accounts in the future.[11]

Of course, not all of Halifax's manufacturers and merchants needed so much prompting as Sutcliffe; men such as Hill had their own internal imperatives for keeping good accounts. Yet if the changes in practices and attitudes resulted from a combination of internal and external influences, they took on particular meanings in Halifax's social and economic context. There is evidence, for instance, that involvement in

---

8. CDA/FH/437, Hill ledger, 1736–41.

9. To give but one example of an increasingly common practice, George Stansfield of Sowerby paid off his debt of £50 to Samuel Stead of Halifax, incurred for wool that Stead had supplied to him, by bill: CDA/FH/396, Stansfield letter book, 2 July 1728.

10. CDA/STA/81, Stansfield receipts, a payment to a York tea merchant of two bills of £10 each; CDA/HAS/327 (33), Howarth ledger, 1755–66, and HAS/346 (15), Howarth cashbook, 1762–63.

11. CDA/HAS/449 (714), Sutcliffe memorandum book, Sutcliffe to W. W. Richardson, 1769.

a national web of credit served to identify the users of bills of exchange to one another as a group and to demarcate them from the social groups that did not use such instruments. There was surely a difference between the worldview of a manufacturer who used an early form of double-entry bookkeeping and that of a simple artisan who kept only rudimentary accounts. Certainly the involvement of the manufacturers in the national web of credit gave them a very different view of the Halifax Coiners crisis of the later eighteenth century. As John Styles's analysis of the event shows, the coiners—who clipped English coins and recast the shavings as Portuguese miodores—were tolerated and even encouraged by the small domestic clothiers of the region, who benefited from an increase in the scandalously short supply of coins. The manufacturers and merchants who had to trade outside of the region, in contrast, were risking their valuable creditworthiness by dealing with the doctored coins. The result was the formation of a society of manufacturers and merchants to secure government help in fighting the coiners. This society was only partly successful in its primary aim, but it did identify a very real division in Halifax based on involvement in the national web of credit.[12]

The development of Halifax's capital market follows a chronology similar to that of commercial credit. Although precise measurement is impossible, all the evidence suggests that the relatively small and unsophisticated market for capital that existed at the end of the seventeenth century grew rapidly in the first half of the eighteenth century.[13] The records of the Manor of Wakefield show that the number and value of the mortgages of copyhold land in the township of Sowerby increased between 1680 and 1740, especially after 1730. The use of a collusive legal procedure that gave the owner of a copyhold property a clear title also increased from 1730; although the legal procedure was invented to break entails, in Sowerby it was usually a prelude to a mortgage, for lenders wanted to know the property had no other encumbrances.[14] Unfortunately, the transactions recorded in the West Riding

---

12. Styles, "Our Traitorous Money Makers," 214–17, 248–49.
13. For the provinces as a whole see B. L. Anderson, "The Attorney and the Early Capital Market in Lancashire," in Crouzet, *Capital Formation*; "Law, Finance, and Economic Growth," in *Great Britain and Her World*, ed. B. Ratcliffe (Manchester, 1975); and "Provincial Aspects."
14. Yorkshire Archaeological Society, Leeds, Wakefield Court Rolls. The court rolls are extant for the period after 1740 but are too fragile to use. A good example of this procedure and the following mortgage is the transaction by Timothy Normanton, 1730, docket no. 85. Between 1680 and 1730, in a period when the number of transactions recorded in the court

TABLE 2. Mentions of mortgages and of money loaned at interest in sample wills probated, Halifax, 1690–1785

	1690–1709 (N = 220)		1710–1729 (N = 147)		1730–1749 (N = 186)		1750–1769 (N = 180)		1770–1785 (N = 173)	
	No.	%	No.	%	No.	%	No.	%	No.	%
Mortgage owed by or to testator	2	0.9%	3	2.0%	8	4.3%	11	6.1%	15	8.7%
Money loaned at interest	18	8.2	19	12.9	24	12.9	38	21.1	63	36.4

Source: Probate Records, Borthwick Institute of Historical Research, Pontefract Deanery and Prerogative Court.

Registry of Deeds, which was set up for the specific purpose of providing lenders with a clear title to freehold land, are not detailed enough to allow a calculation of the number or value of mortgages. It is perhaps worth noting that although the registry began in 1704, it did not really become heavily used until the 1730s and 1740s; this increase is attributable to more than an increasing number of mortgages, but that was undoubtedly an important component of the registry's business.[15]

Probate records also show the development of a market for capital. Table 2 shows increases in the number of wills that mentioned mortgages owed to or by the testator and in the number of wills that mentioned money put out to earn interest.[16] Since most mortgages were relatively short-term loans of one or two years, the number of mortgages mentioned in wills was only a small fraction of the total. Essentially, these figures measure the growing probability that a testator would die while party to a mortgage. The increase in the number of wills that mention money out at interest indicates the expectation among Halifax's testators that capital sums could be easily and securely invested. Indeed, the expectation that money was going to earn interest was so prevalent that in the 1760s William Foster thought it necessary

---

rolls remained steady at about 200 per decade, the proportion of mortgages increased (with some fluctuation) from just over 7 percent to almost 15 percent, and the average value of those mortgages increased from £68 to £148.

15. W. E. Tate, "Five English District Statutory Registries of Deeds," *Bulletin of the Institute of Historical Research* 20 (1943–45): 100; Hudson, *Genesis of Industrial Capital*, 96.

16. Perhaps the most common context in which interest payments were mentioned was a bequest of money to a legatee with instructions that the gift was to accrue interest until it was paid; see BIY/OW, Thomas Thompson, Skircoat, September 1751. Also relatively common were bequests that specifically mentioned that the testator was owed money with interest due.

TABLE 3. Number of wills instructing sale of real estate, Halifax, 1690–1785

Reason for selling	1690–1709	1710–1729	1730–1749	1750–1769	1770–1785
Payment of debts	6	6	3	2	2
Provisions of cash for younger children	3	5	4	9	17
Provision of cash for all children	2	1	1	4	8
Provision of maintenance for widow or underage children	–	1	3	–	1
All reasons	11	13	11	15	28
Wills mentioning land	134	98	115	111	108
Land sales as a percent of testators with land	8.2%	13.3%	9.6%	13.5%	25.9%

Source: Probate Records, Borthwick Institute of Historical Research, Pontefract Deanery and Prerogative Court.

to specify that a bequest to his daughter of £200, to be paid when she reached 24, was *not* to accumulate interest.[17]

A different measure of the development of a capital market in Halifax is the increase in the number of testators who instructed their executors to sell land in order to procure a cash sum and the uses that they specified for this money. Table 3 shows that up to 1730, the most common reason for selling land was to cover debts; in these cases, the testator typically specified that only a portion of his estate be sold. After 1750 selling land to pay off debts was rare. If land was sold, as it increasingly was, it was to provide cash portions for younger children or even, if all of the land was sold, for all of the children. By the third quarter of the eighteenth century, then, the capital market made it possible for a testator to transmit some or all of his property to his children in the form of cash.

Halifax's capital market changed in character as well as in size in the first half of the eighteenth century. At the turn of the century, bonds and mortgages were typically made between members of the same family; the account books of Samuel Lister, for instance, show that he borrowed several sums from cousins and uncles.[18] Such familial borrowing continued throughout this period, but developments in

17. BIY/OW, William Foster, Wadsworth, October 1760.
18. CDA/SH/AB:24, Lister family bonds.

the market made loans between unrelated and even unacquainted people possible. Local attorneys, for instance, were instrumental in obtaining mortgages for their clients, either as lenders or as borrowers, and they also remortgaged properties or transferred mortgages from one lender to another.[19] The geographical scope of the capital market also broadened to encompass the whole West Riding. This regional capital market gave rise to brokerage services such as the one that which Benjamin Worsdale of Leeds advertised in the *Leeds Mercury* in the 1730s and 1740s: "Several £50 to be lent on good bond; —several £100 on bond or mortgage; —several £150 to be lent on land security or other good mortgage; several £200, £300 on land or mortgage; —£400, £600, £800 on land security; —£1000, £2000, £3000 lent on land...."[20]

In Halifax, as in the rest of the country, the eighteenth century also saw an increase in the types of loans available. Although the practice was relatively uncommon, some Halifax residents owned shares in the national debt: Samuel Lister owned £1,000 worth of stock in the 4 percent consolidated fund at his death in 1766. Much more common were investments secured by the income of turnpikes, canals, or civic improvements. Sara Aked owned a mortgage of £220 in Halifax's waterworks when she died in 1781, and Elizabeth Barber bought £200 in shares in the Calder Navigation when it was launched in 1758.[21]

While the scope and nature of Halifax's capital market in the eighteenth century developed in a regional and national context, the significance of the changes lie in the meanings these new practices acquired in the local context. A Halifax testator who chose to sell all

---

19. Samuel Fenton billed Japhet Lister for procuring a mortgage on one of his properties in 1760: CDA/SH:3/B/1/1, Lister family bills. John Howarth presented a bill to John Wells that included a charge for arranging a mortgage: CDA/HAS/330 (759), Howarth bill book, f. 35–36. For a remortgage see Musgrave Brisco's purchase of a mortgaged property in 1752; the owner had made two mortgages to one person, both of which were transferred to a second person, who then was paid off by Brisco: HAS/371 (517), Howarth legal papers, 14 December 1752. The network created by such lawyers is described in M. Miles, "The Money Market in the Early Industrial Revolution: The Evidence from West Riding Attorneys, c. 1750–1800," *Business History* 23 (1981): 127–46.

20. *Leeds Mercury*, 7 September 1736.

21. BIY/OW, Samuel Lister, Southowram, Prerogative Court, November 1766 (he also owned £100 in the 3 percent funds); Sara Aked, Halifax, December 1781; CDA/FH/375, Stansfield navigation papers. The absence of investment in government funds and the importance of local statutory bodies were typical of provinces: Anderson, "Law, Finance," 108–9, and "Provincial Aspects," 21.

of his land to provide cash portions for his children could do so because of the development of a secure and accessible market for capital, but the choice itself has to be understood in the context of the developments in Halifax's textile industry which made a capital sum necessary for a son's start in trade. As the example of John and Samuel Lister suggests, before the early eighteenth century no one needed "capital"—conceived of as a sum of money that one invested in trade with the intention of making a profit—to begin trading as a manufacturer. Indeed, it does not appear that these people thought of their activities in terms of an investment of resources that could have been used elsewhere.[22] One of the effects of the emergence of manufacturing was an increasing need for capital as capital. As Pat Hudson has shown, clothiers increasingly began to use their estates as a way of securing the capital necessary for expansion or for surviving a depression.[23] Another sign of such new attitudes was the increasing number of partnership agreements in the eighteenth century, one of whose purposes was to pool a sufficient amount of capital to make a concern viable. Changing economic practice thus changed the set of cultural assumptions surrounding money, creating, in the context of Halifax's textile industry, a concept of capital as money to be invested in trade. As Samuel Lees's instructions that his money be left in the trade only as long as the yield was good suggests, this was money they were aware could be invested elsewhere.[24]

This concept of capital was not limited to textile entrepreneurs. Land, for instance, did not cease to be important as an investment. Even in the last twenty-year period shown in Table 3, only 25 percent of landowners instructed that even some of their land be sold. There is evidence, however, that the meaning of land as an investment had changed; rather than being part of the family patrimony, a safe and secure fallback from the uncertainties of the textile industry, land increasingly became an active investment, a commodity to be bought, sold, and, most important, improved.[25] When George Ramsbottam died in 1785 he was building cottages on a parcel of land he had recently

---

22. John Smail, "Manufacturer or Artisan? The Relationship between Economic and Cultural Change in the Early Years of Eighteenth-Century Industrialization," *Journal of Social History* 25 (1992): 791–814.

23. Hudson, *Genesis of Industrial Capital*, 85–86, 96–97.

24. BIY/OW, Samuel Lees, Skircoat, Prerogative Court, June 1761.

25. Charles Steffan, "Gentry and Bourgeois: Patterns of Merchant Investment in Baltimore County, Maryland, 1658–1776," *Journal of Social History* 20 (1987): 531–48.

purchased with money raised by a mortgage. His will instructed that the cottages were to be finished, and he authorized his executors to take out an additional mortgage on the property if it was necessary. Once the cottages were built, the rent from them was to pay the interest on the mortgages and support his widow. When she died, the cottages were to be sold, the mortgage was to be paid off, and the residue was to go to Ramsbottam's five daughters.[26] Ramsbottam saw these cottages as a moneymaking proposition, and the initial purchase of the land, made possible by a mortgage, was only a way for Ramsbottam to take advantage of Halifax's growing population to provide, ultimately, cash portions for his daughters.

Lenders, too, were adopting new concepts of capital. The more anonymous exchanges made possible by the developing capital market required lenders to evaluate the potential security of their investment in more abstract terms than was necessary for a late-seventeenth-century widow lending money to her nephew. They also had to choose among a wide variety of investments. Here, too, the local context was important. Some people preferred the security of stocks in the national debt or in local statutory authorities, but these options were never so popular as personal loans and mortgages.[27] One reason that mortgages were preferred may have been the greater liquidity that was available in the mortgage market. A bequest intended for an underage son might be put out at interest to provide for his education and apprenticeship, but it had to be available as capital when he reached his majority and could begin in business for himself.[28]

Lenders in Halifax's capital market, no less than borrowers, increasingly thought of their financial resources in terms of capital that could be employed in a variety of ways to yield a profit, and increasingly managed it to maximize that profit. For both lenders and borrowers, these cultural changes came about because of a combination of forces, internal and external to the parish, and as they were adopted, these practices acquired particular meanings in that context.

26. BIY/OW, George Ramsbottam, Stansfield, April 1785.

27. John Roydes, one of Halifax's wealthiest merchants, left money for the annuities that were to provide for one of his daughters and his housekeeper/governess in the "public funds" since he wanted no problems with the payment of these annuities: BIY/OW, John Roydes, Halifax, Prerogative Court, July 1781.

28. John Emmet, a Halifax iron founder, left his young son Samuel £2,000, the interest on which was to pay for his maintenance and education and "bringing up to some trade or business" until he was 21: BIY/OW, John Emmet, Halifax, July 1785.

CONSUMPTION

Changes related to but not derivative of the economic and cultural developments in the textile industry occurred on the other side of the merchants' and manufacturers' account books: not their demand for capital but their growing spending power. Merchants and manufacturers did not reinvest all of their profits in business. Some of the money was siphoned off to support a more luxurious lifestyle, and this development was reflected in the demand for services and goods in the parish. As with Halifax's developing money market, the changing patterns of consumption have to be seen in a national context, for the fashions of the metropolis were copied in the provinces—often selectively, but with increasing rapidity as the century progressed.[29] Once again adoption operated alongside appropriation, for Halifax's emerging elite gave these new practices and fashions meanings that were relevant to the local context.

One side of the changing patterns of consumption was the growth in the range of services available. A town of local and even regional importance, Halifax had had lawyers of some description throughout the early modern period, but during the eighteenth century the numbers of lawyers practicing in the parish increased dramatically and so did the range of services they offered. In the seventeenth century the main business of local lawyers, many of whom would be more accurately described as scriveners, was conveyancing and wills. For instance, a father and son, John Hargreaves Sr. and Jr., were very active in the late seventeenth century making wills and deeds; they did not do more complicated work, nor did they undertake cases in London, for they were not qualified to do so.[30]

---

29. For the spread of fashion to the provinces see Alan Everitt, "Country, County, and Town: Patterns of Regional Evolution in England," *Transactions of the Royal Historical Society*, 5th ser., 29 (1979): 79–108; Peter Borsay, *The English Urban Renaissance: Culture and Society in the Provincial Town, 1660–1770* (Oxford, 1989); Penelope Corfield, *The Impact of English Towns, 1700–1800* (Oxford, 1982); Amanda Vickery, "Women and the World of Goods: A Lancashire Consumer and Her Possessions, 1751–81," in Brewer and Porter, *Consumption and the World of Goods*, 274–301; Lorna Weatherill, *Consumer Behavior and Material Culture in Britain, 1660–1760* (London, 1988). For the history of consumption in general, Neil McKendrick's work remains an important starting point. See, e.g., "Commercialization and the Economy," in McKendrick, John Brewer, and J. H. Plumb, *The Birth of a Consumer Society* (London, 1983), 9–194. However, many of the essays in Brewer and Porter, *Consumption and the World of Goods*, are critical of all or parts of McKendrick's analysis.

30. Webster, "Halifax Attorneys," pt. 1, 82, 84.

During the eighteenth century, conveyancing continued to provide the bulk of the local attorneys' trade, but it was usually supplemented by a much broader range of services. Robert Parker and John Howarth, two of Halifax's more prominent attorneys in the second half of the eighteenth century, made most of their money by making deeds, but they also did bankruptcy proceedings, chancery cases, partnership agreements, marriage settlements, and local government work.[31] Even the wills and deeds drawn up in Parker and Howarth's time were more complex than those of half a century earlier; for example, preexisting mortgages and the proliferation of trusts made deeds and wills so much longer and more complex that they required the services of a fully qualified attorney instead of a scrivener.

Developments in other professions are more obscure. The church experienced no significant growth, but more doctors were practicing in mid-eighteenth-century Halifax than there had been earlier. The numbers of bookkeepers and schoolmasters also increased. It is not until the late 1730s that any of the surviving commercial account books show the influence of a bookkeeper's diligence, but thereafter it becomes more common. Advertisements in Halifax's only newspaper, the short-lived *Union Journal,* provide a sense of the numbers of schoolmasters in the parish by midcentury and the range of subjects they taught: in addition to the traditional grammar school subjects, students could learn modern European languages, account keeping, dancing, and music. Indeed, people in the lesser professions might often wear several hats. William Norris, for instance, was appointed as the clerk to the Calder Navigation committee and supplemented his salary by teaching writing, accounts, and the "true Italian method of bookkeeping." Similarly, the organist at the parish church was expected to supplement his salary of £20 a year "by teaching scholars, tuning instruments, and other perquisites that may arise from his situation."[32]

Related to the development of a service industry in the parish was the growing range of consumer goods that its residents bought. The extent of the growth in this sector of Halifax's economy is suggested by an increase in the number of nontraditional craft occupations recorded in wills. In the 1690s, only 8.9 percent of the people whose occupations were recorded worked outside of the textile industry or

31. CDA/RP/various, Parker legal papers; CDA/HAS/332 (1), Howarth daybook, 1749–83.
32. The *Union Journal or Halifax Advertiser,* 29 July 1760 and 15 June 1760; BIY/CP, I/1449, Halifax organ case, testimony of Henry Bates, 12 December 1764; J. W. Houseman, "The History of the Halifax Parish Church Organ," *THAS,* 1928, 77–112.

the basic craft and provision trades, such as carpentry, masonry, and baking. These were a chapman, a nailer, a clockmaker, two innkeepers, two linen drapers, two mercers, and three each of apothecaries, shoemakers, and tailors. By the 1720s and 1730s, that proportion had increased to 10.1 percent, and by the 1760s and 1770s the figure rose to 20 percent. Occupations such as innkeeper, cordwainer, linen draper, grocer, and shopkeeper were relatively common by the mid-eighteenth century, but more unusual trades such as breeches maker, saddler, and staymaker were also making an appearance.

These more exotic trades were supplying a fairly exclusive market, one that had not existed half a century earlier. The scope of this luxury market can be gauged from advertisements in the *Union Journal*. Alex Smith, bookseller, advertised an auction of books. An anonymous entrepreneur informed the public of the opening of "commodious cold baths" in Ovenden. William and Robert Appley, joiners, advertised that from their shop opposite Mr. Caygill's square in Halifax they would undertake all kinds of joinery, "in the neatest manner, suitable for gentlemen and ladies and all others of the smaller abilities, at lowest prices"—a comment that suggests an awareness of the different markets that were developing in Halifax.[33] The first directory that included Halifax, William Bailey's *Northern Directory* of 1781, shows a similar trend. It was mostly concerned to list the large merchants and manufacturers of the town, but several men in the luxury trades were also included. There were five grocers, four drapers, four druggists, three ironmongers, a brass founder, an iron founder and boxmaker, a silk merchant, a watchmaker, and an innkeeper at "an excellent house."[34]

The existence of these shopkeepers and craftsmen is but one sign of a fundamental change in consumption patterns in Halifax in the first half of the eighteenth century. As we saw in Chapter 2, the striking feature of the household inventories of the late seventeenth and early eighteenth centuries is the overall similarity in the quality of the goods in the houses of the poor, the middling sort, and even the relatively rich. The lack of important distinctions in the types of goods found in the households of Halifax's broad middling sort is not surprising. The growth in consumption that was to transform eighteenth-century society was only just beginning, and in Halifax, as in much of the rest of

---

33. *Union Journal*, 3 April 1759, 29 July 1760, 29 April 1760, and 24 April 1759.
34. William Bailey, *Northern Directory* (Warrington, Lancs., 1781), 200–203. Other suggestive occupations that appeared in increasing numbers were doctor, surgeon, and bookseller.

England, household furnishings were locally made and were not yet subject to the dictates of fashion. Nor is it possible to distinguish the lack of means from the lack of desire. The middling sort might buy a feather bed to replace one of straw, or pewter and brass to replace wooden trenchers, but these things were comforts, not significant statements of a new social distance.[35]

Even around the turn of the century there were exceptions to this pattern. The "russia leather chairs" in John Wainhouse's parlor were significantly more valuable than other chairs listed in inventories of the same period; they were a luxury that would have set his house apart from those of his neighbors.[36] In the late seventeenth century, however, such instances were rare and such luxury goods were out of place even in the inventories of the people who owned them: John Wainhouse's russia leather chairs were in the same room as goods that could have been found in the house of any moderately well-to-do yeoman. During the eighteenth century both of these patterns began to change. Not only did the possession of luxury goods become common among an identifiable group, but these families tended to own a range of such goods and to place them in a single room or two. Although probate inventories become increasingly less common after 1730, the few inventories of wealthy decedents made in the 1740s all contain luxury goods of one sort or another, and these goods tended to be grouped in one or two rooms, suggesting the emergence of the "front parlor" with its attendant social implications. Francis Priestly, for example, a yeoman from Hipperholme, had a room described as the "best chamber" with a carpet, an oval table, a screen, and an expensive bed, and he also had a room described as the "lower parlor" with a turn-up table valued at 14 shillings, curtains, a mirror, and five little pictures. Similarly, Jeremiah Drake, a druggist, had a parlor that contained a tea table, a chimney glass, two family portraits, floor mats, and six china plates.[37]

By the 1780s, when inventories become somewhat more common

---

35. McKendrick, "Commercialization and the Economy"; Weatherill, *Consumer Behavior*. Weatherill's extensive sample of inventories suggests that between 1675 and 1725 most "advances" in the ownership of material goods were concentrated in the realm of comforts rather than luxuries.

36. BIY/OW, John Wainhouse, Skircoat, April 1693.

37. BIY/OW, Francis Priestly, Hipperholme (outsized will), May 1745; Jeremiah Drake, Northowram, March 1745/46. See the discussion of "fronstage" activity and its implications for material culture in Weatherill, *Consumer Behavior*, 9.

again, a change in the goods available and in their display is evident. John Sutcliffe, who lived in the western extremity of the parish, had a parlor with an oak snap tea table, six china cups and saucers, six silver teaspoons, silver tongs, a glass decanter, and some china and delftware cups. The only thing that marred this room's status as the front parlor were the two beds that were also listed. Nathaniel Aked must have been a lodger in someone else's house when he died in 1785, for only one room is listed in his inventory, but it was filled with luxury goods, including an oak tea table, a mahogany tea table, and an eight-day clock in an oak case.[38] Sutcliffe and Aked, moreover, were by no means among the wealthiest residents of the parish who died during this period.

Surviving household account books confirm the impression given by probate inventories. John Howarth's cashbook records the payments this prominent attorney made for such ephemeral luxuries as a satin hat for his daughter (3/6d), a hat for his son (6s), and gingerbread (1s) bought while on a visit to Wakefield.[39] Among such mundane items as a chest of drawers, a water tub, and a large chest that Catharine Lister inventoried in 1761 were such luxuries as a large glass dressing case, a black ebony table, a card table with black velvet, half a dozen "madgena" chairs, a japan box, a mahogany tea table, china dishes and plates, teacups and saucers, and a japan plate warmer.[40] Arranging interiors in the new style was not just a question of furniture; some of Halifax's wealthier residents went so far as to rebuild their houses, and when they did so they invariably included substantial luxuries. During the time that George Stansfield Jr. was building a new mansion, he made notes of where he could get such things as mahogany planks and marble. The marble was presumably for a fireplace like the one that was mentioned in one of the Lees family's partnership agreements.[41] Perhaps the most extravagant of these new mansions was the house of the Roydes family, which was grand enough to allow Roydes to serve as host to the king of Denmark when he visited the parish in 1768.[42]

The particular importance attached to articles associated with the consumption of tea, coffee, and chocolate, helps us to reconstruct their

38. BIY/OW, John Sutcliffe, Stansfield, April 1785; Nathaniel Aked, Halifax, April 1785.
39. CDA/HAS/346 (15), Howarth cashbook, 1762–63.
40. CDA/SH:3/AB/17, Lister account book, 1761.
41. CDA/FH/399, Stansfield accounts, n.d. (mid–eighteenth century); CDA/RP/897, 1773.
42. T. W. Hanson, "The Roydes of George Street, Halifax, and Bucklersbury, London," *THAS*, 1941, 76.

diffusion through the parish. The earliest references to tea drinking found in the Halifax probate records are in two inventories in the 1720s, both of men of the upper ranks of Halifax society. George Mewson, a local attorney, had a tea table and a silver teapot worth £12/2, and also a small amount of chinaware. James Kitson, a stapler from Halifax town, owned sixty-seven pieces of "china ware," a "tea table tray," and a tea kettle when he died in 1725.[43]

By mid-century, all of the surviving household accounts show payments for tea or coffee, and teacups and other chinaware appear more frequently in wills. Nathaniel Chadwick, a yeoman active in the cloth trade, left to Elizabeth, his "dear and loving wife," £500 out of his personal estate, and all the silver, linen, and household goods that she had brought to the marriage. He also left her the rents and profits of his real estate and goods sufficient to furnish a room, including a bed, clock, and silver cup, two silver salters, and the cups and furniture that went with the tea table. Such bequests were never common, but they were usually mentioned in such a way as to emphasize their importance and to suggest that the owners were beginning to value such social refinements and had the leisure necessary to use them. When John Sutcliffe, a stuffmaker of Sowerby, bequeathed his wife a freehold estate in the neighboring township and the goods necessary to furnish a room, the only items he mentioned specifically were "the bed that we usually sleep on" and "my china ware and other things used in and about drinking of tea."[44]

Bequests of tea and coffee paraphernalia were usually made to women. Like Chadwick and Stucliffe, many husbands left such goods to their wives, who in turn often left them to their daughters. Ann Smith, for instance, left a damask table linen, silver coffeepot and stand, and six silver spoons to her daughter Elizabeth, and another damask table linen and a mirror to her daughter Jane. Male heirs received other things. Nathaniel Priestly left his repeating clock, two silver sauce-

43. BIY/OW, George Mewson, Hipperholme, April 1721; Thomas Kitson, Hipperholme, July 1725. In view of the high quality of inventories before the 1720s, these are almost certainly the first instances of tea paraphernalia in the parish. McKendrick comments that tea consumption increased fifteenfold during the course of the eighteenth century: "Commercialization and the Economy," 29, 104. See also Weatherill, *Consumer Behavior*, 37.

44. CDA/STA/81, Stansfield receipts, 1763; CDA/SH:1/SHA/3a, Lister account book, c. 1756; CDA/HAS/307 (322), Firth daybook, 1750, and HAS/346 (15), Howarth cashbook, 1762–63; BIY/OW, Nathaniel Chadwick, Halifax, November 1746, and John Sutcliffe, Sowerby, April 1771. On tea drinking as an important marker of social status during this period, see Weatherill, *Consumer Behavior*, 187–89.

Loans and Luxuries 99

boats, and a silver coffeepot to his daughter, while his son and son-in-law received parts of his library. Hannah Sutcliffe left her new bed and curtains, her pinchbeck watch, and silver teaspoons to her mother for her life, but after her mother's death the bed was to go to her brother, while the watch and spoons were to go to her niece.[45] The unequal distribution of luxury goods within the family suggests that women played a crucial role in the creation and maintenance of the social distinctions that went along with these items. The use of these goods, and thus the social conventions and practices that revolved around the serving of tea or coffee or of a meal on china plates, were necessary parts of the distinct material culture these men and women were creating.[46]

As in the case of the money market, this developing material culture had its origins in the world outside of Halifax. The point is perhaps obvious, but it is seen with particular clarity in the accounts of Jonathan Hall. Hall left Halifax for London in 1701 to serve an apprenticeship as an upholsterer, and after taking his freedom of the city he remained in the metropolis into the 1740s. In the 1720s and 1730s, the period for which detailed accounts survive, Hall's business was varied. As well as making and repairing chairs and curtains, he worked as an interior decorator, decking out a church in mourning for the funeral of the "honorable Lady Martin" in 1723, or, more mundanely, finishing several rooms in the house of Mr. Robert Rogers. Hall also operated as a merchant, supplying customers in the provinces with the range of goods available in London. Hall maintained contact with his native parish, for one of his accounts was with a William Wood of Halifax. A typical shipment, sent in June 1726, included "a large looking glass in a walnut frame, a pair of glass arms and a pair of brass arms, a swinging glass in a walnut frame, 6 Dutch tables, 4 square and 2 oval, 12 chairs with India backs, French feet and fine cane bottoms, and three sets of gilt cornices." Some six months later, Hall sent Wood still more chairs, a settee bed, four tea tables, and a large selection of hats.[47]

---

45. BIY/OW, Ann Smith, Halifax, September 1770; Nathaniel Priestly, Halifax, May 1781; Hannah Sutcliffe, Halifax, July 1782. Amanda Vickery has shown that table china and silver were usually selected by the wife, who instructed her husband about what to buy: "Women and the World of Goods," 276–81.

46. Leonore Davidoff and Catherine Hall, *Family Fortunes: The Men and Women of the English Middle Class, 1780–1850* (London, 1987). I discuss the changing place of women in household production in detail in Chapter 6.

47. CDA/SH:3/AB/11, Hall account book.

Hall's shipments provided Halifax's residents with household goods from London, goods selected by a man whose work for the titled elite kept him in touch with changing fashions.[48] Needless to say, Hall's shipments were not the only contact that Halifax's residents had with the new material culture of the eighteenth century. Almost everyone of any status in eighteenth-century Halifax had a friend or relative in London, and the men, at least, often went there themselves. Nor did one have to go all the way to London to be exposed to these new goods.[49] Leeds, Wakefield, and Pontefract were a day's journey from Halifax, and York was only a little more distant. The markets in all three towns, not to mention the necessity of legal business, ensured that most of Halifax's elite made regular visits to these places.[50]

On one level, then, a more sophisticated consumer culture emerged in Halifax as the commercial and professional elite adopted practices and fashions generated outside their community. As these new practices and goods were appropriated, however, they acquired or were given meanings shaped by the local context. Of particular importance were the social implications of this material culture. In the first place, the use of certain services and the possession of certain goods helped to define the members of an increasingly distinct group. Halifax attorneys, for instance, drew most of their clients from this new group of merchant and manufacturing families, more and more of whose lives, from simple conveyancing to partnerships, trusts, and marriages, became transactions undertaken by their lawyers.[51] The lesser professionals also offered services, whether keeping a partnership's accounts or teaching accounting or music, the use of which also defined a distinct group. The possession of certain kinds of consumer goods served an equivalent function and suggests that new practices and attitudes spread beyond the narrow commercial world of the merchants and manufacturers. The families of doctors, lawyers, and clerks all shared the comforts and refinements that prosperity brought, and they developed, along with the merchant and manufacturing families, new cul-

---

48. CDA/SH:3/AB/10, Hall account book, draft letter, 5 August 1716, mentions two china glasses he had just seen that he thought the recipient might be interested in.

49. In her analysis of the purchases of a Lancashire gentlewoman Amanda Vickery has shown that the world of fashion had local and regional as well as national dimensions: "Women and the World of Goods," 288–91.

50. Borsay, *English Urban Renaissance*, argues that York in particular was the center of polite society in the North.

51. CDA/HAS/327 (33), Howarth ledger, 1755–66.

tural expectations about the goods and services necessary for the life they wished to lead.

As well as identifying the members of an increasingly distinct group to one another, the use of these services and goods informed this group's relations with other groups. On one hand, implicit in the very genesis of the eighteenth-century consumer culture was the attempt by middling people to demonstrate their social worth by purchasing goods associated with a higher status. Recent work on the history of consumption shows that in doing so middling people were not slavishly emulating their social betters. If, however, they bought new goods not to become aristocrats but to enhance their lives as merchants or lawyers, they did so in part with the intent of establishing their social credentials.[52] Equally important was the way Halifax's merchant, manufacturing, and professional families appropriated this material culture to distinguish themselves from their social inferiors. Of course, it was not difficult to derive this particular message from the possession of a distinct set of goods. However, in a social and economic context increasingly shaped by large-scale production, this message made sense, and was thus emphasized, by the people who owned china teacups and had their sons taught the "true Italian method of bookkeeping."

Yet the meanings that Halifax's merchant, manufacturing, and professional families gave to the use of certain services and the possession of certain goods have to be understood in the context of a changing social structure and the new relations of production that gave rise to it. The impact of the development of large-scale manufacturing on Halifax's society was profound, extending far beyond the new social relations that emerged between manufacturer and worker. Perhaps the most important result of this economic process was an increasingly polarized social structure that no longer corresponded to the social world of the middling sort. While the hearth tax returns of 1664 suggest that the residents of Halifax were ranged along a social continuum, the land tax returns of 1782 show that the parish's social structure had become more lopsided. In 1782 we find many more poor households and more

52. Jean-Christophe Agnew, "Coming Up for Air: Consumer Culture in Historical Perspective," 19–39; Colin Campbell, "Understanding Traditional and Modern Patterns of Consumption in Eighteenth-Century England: A Character-Action Approach," 40–57; Lorna Weatherill, "The Meaning of Consumer Behavior in Late Seventeenth- and Early Eighteenth-Century England," 206–27; and Vickery, "Women and the World of Goods" all in Brewer and Porter, *Consumption and the World of Goods*. See also Ben Fine and Ellen Leopold, "Consumerism and the Industrial Revolution," *Social History* 15 (1990): 151–79.

TABLE 4. Exemptions from hearth and land taxes in selected Halifax townships, 1664 and 1782

	Hearth tax, 1664			Land tax, 1782		
	Household	No. exempt	Percent exempt	Households	No. exempt	Percent exempt
Halifax	502	209	41.7%	1,514	1,257	83.0%
Skircoat	85	28	33.0	321	218	67.9
Southowram	148	54	36.5	540	346	64.1
Northowram	328	157	48.0	741	476	64.2
Hipperholme	199	67	33.7	377	213	56.5
Shelf	83	29	34.9	200	144	72.0
Warley	256	83	32.5	502	288	57.4
Midgley	95	25	26.3	225	132	58.7
Ovenden	308	117	38.0	706	480	68.0
Sowerby	468	140	29.9	640	371	58.0

Sources: PRO/E.179/210/393; WYAS/Wakefield, QE/13/7/various. Figures for the number of households in 1782 are from the curate's census, 1776: CDA/MISC/118.

very wealthy ones. Any comparison between the hearth tax and the land tax must be made with caution, of course, but evidence on the numbers of exemptions from payment is the most reliable and the most revealing. As Table 4 shows, the proportion of exempted households—those living at or below the poverty line—was almost twice as high in every township for which figures can be calculated, having risen from around one-third to almost two-thirds.[53] Unfortunately, the different characters of the two taxes makes comparison at the other end of the social spectrum more problematic. Although both taxes measured the value of the property that the family actually occupied, they did so in different ways, particularly since the land tax assessed the property's agricultural land as well as the house itself. A comparison of the number of households that were wealthy as opposed to merely comfortable, if not conclusive, is certainly suggestive. In Halifax, the wealthiest township in the parish in both periods, just over 12 percent of the assessed households

---

53. The ecclesiastical "census" from which I calculated the number of exempted households in 1782 (CDA/MISC/118) was prepared by an Anglican curate and probably gives fairly accurate estimates of the populations of those townships, because the Church of England collected tithes from all residents. Moreover, the figure for the township of Sowerby is in agreement with a very accurate "census" made of that township's residents (of all denominations) in 1764: CDA/STA/215/3. Both taxes exempted not only householders on parish relief but also those too poor to pay local rates: Roger Howell, "Hearth Tax Returns," *History*, n.s. 49 (1964): 42–54.

had six or more hearths in 1664, but in 1782 over 30 percent of houses were assessed more than £20 a year.

Thus the new consumer culture contributed to the reciprocal relationship between economic and cultural change in the textile industry. Already constructing a new set of economic and social relations that turned artisans into workers, Halifax's manufacturers appropriated aspects of the eighteenth century's consumer culture to articulate more broadly the social differences that separated them from these workers. They were, in essence, constructing a new map of the changing social order. Moreover, just as the attitudinal changes discussed in Chapter 3 caused and were caused by changes in economic practices, the emergence of these new social relations in this much broader sphere, and the assumptions that underlay them, caused and were caused by the trend toward large-scale production and the emergence of the objective category of "worker." Attorneys and merchants and the families of the manufacturers—people who did not themselves employ large numbers of laborers and who were outside of the developing wage nexus—were nonetheless active agents in this process of social polarization, for they too constructed a map of their changing social world on the basis of new patterns of consumption. These cultural changes had the cumulative effect of emphasizing the social barrier between the poor and their betters and of shifting its location. The boundary that had separated the middling sort from the laboring poor was replaced by a more exacting standard that separated merchant, manufacturing, and professional families from the laboring poor *and* the parish's artisanal population.

Consumption was not the only arena in which these new social relations were articulated. Changing structures of local government, and in particular poor relief, also suggest the emergence of a new set of social relations that allowed the elites to treat the poor as members of a distinct social group. The work of historians such as William Hunt, David Underdown, Keith Wrightson, and David Levine shows that the starting point of this process of change was not a preindustrial golden age of harmonious social relations, but the parish's egalitarian Puritanism and the absence of any evidence of a concerted attempt at Puritan social control before the outbreak of the Civil War or during the interregnum seems to suggest that the "poor" in Halifax were not culturally distinct from their more fortunate neighbors.[54] Of course

---

54. William Hunt, *The Puritan Moment: The Coming of Revolution to an English County* (Cam-

seventeenth-century elites saw themselves as socially distinct from the laboring poor, but the nature of the social differences expressed changed dramatically between the seventeenth and eighteenth centuries. The impulse of the Puritan reformers described in the works of Hunt, Underdown, and Wrightson and Levine was directed at moral control of the poor. Hunt, in particular, makes it clear that yeomen and gentlemen in Jacobean Essex saw the poor and their sins as but one of the many fronts on which the Antichrist was threatening their world. Thus seventeenth-century poor relief, though informed by a real social distance, was still "personalized" in that it attempted to correct the poor. As Gertrude Himmelfarb has shown, the concept of poverty based on the moral economy was replaced in the eighteenth century by one based on political economy.[55] In the discourse of the dominant elite, the poor were objectified; they became an inevitable feature of the system, and their control required the formation of rigorous and rational institutions.

One indication of the Halifax elites' increasingly rational management of the poor is the change in the style in which township accounts were kept. The haphazard accounts of the seventeenth and early eighteenth centuries gave way to more rigorous systems in all but the smallest townships from the 1730s. A separate account book was often kept for each officer, and the debit and credit sides of an account for a given year were entered on opposite sides of an open page, with balances carried over to the next page. Perhaps most significant, the accounts were examined by the vestry—which included professionals and landowners as well as merchants and manufacturers—at least once a year and often more frequently.[56] Accounts had to be kept meticulously, as the Sowerby workhouse account book stated, "to know what the house uses every month and every year."[57]

---

bridge, Mass., 1983); David Underdown, *Revel, Riot, and Rebellion: Popular Politics and Culture in England, 1603–1660* (Oxford, 1985); Keith Wrightson and David Levine, *Poverty and Piety in an English Village: Terling, 1525–1700* (New York, 1979). The one instance of "social control" in the prewar period was the Halifax workhouse, established in 1635, whose governors had extensive powers to regulate the local poor. Established on the basis of letters patent signed by Charles I, the workhouse collapsed within a few years because of a lack of support from this staunchly Puritan parish.

55. Gertrude Himmelfarb, *The Idea of Poverty* (New York, 1984), 3–41.

56. This transition can be seen in two account books that are extant for the entire period under discussion: CDA/MIC/9, Halifax churchwardens' accounts, and CDA/SPL/143, Sowerby constables' accounts.

57. CDA/SPL/32, Sowerby overseers' accounts, 1758–73, instructions for taking accounts on the first page.

A new rationality is also evident in other aspects of the eighteenth-century system of poor relief. Pat Hudson's analysis of the pauper apprenticeship records for the township of Sowerby suggests that from the mid–eighteenth century, this aspect of poor relief was managed with an eye to giving the manufacturers and merchants who controlled local government every possible advantage in the industrial labor market.[58] The administration of the settlement laws also indicates the shifts in these social relations.[59] A statute of 1697 allowed the townships in the parish to collect a "settlement certificates" from any immigrant deemed to be potentially in need of relief, but none made extensive use of this provision until the second quarter of the eighteenth century. The dramatic rise in the use of this aspect of the settlement laws between 1725 and 1745 indicates the parish elites' increasing willingness to use the law against the laboring poor, which in turn suggests the emergence of new cultural attitudes that encouraged such rigorous treatment of a group that encompassed the artisanal population.[60]

There were other reasons for the observed rationalization in the elite's control of the poor, not least the spiraling poor rates.[61] It is worth noting, however, that the changes, particularly those in the account books, paralleled the emergence of new accounting methods among merchants, manufacturers, and professionals. In a sense, the appearance of precise bookkeeping in the township accounts is to be expected as the task of running a township became more complicated. If only because more money was involved, more exacting methods were needed to keep track of the finances. The significance of this development for the emergence of a middle-class culture in Halifax lies in the way merchants and manufacturers took the cultural expectations they were developing in a business context and applied them to local

58. Pat Hudson, address to the Halifax Antiquarian Society, 17 October 1991.
59. James S. Taylor, "The Impact of Pauper Settlement, 1691–1834," *Past and Present* 73 (1976): 48–52; Philip Styles, "The Evolution of the Law of Settlement," *University of Birmingham Historical Journal* 9 (1963–64): 33–63; E. M. Hampson, "Settlement and Removal in Cambridgeshire, 1662–1834," *Cambridge Historical Journal* 2 (1926): 273–89.
60. The application of these settlement laws can be followed in six of the parish's townships: Halifax (CDA/MISC/93/1–4, CDA/OR/97, and CDA/HAS/154 [672]), Sowerby (CDA/SPL/92–94), Elland (CDA/EG/A/3/1–193 and EG/A/34, 37, 39, 40, 81, 86), Heptonstall (CDA/HPC/A/11), Shelf (CDA/MISC/374/2/1–2), and Ovenden (CDA/HAS/110 [241], HAS/106 [255], HAS/107 [239], HAS/94 [240]). After a peak in the 1730s and 1740s, use of the laws fell off as rapidly as it had grown, probably because the system was too clumsy to maintain.
61. Surviving overseers' accounts show that poor rates in the parish rose by a factor of 2 or 3 between the beginning and the middle of the eighteenth century: Halifax, CDA/MIC/9; Hipperholme, CDA/HAS/65 (767); Ovenden, CDA/HAS/200 (70); and Sowerby, CDA/SPL/31.

government. No doubt many of the officers who carried out poor relief and highway repair in the 1750s kept accounts very much as their predecessors of the later seventeenth century had done—by making a detailed but unorganized list of the payments made and the tax assessments received. In the seventeenth century, the vestry simply entered these accounts, as they were, in the town's account book. In the mid–eighteenth century, the vestry took these accounts and calculated a more regular, if more abstract, version of the year's expenditures and entered that in the book. These forms of accounting seem to have been carried over to the sphere of poor relief from the business world. Once in the new arena these new practices had cultural implications that affected the social relations between the poor and their betters. These new accounting procedures, implying the ability to perform profit/loss calculations concerning the poor, also imply a significant objectification of the problem of poverty.

CONCLUSION

The developments in the textile industry were contemporaneous with a much broader transformation of Halifax's economy, society, and culture. A new money market, involving bills of exchange and investment credit, developed and began to transform the way everyone from a manufacturer to a lawyer's widow perceived money, credit, and land. At the same time, the full purses of merchant and manufacturing families introduced the consumer society into Halifax and brought with it new professionals: both the providers of these luxury goods and the managers of an increasingly complex financial world. Silk merchants, doctors, and lawyers were ancillary to the textile industry in one sense, since their livelihoods depended on the merchants' and manufacturers' profits; but they moved in the same social circles and shared the same culture, one that was becoming increasingly distinct. The merchants and manufacturers, then, made more of their own kind.

These developments transformed both the objective structures of Halifax's economy and society and the mental worlds of its elite in ways that made the emergence of a middle-class culture possible. The new money market, which hinged on and encouraged new perceptions of how money and land could be used, formed the basis for the economic interactions characteristic of capitalist market relations. The new consumer society, which hinged on and encouraged new perceptions of how social distance could be measured and enforced, brought new goods and services to the parish. Thus the new economic structures that developed in Halifax's textile industry between the late seventeenth and mid–eighteenth centuries were associated with changes with much wider implications. The emergence of merchants and manufacturers out of the ranks of the yeoman clothiers was part of a more fundamental process of cultural transformation from the world of the middling sort to that of the middle class.

The differences between the lives of Jonathan Baumforth and George Stansfield Jr. provide a specific example of this process. Baumforth, a clothier in the township of Southowram, was worth about £1,000 when he died in 1720, yet as we saw in Chapter 2, his relations with his neighbors and workers were very convivial. To be sure, status distinctions were made. Young people and servants received less respect than older people and independent artisans, but no hard line, no great division in the social order separated servants, artisans, and yeoman clothiers. Yeomen such as Baumforth were typical of Halifax's middling sort. They lived in an economic world where personal, reciprocal credit was the rule, and in which luxury goods were not very important. Theirs was a world defined by neighborhood and by a shared culture that was recognizably connected to their essentially artisanal economy.

In the life of George Stansfield Jr. of Fieldhouse in Sowerby we see equally vividly the social implications of middle-class culture. Born as Baumforth lived out the last year of his life, George Stansfield, the son of an already wealthy manufacturer, went on to become one of the largest producers of cloth in the parish. No testamentary dispute survives to reveal the social relations that patterned Stansfield's world, but they can be pieced together from an analysis of domestic architecture.

Jonathan Baumforth almost certainly lived in one of the typical yeoman clothier's houses that dotted the hillsides of Halifax parish—houses that reflected the social relations of Baumforth's middling sort (photos 1 and 2). Large enough to provide room for the few luxuries that such families indulged in, these houses were also well suited to the clothier's business. The Baumforth house probably had a workshop attached to it, and the chamber above it would have been the sleeping place for the journeymen and apprentices who worked for the clothier in this house and lived with him as part of the family.[62]

---

62. Colum Giles, *Rural Houses of West Yorkshire, 1400–1800* (London, 1986), 152–55. The

1. Lower Scout, a typical clothier's house, Sowerby, 1693. (Author's photograph.)

2. Hollinghey, a typical yeoman clothier's house, Sowerby, 1577. (From John Leyland, *The Ancient Buildings of the Parish of Halifax* [1879]; reproduced by permission of the Reference Department, Halifax Central Library.)

Contrast this house with the one that George Stansfield built for himself in Sowerby, in 1749, shortly after his father's death (photo 3). Fieldhouse is an imposing neoclassical mansion, complete with frame windows, colonnade, and a sweeping entrance drive. Stansfield built his house according to the double-pile plan that was becoming popular at this time—symmetrical bays framing a central section—a considerable contrast to the hearth-passage plan common to yeoman clothiers' houses of the seventeenth century. An architectural historian of the West Riding remarks: "The success of the double-pile house lay in the way it permitted two entirely separate systems of circulation to operate in complete independence. The hall and main staircase were the pivots in the system which served the polite society within the house, but the house also sheltered another world, that of the servants operating in their own domain."[63] In the very design of his house, then, Stansfield was making a statement about the distance he wanted to put between his family and the world of artisans and servants. Stansfield's workers, for instance, were no longer part of the household; they lived out— hardly surprising, since there were more than 250 of them.[64] Stansfield lived in an economic world dominated by the idea of interest credit and in which land was easily interchangeable with its cash value. Luxuries were important to such families, as were the professional services that greater wealth brought into being, and their social world was populated by business associates rather than neighbors. The banquet held at Fieldhouse in 1758 to celebrate the opening of the Calder and Hebble Navigation, for which Stansfield had commissioned a glass service etched with scenes of the new navigation, would hardly have been attended by his makers.[65]

It is hard to imagine George Stansfield inviting colliers and weavers into his house to share a beer, as Jonathan Baumforth did, for an increasingly distinct socioeconomic experience and cultural construction of that experience erected a social barrier between manufacturers and artisans—a barrier that was itself a sign of the emergence of a distinct middle-class experience.

That barrier, and indeed the whole set of economic, social, and cul-

---

workshop was usually located across a passage from the main body of the house; hence the name for this architectural style: the "hearth passage plan."

63. Ibid., 99.
64. CDA/FH/409/2-3, Stansfield stocktaking, 1764.
65. H. P. Kendall, "Antiquarians at Sowerby," *THAS*, 1901 (unpaginated).

3. Fieldhouse, the mansion built by George Stansfield Jr., Sowerby, 1749. (Photo by Andrew Caveney.)

4. Old Fieldhouse, the house of George Stanfield Sr., Sowerby, seventeenth century. (Reproduced from an early twentieth-century slide by kind permission of Dr. J. A. Hargreaves, Hon. Secretary of the Halifax Antiquarian Society.)

tural changes that its existence assumed, was erected gradually. Consider George Stansfield Sr., who stands midway between Baumforth and his son. As a result of his new economic practice as a large-scale manufacturer, George Sr. was developing cultural attitudes that would come to destroy the social world that Jonathan Baumforth had known. He understood problems of profit and loss; he followed, a bit haphazardly, new accounting procedures; and he recognized, if a little reluctantly, that he could no longer protect the makers who worked for him from fluctuations in the markets.[66] But if George Sr. had left Baumforth's social world behind, he had not yet arrived at that of his son. His house was the house of a seventeenth-century yeoman clothier (photo 4). It was admittedly large, for George Sr. was a wealthy man, but it was a yeoman's house all the same, and in the 1720s and 1730s, living in a house with an attached workshop still implied certain social and cultural relations.

It is not difficult to identify the distinct cultures of the middling sort and middle class, but understanding how that middle-class culture originated requires an explanation of the transition between them. That explanation is provided by an attention to process, for I have argued that the transformations in practice and culture that led to the emergence of a distinct middle-class experience accumulated over time as the result of interactions between structure and action. If neither Jonathan Baumforth nor George Stansfield Sr. set out to become middle class, the implications of the changes they made led in that direction. Yet this process cannot be reduced to the economic transformation in the parish's woolen industry; equally important was the appropriation of cultural forms from outside the parish and the incorporation of a broader social elite.

66. CDA/FH/396, Stansfield letter book.

PART II

Crystallization: The Making of a Middle-Class Consciousness

Between the late seventeenth and mid–eighteenth centuries the shifting structures of practice of a new commercial and professional elite created an increasingly coherent middle-class experience in the parish of Halifax. The emergence of this class experience was not a predetermined outcome of the new relations of production in the parish's textile industry, for those changes were part of a complex and comprehensive process of cultural transformation. Moreover, the ways in which Halifax's elite construed their changing world were also shaped by features of eighteenth-century society not directly related to the textile industry with the result that this class experience was shared by a group wider than the merchants and manufacturers alone. Class experience, however, is not the same as class; class consciousness is also necessary. Thus it remains to explain how the merchants, manufacturers, and professionals of mid-eighteenth-century Halifax who shared this class experience came to "feel and articulate the identity of their interests as between themselves, and as against other men."[1]

The nature of the distinction between class experience and class consciousness can be seen in the case of George Stansfield Jr., the giant merchant/manufacturer of Sowerby. During the first half of the eighteenth century, Stansfield, and others like him, developed a new set of social relations, a new set of economic practices, a new set of tastes and desires—in short, a new culture. Of course, class identity,

---

1. E. P. Thompson, *The Making of the English Working Class* (Harmondsworth, 1968), 8.

specifically middle-class identity, was implicit in many aspects of the new culture of this group: in the way they did business, understood capital, and dealt with their workers. Yet it would be wrong to characterize this culture as a *class culture*, because nothing about the practices associated with it made these families consciously constitute themselves as a group vis-à-vis other groups in the social order. Nor did they explicitly define their interests as a group as opposed to those of other groups. The class identity that was implicit in the culture through which manufacturers such as George Stansfield Jr. related to the world had to be made explicit before a middle-class culture could exist.

It is helpful to think of the transition from the class implicit in socioeconomic experience to the class explicit in class consciousness as a crystallization.[2] First, this term suggests that the cultural changes associated with the emergence of class consciousness occurred not by the laborious creation of wholly new cultural patterns but by a reorganization, a "reconstruing," of practices and ideas that were already present. As Part I shows, the creation of new cultural patterns takes time, but their reorganization may happen in a relatively brief period, in a moment of crystallization.[3] In Halifax this moment came in the 1750s and 1760s, when the largely *unconscious* changes in structures of practice that had been going on as part of an evolutionary process became part of a group's *conscious* understanding of the world and their place in it.

Second, it emphasizes that class formation was a collective process: individuals do not have a class culture, groups do. The shifting structures of practice of a George Stansfield Jr. tell us nothing about class unless they were shared by a larger group. It is only the awareness of the political implications of a set of socioeconomic practices shared by many people that makes a class culture. Thus while the process of cultural transformation that gave rise to a middle-class experience took place through largely unconscious changes in the social and economic practices of individuals, the making of a class culture of which these

---

2. As Stuart Blumin has pointed out, the concept of crystallization is in some sense inappropriate for history because it implies that an "event" such as crystallization is inevitable and that its product takes a determinate form: *The Emergence of the Middle Class: Social Experience in the American City* (New York, 1989), 258. Like Blumin, however, I feel that the term has its uses.

3. William Sewell suggests that much the same kind of process was at work in the case of the working class: "How Classes Are Made: Critical Reflections on E. P. Thompson's Theory of Working-Class Formation," in *E. P. Thompson: Critical Perspectives*, ed. Harvey Kaye and Keith McClelland (Cambridge, 1990), 70.

individuals were conscious, as a group, requires a broader view. We must look beyond social and economic practices and also beyond the individual to concentrate on those fields of action that brought people together in the pursuit of common goals. It was through such actions that Halifax's merchant, manufacturing, and professional families came to share a class identity.

Historians have tended to focus on two fields of action in which class consciousness was formed. Some emphasize the role of political struggle in the emergence of class identity, and recent work on the middle class has emphasized the local level of much of this political action. Anthony Howe argues that the political authority that the cotton magnates of Lancashire established locally was probably more important than their involvement in national politics in creating the bonds of class identity.[4] Theodore Koditschek and Robert Morris also stress the role that common political action played in the articulation of a middle-class consciousness in the Yorkshire towns of Bradford and Leeds.[5] Both show how the proliferation of voluntary associations provided outlets for the nascent middle class's political ambitions as well as a focus for their emerging class consciousness.

Politics has also been important for historians interested in a linguistic approach to the problem of class formation. Gareth Steadman Jones's study of Chartism, for instance, explains this "working class" movement in terms of the radical tradition within English politics, for it was the common political language that shaped participants' perceptions of their experience in the new industrial mode of production rather than the other way around.[6] Dror Wahrman's work on middle-class formation takes a similar perspective; he argues that middle-class identity was essentially a political rhetoric.[7] Both of these historians

---

4. Anthony Howe, *The Cotton Masters, 1830–50* (Oxford, 1984).

5. Theodore Koditschek, *Class Formation and Urban-Industrial Society: Bradford, 1750–1850* (New York, 1990); R. J. Morris, *Class, Sect, and Party: The Making of the British Middle Class, Leeds, 1820–1850* (Manchester, 1990).

6. Gareth Steadman Jones, "Rethinking Chartism," in *Languages of Class: Studies in English Working-Class History, 1832–1982* (Cambridge, 1983), 90–179. For a very rigorous, perhaps too rigorous, critique of Jones on this score, see David Mayfield and Susan Thorne, "Social History and Its Discontents: Gareth Steadman Jones and the Politics of Language," *Social History* 17 (1992): 165–88.

7. Dror Wahrman, "National Society, Communal Culture: An Argument about the Recent Historiography of Eighteenth Century Britain," *Social History* 17 (1992): 43–72; and "Virtual Representation: Parliamentary Reporting and Languages of Class in the 1790s," *Past and Present* 136 (1992): 83–113.

underplay the socioeconomic determinants of class. This is a mistake, but I believe they are correct to give language a central place in their analyses. Like Patrick Joyce, I hold that the two are not mutually exclusive;[8] indeed, class consciousness depends on the relationship between linguistic and economic factors.

Other historians have identified the adoption of a distinctive set of values and behaviors as the arena in which class identity was formed. Leonore Davidoff and Catherine Hall see family and religion as forming the basis for the emergence of a middle-class consciousness between 1780 and 1850.[9] Margaret Hunt concentrates on how the responses of middling families to the uncertainty of the eighteenth-century business world led them to adopt a distinctive set of values and practices.[10] In some ways, this approach offers advantages over a focus on the political arena. Obviously the values and attitudes on which these historians concentrate were crucial to the identity of individuals and groups, for they were part of day-to-day life in a way that even local politics was not. This approach also makes it possible to examine the role that gender relations played in class formation, again something that is not so evident in the political arena. This approach, however, has some disadvantages. Unlike political action, the adoption of a set of values and attitudes does not obviously constitute the kind of conscious act that is necessary for class formation. It is also not clear why the outcome of such an act would necessarily be class consciousness, for the adoption of a set of values does not require one to define one's identity in opposition to that of another group, and it is difficult to equate with a particular socioeconomic experience. Catherine Hall's analysis of the different ways in which Samuel and Jemima Hall experienced the Peterloo Massacre, for instance, suggests that this working- class couple structured their relationship on the basis of a domestic ideology in many ways indistinguishable from that of the middle class.[11]

Curiously, most historians of class adopt just one of these approaches,

---

8. Patrick Joyce, *Visions of the People* (Cambridge, 1991).

9. Leonore Davidoff and Catherine Hall, *Family Fortunes: Men and Women of the English Middle Class, 1750–1850* (London, 1987).

10. Margaret R. Hunt, *The Middling Sort: Commerce, Gender, and the Family in Eighteenth-Century England* (Berkeley, forthcoming).

11. Catherine Hall, "The Tale of Samuel and Jemima: Gender and Working-Class Culture in Nineteenth-century England," in Kaye and McClelland, *E. P. Thompson*, 78–102. My thanks to Dror Wahrman for this insight. In a forthcoming book, Anna Clark analyzes just what those differences were: *The Struggle for the Breeches: Gender and the Making of the British Working Class* (Berkeley, forthcoming).

to the exclusion of the other.[12] This choice is unnecessary, however, for the alternatives are by no means contradictory. In Chapters 5 and 6 we shall see that politics and family relations were part of the same moment of class formation. The middle-class consciousness that developed in Halifax in the decades after 1750 had two faces, one public and the other private. Each provided a means through which members of Halifax's nascent middle class could feel and articulate the identity of their interests as a group and as against other groups.

Chapter 5 explores the making of this middle-class consciousness in the way Halifax's merchants, manufacturers, and professionals constructed the public sphere. It is largely about politics, for the class identity of Halifax's elites emerged as a result of their demands for local recognition and power. Collectively the episodes in which they expressed those demands define a moment of class formation, for they all involved the articulation of a political culture unique to the middle class. This political culture included both the institutions in which Halifax's merchants, manufacturers, and professionals met on a regular basis and the common goals in pursuit of which this new elite forged their middle-class consciousness.

Chapter 6 explores the making of this middle-class consciousness in the way the families of Halifax's merchants, manufacturers, and professionals constructed the private sphere. Although less visible and less abrupt than corresponding developments in the public sphere, the making of the private sphere played no less a role in the emergence of a middle-class consciousness. Like parish politics, it involved the development of shared and exclusive practices and values that distinguished this group from other groups in the social order. A crucial aspect of these values and practices was a new set of gender relations, for the private sphere was quite distinct from the male worlds of business and politics.

12. Koditschek, *Class Formation*, is a partial exception to this generalization.

Chapter 5

Constructing the Public Sphere: Associations, Disputes, and Parliamentary Politics

One of the most striking features of Halifax's history in the decades after 1750 is the host of associations that were formed to accomplish specific projects—to reorganize a workhouse, build a canal, start a library. As John Brewer has noted, such voluntary associations were a new political form in the eighteenth century, and they enabled provincial merchants, tradesmen, and professionals "to exercise collectively an influence in the community far beyond that conferred by their individual incomes." They were therefore a form particularly suited to the needs of the commercial and professional elites in places such as Halifax.[1] Since English society denied this group structured opportunities to exercise their influence and meaningful acknowledgment of their social prestige, they had to create their own institutions and these institutions helped to create class identity.[2] Other efforts to wield influence can be seen in the series of disputes that racked the parish in the third quarter of the eighteenth century. These disputes—over church

---

1. John Brewer, "Commercialization and Politics," in Neil McKendrick, John Brewer, and J. H. Plumb, *The Birth of a Consumer Society* (London, 1983), 224–25.
2. The role that such institutions played in the development of middle-class culture is discussed in R. J. Morris, "Middle-Class Culture, 1700–1914," in *A History of Modern Leeds*, ed. Derek Fraser (Manchester, 1980), 200–222, and his *Class, Sect, and Party: The Making of the British Middle Class, Leeds, 1820–1850* (Manchester, 1990). Also relevant are Leonore Davidoff and Catherine Hall, "The Architecture of Public and Private Life: English Middle-Class Society in a Provincial Town, 1780–1850," in *The Pursuit of Urban History*, ed. Derek Fraser and Anthony Sutcliffe (London, 1983), 340; and Theodore Koditschek, *Class Formation and Urban-Industrial Society: Bradford, 1750–1850* (New York, 1990).

rates, a workhouse, a chapel, an organ—between factions of the parish's commercial and professional elite demonstrate that class identity can be defined by conflict—by shared assumptions concerning what the fight was about and how to manipulate the political system to gain those ends. A final set of efforts—obtaining an act of parliament, petitioning on behalf of the trade, and elections—demonstrate how Halifax's inhabitants and the elite in particular saw themselves in the national political context.

Taken together, these episodes suggest that the mid–eighteenth century was a period of fairly intense political struggle that transformed perceptions of the social order and the political culture. The associations, the disputes, and involvement in national politics were means by which Halifax's commercial and professional elite at once constructed their middle-class consciousness and expressed this class identity vis-à-vis other groups. They were, in short, part of a moment of class formation.

Political actions transformed the social order because they established and confirmed Halifax's merchants, manufacturers, and professionals as the dominant social group in the parish. Of course, this group was already dominant in the parish simply by virtue of their economic and social influence, but these episodes gave that dominance explicit institutional form. Note that these men exerted their dominance as a group, for their efforts to achieve their common goals required them to work together. Moreover, the common identity that was at once the impetus behind and the result of these events was not limited to the episodes themselves nor to the economic self-interest of the individuals involved.

In making explicit their claim to even local political power, Halifax's merchants, manufacturers, and professionals also explicitly differentiated themselves from other groups in the social order. Most obviously, given the nature of Halifax's social structure, the elite's claims to power were directed against the respectable middling sort—yeoman farmers, independent artisans working in the textile industry. This group, which had had a political voice at the beginning of the century, found itself increasingly marginalized as the century wore on. Equally important were the implications of these episodes for the local gentry. The gentry had never had particularly strong claims to local political power, so it would be a mistake to imagine that the class identity of the merchants, manufacturers, and professionals was constructed in explicit opposition to them. Though real power was not at stake, however, this new elite usurped the social prestige that the local gentry had formerly enjoyed by right, and the ways in which they conceptualized their political leadership created a different basis for local political power. Through their political activities, then, Halifax's merchants, manufacturers, and professionals constructed not just a group identity but a class identity.

Although the concept cannot be used uncritically, the transformation in Halifax's political culture is an instance of what Jürgen Habermas has described as the formation of a "public sphere" in the eighteenth century. Habermas's *Structural Transformation of the Public Sphere* has been subjected to numerous critiques, most of them focused on the stark contrast Habermas presents between the government and the bourgeois public sphere.[3] With the exception of the relationship between the public and private spheres, however, critics substantially agree with Habermas on the key features that identified the public sphere as a distinct form of political discourse. Three of these features are particularly relevant to our concerns here. First is the exercise of reason to arrive at critical judgments in the public sphere. Second is a degree of freedom of information and an openness in discussion which was guaranteed, in part, by the existence of the press. Third is the assumption of a fundamental equality of individuals within the public sphere.[4] All of these elements of Habermas's grand process are evident in the political struggles that stirred the small world of mid-eighteenth-century Halifax.

The political discourse of the public sphere resonated with the position that Halifax's commercial and professional elite held in the social order. The economic developments of the first half of the century had

---

3. Daniel Gordon, "Philosophy, Sociology, and Gender in the Enlightenment Conception of Public Opinion"; David A. Bell, "The 'Public Sphere,' the State, and the World of Law in Eighteenth-Century France"; and Sara Maza, "Women, the Bourgeoisie, and the Public Sphere: Response to Daniel Gordon and David Bell," all in *French Historical Studies* 17 (1992): 882–950; Anthony LaVopa, "Conceiving a Public: Ideas and Society in Eighteenth-Century Europe," *Journal of Modern History* 64 (1992): 79–116; Dena Goodman, "Public Sphere and Private Life: Toward a Synthesis of Current Historiographical Approaches to the Old Regime," *History and Theory* 31 (1992): 1–20.

4. Jürgen Habermas, "The Public Sphere: An Encyclopedia Article," *New German Critique* 1 (1974): 49–55, and *The Structural Transformation of the Public Sphere: An Inquiry into a Category of Bourgeois Society* (1962), trans. Thomas Burger (Oxford, 1989), esp. 24, 27, and 34–37. The emergence of politics into the public sphere was undoubtedly very closely related to the middle class's separation of their world into the public realm of politics and commerce and the private realm of the home, a concept developed most clearly in Leonore Davidoff and Catherine Hall, *Family Fortunes: Men and Women of the English Middle Class, 1780–1850* (London, 1987), 13, 29–33. I discuss this aspect of the making of Halifax's middle class in Chapter 6.

increased the wealth of individual members of this elite and expanded the group has a whole, but the traditional political discourse of the eighteenth century, which was cast in terms of hierarchy and deference, did not provide a promising basis on which such a group could exert influence. With its stress on the equality of individuals within the group and on reason as the correct approach to the world, the political discourse of the public sphere was attractive because it provided this new elite with a language in which they could articulate their demands. This language was at odds with the local gentry's assumptions about the basis of their authority and prestige. Thus the making of a public sphere through associations and disputes identified this group of merchants, manufacturers, and professionals vis-à-vis those below them in the social order by excluding them from power, and at the same time it provided the discourse that defined their identity vis-à-vis those above them in the social order.[5]

THE CAST

The most important members of the cast of characters involved in these episodes were the sixty to seventy substantial merchants and manufacturers who dominated Halifax's economy and in particular its textile industry. They were joined by about fifteen professionals: doctors, lawyers, the vicar, and a few of the curates.[6] Families and individuals in the two groups were linked through social and business ties.[7] John Howarth, for example, sent his children to a dancing school in Halifax whose other patrons could only have been wealthy merchants and man-

---

5. Although she does not make explicit reference to the public sphere, Linda Colley makes a very similar argument about the way commercial people felt their exclusion from the political process and articulated their demands for political power: *Britons: Forging the Nation, 1707–1837* (New Haven, 1992), chap. 2, esp. 98–100.

6. It is impossible to arrive at a precise figure for the number of people in this group. I have relied on linkages between probate records, deeds, and a variety of local records. In addition, I have examined the numbers of Halifax residents who insured property with the Sun Fire Insurance Company before 1785 and with the Royal Insurance Company before 1787; altogether forty individuals or companies insured some commercial property, either goods or real estate, to a total value of £62,945: Guildhall Library, London, Sun Fire Insurance, Ms. 11936, and Royal Insurance, Ms. 7253.

7. John Seed, "From Middling Sort to Middle Class," in *Social Orders and Social Classes in Europe*, ed. M. L. Bush (London, 1992), 120.

ufacturers.[8] Dr. Cyril Jackson was a close friend of the Caygill family and was involved as one of the trustees in Ann Caygill's marriage to the Reverend Mr. Robert Charlesworth.[9] Charlesworth was not the only member of the parish's clergy to move in the same social circles as the commercial elite; the Reverend Mr. John Watson, Halifax's antiquarian, had an annual salary of £100 as the curate of Ripponden, and he corresponded and visited with Halifax's leading commercial families almost as an equal.[10] The activities of Joseph Hulme, M.D., suggest that the connections between the commercial and professional elites were not merely social. Hulme had close social connections with the Pollards, Cookes, and Kershaws, three of Halifax's leading Dissenting merchant families; he served as one of the trustees for David Stansfield's will, along with George Stansfield Jr. of Sowerby; and he had business connections within this group as well. He loaned £3,000 to another merchant family, the Martins, in connection with their business, and he appears as an active investor in the building of Halifax's canal.[11] Halifax's commercial and professional elite, then, were a more unified group than the distinction between their sources of income might imply.

The players who supported these luminaries included between 50 and 150 smaller manufacturers, especially those in the worsted industry—men such as John Sutcliffe, Luke Greenwood, Jonathan Ackroyd, and John Firth.[12] Although they were manufacturers and not domestic clothiers, these men were not in the same league as Samuel Lees or Samuel Hill either in the scale of their business or in their lifestyle, but they shared important cultural attributes with their betters. Also on the

8. J. H. Priestly, "John Howarth at Home," *THAS*, 1947, 11.

9. CDA/CN 95, marriage settlement, 1761.

10. S. L. Ollard and P. C. Walker, eds., *Archbishop Herring's Visitation Returns, 1743*, Yorkshire Archaeological Society Record Series 72 (Leeds, 1928); the return for Halifax lists the curate of Ripponden's income as £100.

11. BIY/OW, David Stansfield, Prerogative Court, July 1770; PRO/C.12/896/2, Chancery, Edwards v. Martin for debt, 1769; C.12/424/12, Banks v. Stansfield re Calder Navigation, 1769.

12. If the members of Halifax's elite are difficult to identify, the members of this group are even more obscure. It appears that in the township of Sowerby, where extensive records have survived, there were fifteen to twenty-five men, manufacturers of one sort or another, below the top rung but well above the level of a simple yeoman or craftsman. That Sowerby was somewhat typical in this regard is suggested by the records of West Riding merchants who traded in Halifax, which reveal the names of a few men who do not appear in other records but who were trading on a fairly substantial scale. See, for example, the ledger of R. J. Lister, worsted yarn dealer of Frizing Hall near Bradford: University of Leeds, Brotherton Library, Business Archive, Marriner Records, no. 33.

fringes of the commercial and professional elites were the people who supplied them with the goods and services that gave them an increasingly distinctive lifestyle—shopkeepers, skilled artisans, and the lesser professionals such as bookkeepers and teachers. It is difficult to establish the extent to which the members of this group participated in the cultural world of Halifax's merchants, manufacturers, and professionals. The annual salary of the bookkeeper engaged by the firm of Lees and Edwards was £60 plus room and board. This was a decent amount, on a par with the incomes of most of the parish's curates and roughly twice what Richard Hill paid to a highly skilled artisan responsible for overseeing the finishing of his cloths.[13] Although bookkeepers might go on to become merchants in their own right, they were salaried employees, and, like teachers, they must have been hangers-on at the fringes of an increasingly exclusive social group.

Shopkeepers and skilled craftsmen (bookbinders, clockmakers, and the like) had even less claim to inclusion in the emerging social world of Halifax's elites, for they were never anything but suppliers of goods. Yet theirs was an experience distinct from that of the increasingly proletarianized "makers" in the textile industry, and they probably participated vicariously in the emerging political power of the commercial and professional elite.

ASSOCIATIONS

It would be absurd to assert that there were no associations in Halifax before the mid-eighteenth-century moment of middle-class formation, for voluntary associations can be found in late-seventeenth-century Halifax. Township government, although it was not an entirely voluntary form of association, can be included in this category. More obviously, the Nonconformist chapels that sprang up in the parish after the Restoration continued the middling sort's tradition of seeing to their own religious needs.[14] Thus it is the timing and nature of the associations in the mid–eighteenth century that are significant.

First, the sheer numbers of associations formed in the mid-eighteenth century is striking. Meetings were held, subscriptions were

---

13. CDA/FH/461a, Hill to Stansfield, 31 January 1775.
14. William Sheils, "Oliver Heywood and His Congregation," in *Voluntary Religion*, ed. Sheils and Diana Wood (Oxford, 1986).

raised, committees were appointed, all at the drop of a hat.[15] Second, the mid-eighteenth-century associations differed significantly from earlier ones in their organization, methods, and aims. Whereas the earlier associations restricted their activities to local government and the maintenance of congregations, the crop of associations formed in midcentury assumed competence in almost all fields of social life, from commerce to religion to entertainment. They were also much more socially exclusive and more explicitly public in their orientation. They aimed at the exercise of power, and they relied on the strength of the group to achieve their ends. They were, in short, characteristic institutions of the middle-class public sphere.

Two associations formed in the township of Sowerby demonstrate the timing and nature of these new groups. The first began with a special vestry meeting held in the township in 1749 to investigate a complaint that "the several officers of the town stand in need of frequent advice," and that the "principal inhabitants [are] being frequently and unseasonably visited and called off to the neglect of their own private business by the said officers and poor of the said town." The meeting resolved that since the town's business was intricate, especially with respect to the distribution of charity money, "a meeting of the subscribers, the said principal inhabitants of Sowerby, shall be established and constantly held on the first Tuesday of every month." In 1755 the "principal inhabitants" consolidated their hold on township government by reforming the administration of the township's most expensive charge, poor relief. They appointed twelve of their number as overseers of the poor, reestablished the township's workhouse, and hired a master to oversee the actual work of poor relief at a salary of £12 a year.[16] Although this group's capture of the machinery of local government did not create a voluntary association in the strict sense of the term, its import was the same, for it required the group to identify, consciously, both their goals and their unity of purpose.

The second example from Sowerby township was without question a

---

15. Among the associations not discussed here were ones formed to prosecute legal cases (CDA/RP/268, Sowerby mills suit, and CDA/RP/144, Hull harbor dues suit); groups formed to procure enclosure awards (CDA/CN/99/1, Northowram enclosure); and prosecution societies (CDA/HAS/B:11/10/1, 1757; CDA/HAS/B:11/10/2, 1766; and HAS/b:11/10/4, prosecution society deed, 1785).

16. CDA/SPL/30, Sowerby chapel wardens' account book, special vestry meeting, 5 December 1749; CDA/HAS/378 (425), Sowerby workhouse agreement, 1755; CDA/SPL/31, 32, Sowerby overseers' accounts, 1737–58, 1758–73.

TABLE 5. Indications of sociopolitical status of the principal inhabitants of Sowerby, 1749–1770

	Vestry signature[a]	Window tax[b]	School trustee[c]	Land tax	Work- house[d]	PI[e]	Chapel fund[f]
Mr. George Stansfield	20	19	x	£5	x	x	£300
Mr. Israel Wilde	6	13	x	5	x	x	100
Mr. John Priestly	15	13	x	5	x	x	100
Mr. Richard Thomas	10	14		5	x	x	60
Mr. John Lea	6	16	x	1+	x		50
Mr. Joseph Wells	5	14	x	1+	x	x	50
William Moore	8	14	x	5			50
John Walker[g]	1	–	x	5	x	x	20
Mr. Welsh[h]	13	9	x	1+			20
James Greenroyd[g]	1	–		1+			20
William Starkey	3	9		–	x		10
Michael Normanton	2	9		2–4+			10
John Butterworth	9	12	x	?			10
William Sutcliffe[g]	9	–	x	1+	x	x	10
John Sutcliffe[g]	8	–		5	x		10
Mr. Elkhana Holroyd	7	19	x	2–4+	x		10
Luke Greenwood	20	11		?	x	x	10
James Farrer	4	14		1+			10
Mr. Tillotson	2	15		1+	x		10
William Barker	2	11	x	1+	x		10
William Broadbent[i]	–	19		1+			10
David Waterhouse	–	9		–			5
Samuel Wood	3	18		?			5
Edward Wilde	–	14		?	x		5
Cornielius Haigh	–	13		0			5
John Garnet[i]	–	13		0			5
Elkhana Hoyle	5	9		0			0
Henry Whitworth[g]	5	–		2–4+	x		0
James Broadbent	3	11		1+			0
John Haigh[i]	1	14		0			0
James Heap	1	12		0			0
William Crosley[i]	1	11		<1	x		0
Mr. Dyson[i]	–	15		1+			0
John Hardy	–	13		0			0
Mr. Phillips[i]	–	12		1+			0
Joshua Wadsworth	–	11		0			0
John Bates	–	11		<1			0

Note: All residents who signed the township accounts as members of the vestry five or more times or paid taxes for nine or more windows or subscribed to the new chapel are listed unless they were not residents or were impossible to identify with accuracy. Two additional houses with nine or more windows belonged to widows and a third was unoccupied.

[a]Number of times signature appears on township accounts, 1750–70.
[b]Number of windows taxed, 1758.
[c]Appointed trustee of Sowerby Charity School, 1765.
[d]Overseer of the poor and new workhouse, 1755.
[e]Signed agreement on vestry meetings as "principal inhabitant," 1749.

Constructing the Public Sphere 129

voluntary association. In 1758 "the chapel of Sowerby being greatly decayed in the roof and other parts thereof, some of the principal inhabitants resolved in order to ease the poorer sort of tenant to try whether a voluntary subscription could be procured sufficient, without a particular assessment, to repair the same." The minister posted a notice in the chapel and a "great number of the principal inhabitants" turned out for meetings, where they eventually decided to build an entirely new chapel rather than repair the old one. To this end a substantial subscription was raised, a sum later supplemented by the sale of seats in the new chapel.[17]

Within a decade, then, a group identifying themselves as the "principal inhabitants" had formed associations that established their identity and also their political power in the township. Who were these principal inhabitants? The subscription list for the rebuilding of Sowerby chapel contains the names of the thirty-eight men who subscribed at least £5 toward the rebuilding. Among them were all of the township's important residents with the exception of Dissenters; many of them were manufacturers or merchants. For all intents and purposes, this was the same exclusive group—about 6 percent of Sowerby's householders—who took over the township's government in the same decade. Their social position is confirmed by an analysis of the 1758 window tax assessment, shown in Table 5. Here we can correlate the persons who signed the township accounts more than five times between 1750 and 1770 with those who paid tax for nine or more windows and those who subscribed toward the new chapel. We see that the men who ran the township government and paid for the new chapel— George Stansfield, John Priestly, Luke Greenwood, John Lea, Israel Wilde, and a few others—were the chief taxpayers and were dominant in other aspects of township life.

---

17. CDA/Sowerby register microfilm, unpaginated. The minutes and subscription list for the rebuilding are located at the end of the chapel's mid-eighteenth-century register. See also CDA/STA/215/1, petition to the archbishop of York requesting parochial status for the Sowerby chapel, 1763.

---

[f]Amount subscribed toward new chapel, 1759.
[g]Resident of a part of Sowerby not covered by the window tax assessment.
[h]Mr. Welsh was the curate; hence his relative lack of affluence but great involvement in township affairs.
[i]Nonconformists, hence unlikely to serve on the vestry or support Anglican schools or churches.
Sources: CDA/SPL/30–32, 144 (vestry signatures), CDA/SPL/153 (window tax), CDA/FH/380 (school trustees), CDA/SPL/150/1–2 (land tax), CDA/SPL/31, 32 (workhouse), CDA/SPL/30 (principal inhabitants), CDA/Sowerby register microfilm (chapel fund).

Though these two associations were formed for practical purposes, both reveal something of the new social order that such institutions created. The structure of the chapel subscription list provides a visual clue to this new social world. Heading the list is the name of George Stansfield, probably the principal proponent of the new chapel, and at £200 (with an additional £100 given on behalf of his sisters) the largest single subscriber. Next on the list are Israel Wilde and John Priestly; these two substantial manufacturers each gave £100. Next come Richard Thomas, who gave £60, and John Lea, Joseph Wells, and William Moore, who each gave £50, and the list continues, strictly in order of the amount subscribed.[18] The list can be taken as a very concise expression of these men's sense of community, one that recognized the differences in means within their ranks but also presented an outward face of cooperation and unity.

These associations also redefined the relations of these merchants and manufacturers with people below and above them. Perhaps most important, these two associations allowed Sowerby's merchants and manufacturers to deny authority to anyone outside of a fairly restricted circle. After the workhouse was reorganized in 1755, the township's principal inhabitants served their turns as overseers roughly in order of rank. After all of the eligible men had served a turn, they began a second rotation—a departure from established practice, but necessary to keep the right sort of people in office.[19]

The same exclusion is evident in the financing of the new chapel. Although the ostensible aim of building the chapel by voluntary subscription was to protect the poor from heavy assessments, the minimum subscription of £5 excluded more than just the poor from participation. It is, of course, possible to overstress the elitism of the movement for the rebuilding; there was some support for the scheme among the lesser yeomen, craftsmen, weavers, clothworkers, and laborers of the township. The accounts record, for instance, that the sum of £40/12s was gathered in a house-to-house canvass from people too poor to subscribe a full £5 but solvent enough to contribute something. The township's residents also offered a more tangible contribution to the new chapel. On Easter Sunday in 1761, the curate appealed to the congregation to spend their holidays helping to dig the foundations for the

---

18. CDA/Sowerby register microfilm, subscription list.
19. CDA/SPL/31, 32, Sowerby overseers' accounts, 1737–58, 1758–73. Up to this time it was all but unheard of for an officeholder to serve a second term.

new chapel, and so many people turned up on Monday and Tuesday that the committee didn't have to begin paying workmen until Wednesday. But the form of these contributions to the new chapel emphasized the social gap that separated these people from the township's elite. No manufacturer would have stooped to drop the odd copper in the collection box or spend a day with a spade digging the foundation.

Nor did the contributions made by these casual donors and volunteer laborers confer any rights of ownership in the new chapel. Consider, for instance, the complex method that was adopted to distribute the pews. Although the new chapel had almost the same number of seats as the old, the subscribers—who now "owned" the building—chose to distribute only a portion of them: on average, each farm was allotted four seats in the new chapel for every five seats it had held in the old. This arrangement left the subscribers with a surplus of 198 seats, which they sold to themselves.[20] Cottagers, artisans, and even yeomen who could not afford the £5 subscription or the cost of the pew were left with a reduced number of seats while the township's merchants and manufacturers were able to procure seats in proportion to their wealth and influence. The allotment of seats for George Stansfield's Fieldhouse, for instance, went from seven to six, but he bought a significant number of seats in the galleries, presumably for use by his servants and workers.

If their redistribution of the seats in the new chapel demonstrates the way Sowerby's self-appointed elite saw their relations with the lower orders, the dispute that ensued with Sir William Horton over the same seats demonstrates how they saw their relations with the gentry. Sir William Horton was an influential Lancashire gentleman—a justice of the peace and sheriff in 1764—but the family's roots were in Halifax, and he owned a considerable amount of property in Sowerby. Naturally, Horton was consulted about the chapel, not least because it was located partly on land he owned. From the beginning he had some reservations: in a letter to his steward he commented that he didn't think that his tenants needed new seats, and he certainly was not going to make them spend money on them. He also expressed concern that the seat for Sowerby Hall be "railed" around and distinguished from the common seats, as it had been in the old chapel. Behind these

---

20. CDA/FH/280/1/2, index to the pews in the old and new Sowerby chapels; CDA/Sowerby register microfilm, accounts. The accounts are slightly ambiguous on the exact number of seats in the new chapel; it is possible that 216 seats were sold rather than 198.

demands was Horton's expectation that a gentleman's opinion was to be followed. As he explained in a letter to George Stansfield and Luke Greenwood: "You are pleased to pay me the compliment about your town's affairs; of late I have thought them very well conducted, and whenever I think otherwise, I shall always be ready to give any assistance I can."[21]

The details are hazy, but it seems that the chapel association did not relish this gentleman's presumption of a right to interfere in the affairs of their township. Nor did they intend to let him and his expectation of special treatment get in their way. In 1767, Horton complained to Stansfield and Greenwood about the number of seats allotted to his tenants, claiming that they had been intimidated into accepting fewer pews. The members of the association had a different view of the matter. They wrote to the archbishop of York in 1771 that Horton was being unreasonable in expecting them to pay the costs associated with *his* seats. The dispute between Horton and the Sowerby chapel association dragged on in various courts until the 1780s, delaying the official consecration of the church until a solution was negotiated.[22] No longer was status alone enough to ensure that even a powerful gentleman could have his way over a group of merchants. In the new political discourse of the public sphere there was no room for the kind of influence that Horton expected to exert by right over the township's affairs. If he wanted seats for his tenants or a fancy pew, they expected him to lay out the money himself, just as they were doing.

Indeed, if anyone exerted undue influence on the rebuilding of Sowerby's chapel, it was not William Horton but George Stansfield. Unlike the town of Halifax, where wealthy merchants and manufacturers were numerous, Sowerby was very much dominated by George Stansfield, the giant manufacturer whose mansion at Fieldhouse was one of the grandest residences in the whole parish. Stansfield's influence probably approached that of the resident squire in an agricultural parish. He was, for instance, the moving force behind the chapel: the accounts came to him for payment; he contributed the largest amount of money; and he even had parts of the old chapel erected in the yard of his

21. CDA/STA/215/1/4, Horton to Stansfield and Greenwood, May 1763; STA/215/1/3, Horton to William Whitworth, March 1761; STA/215/2, Horton to Stansfield and Greenwood, April 1761.
22. CDA/FH/282/6, 14 November 1771; FH/282/5, archbishop of York to Rev. J. Welsh, 11 November 1771. Also see PRO/C.12/423/17, Chancery, Stansfield et al. v. Horton, 1777.

mansion.²³ One could argue, then, that the rebuilding of the chapel was not indicative of emerging middle-class consciousness but merely an instance of a much more familiar feature of the eighteenth-century political landscape: interest.

This interpretation, however, would be incorrect for two reasons. In the first place, if we allow that it was perhaps his pet project, even a dominant figure such as Stansfield could not have gotten a new chapel built without the cooperation of other members of his community. Although he was very wealthy by any standard, Stansfield could simply not have afforded to sink £2,000 or £3,000 of his capital in this kind of display; unlike a landed gentleman with a similar income, a manufacturer depended on the circulation of his capital to provide that income. Nor could he simply rely on his economic power to sway his neighbors. Men such as Priestly, Wilde, Lea, Walker, Greenwood, and Holroyd were important manufacturers in their own right, and they too wanted the prestige that a new chapel would bring. If George Stansfield was responsible for the new chapel, it was only as a catalyst; his lead served to make manifest a middle-class community that found expression in the chapel and the subscription list.

In the second place, the men who created this institution intended it to be free of interest politics. At the organizational meeting, the association was established as what Robert Morris calls a "subscriber democracy," for it was agreed that at future meetings "the majority of subscribers of five pounds each or upwards then and there present shall ... have full power and authority to make order and give directions for ... improving the said chapel." As Habermas's discussion of the nature of the public sphere suggests, one of the crucial features of this political discourse was the assumption that within a public context all individuals were equal. Other attributes of the association were also consonant with the discourse of the public sphere. For example, the association's account book was to be kept in a special box at John Garnet's inn, and all subscribers were to be allowed to examine it at their pleasure. The committee also made a point of putting the work for the new chapel out to bid to keep costs down and to ensure that no favoritism was shown.²⁴

23. CDA/STA/215/1/2, chapel accounts, presented to and paid by George Stansfield.
24. CDA/Sowerby register microfilm, minutes, esp. 31 January 1759. For a discussion of "subscriber democracy" and its implications for middle-class culture, see Morris, *Class, Sect, and Party*, 184. Morris also stresses the public keeping of accounts.

Sowerby's are merely two of the better documented associations formed in mid-eighteenth-century Halifax. Many other townships saw a self-selected, exclusive group assume control over township government.[25] In Skircoat, for instance, the workhouse was also reorganized in 1755, perhaps in conjunction with the workhouse in the neighboring township of Southowram: twelve of the wealthiest merchants and manufacturers in the township appointed themselves trustees for "the better management of the workhouse" to ensure that the accounts were kept with "order and regularity." These men included the manufacturers Jonathan Laycock, Samuel Lees, and John Edwards (Lees's father's former partner) and the merchants John and William Greame.[26] In all of these instances, the control established by this new elite prevented yeomen and independent artisans from participating in township government as they had done in the late seventeenth and early eighteenth centuries, and hence emphasized the social distance between respectable householders and the emerging commercial elite.

Other chapels were improved during this period by voluntary associations controlled by merchants, manufacturers, and professionals.[27] The Presbyterian congregation at Northgate End in Halifax town decided in 1762 to build a new chapel instead of repairing the roof, and they raised a subscription to cover the cost. The Congregationalists erected what became known as the Square Chapel in 1772, also by subscription (Photo 5). Subscription lists show that both associations allowed a narrow elite to gain control over existing institutions—in striking contrast to the egalitarian structure of Dissenting congregations in Oliver Heywood's day.[28] Of the 150 to 200 households that

25. CDA/HAS/65 (767), Hipperholme town book, 7 December 1747, 23 August 1750, and 2 September 1752; CDA/MISC/309, Elland town book, meetings of December 1743 and April 1757; CDA/MISC/272, Shelf township book, vestry meeting, 1758; CDA/HAS/142 (770), Skircoat town book, town meeting, 7 May 1760; CDA/HPC/A/3, Heptonstall town book, township agreement, 17 September 1761.
26. CDA/HAS/142 (770), Skircoat town book, vestry meeting, 7 July 1755. A tax assessment of 1773 shows that they were among the wealthiest residents of the township, and many of them were important manufacturers: HAS/609, Skircoat assessment.
27. Repairs to the roof of Oliver Heywood's old chapel in Northowram were paid for by a subscription that was dominated by a narrow elite of merchants and manufacturers: Mark Pearson, *History of Northowram* (Halifax, 1898), 118; and the Presbyterian congregation in Elland built a new chapel in 1756: Albert Rinder, *A History of Elland* (Elland, n.d.), 55.
28. Both Matthew Smith, the minister of the congregation in Warley from the 1680s to the 1730s, and Oliver Heywood seem to have contributed a large portion of the money necessary to build their chapels, the rest being supplied by the congregation at large: H. Armitage, "Mixenden Chapel," *THAS*, 1964, 3–4; James G. Miall, *Congregationalism in Yorkshire* (London,

Constructing the Public Sphere

5. The Square Chapel, the Congregationalists' new meetinghouse in Halifax, 1772. (Author's photograph.)

belonged to the Northgate End Presbyterian Chapel in the mid–eighteenth century, only 67 household heads subscribed toward the new building; less than a fifth (13) of the subscribers provided over three-quarters of the money for the new church.[29] All thirteen, including Richard and Benjamin Cooke, John Kershaw, and William Pollard, were prominent merchants and manufacturers, many of them in partnership with each other; Joseph Hulme, M.D., was also a major contributor. These men, not surprisingly, also dominated the board of trustees of the new chapel that they had paid for, so their influence over the congregation assumed an institutional form. Although artisans

---

1868), 325; Sheils, "Oliver Heywood," 272. For the Square Chapel see CDA/SC/3, accounts and members book, 1772–1900.

29. CDA/NEC/38, Northgate End account book, 1762. The congregation's size can be estimated from the baptismal registers: PRO/RG4/3167, registers of Northgate End Chapel, Halifax.

still attended and may even have contributed small sums, the fact that they did not make an important contribution to the rebuilding of the chapel must have altered their sense of their place within the congregation at the same time that it forged the elite's perception of their leadership role.

As in Sowerby's case, the elite had to work as a group in order to obtain this influence. The largest subscriber to the Northgate Chapel, Richard Cooke, could not possibly have supplied out of his own pocket the £1,000 that was eventually raised—even the largest three or four subscribers together could not have afforded that much—but fifteen or twenty subscribers could. Thus the associations that put up the buildings gave institutional form to the merchants' and manufacturers' perceptions of their common identity while the buildings themselves gave that common identity an enduring physical form.

Given the existing financial and administrative structure, fewer such associations were created in Anglican congregations, but here too Sowerby's case was not alone.[30] In 1764 an association was formed to improve the parish church in Halifax town by installing an organ in the loft. No list of the people who subscribed a total of £1,150 toward this project has survived, but the thirteen trustees appointed to receive the money and oversee the project were all clergymen or prominent members of Halifax's commercial elite, including John Caygill, Nathaniel Holden, John Walker, James Wetherherd, and Robert Roydes.[31]

The organ association, like the associations formed to rebuild the Anglican chapel in Sowerby and the two Dissenting chapels in Halifax town, was explicitly conceived as an institution in the public sphere. Its meetings and subscription were intentionally public, and the trustees were elected "by ball" (a secret ballot) from among the subscribers at a public meeting.[32] Again, two essential features emerge. First, and most obviously, it was only as a group that the elite of Halifax town could have made this improvement. Second, this group adopted the discourse of the public sphere as the natural framework within which they could make claims to power.

---

30. Other associations formed in connection with the Church of England include a subscription for new church bells in the chapel at Lightcliffe in 1787: Pearson, *History of Northowram*, 240; and a subscription to rebuild the chapel at Ovenden in 1777: W. B. Trigg, "Some Ovenden Houses," *THAS*, 1928, 327.

31. BIY/CP, I/1449, Halifax organ dispute; CDA/HAS/B:8/4, documents prepared for the hearing of the organ dispute in King's Bench.

32. See the association's defense against claims of its secrecy: CDA/HAS/B:8/4. All the trustees were elected in this way except the vicar, who sat on the board ex officio.

Both of these features distinguish such associations from earlier efforts toward improvement in the parish, and the differences suggest how this group of merchants, manufacturers, and professionals defined themselves vis-à-vis the local gentry. The changes in this relationship are particularly evident in this instance because the Church of England had traditionally been an object of the local gentry's munificence, as when money was collected in the 1710s and 1720s to augment the incomes of local curates with the assistance of Queen Anne's bounty.[33] Even in a cultural setting where their local power was more apparent than real, such gestures helped to establish the distinctive social position of the parish's gentle families. When they made their own substantial improvement to the church in 1764, Halifax's merchants, manufacturers, and professionals were establishing their power vis-à-vis that of the local gentry by denying them expressions of their social status that they had formerly enjoyed.

ASSOCIATIONS formed in township government or for rebuilding chapels, of course, had a relatively narrow appeal. Many of the other voluntary associations formed in mid-eighteenth-century Halifax, particularly those that were formed to build turnpikes and improve other means of transport in the parish, appealed to much broader groups.[34] The most dramatic and best documented association of this sort was the one formed to extend the Aire and Calder navigation in order to make the river Calder navigable up to Salter Hebble and Sowerby Bridge. Such a canal was vital to the woolen industry in the parish, as it promised manufacturers and merchants direct access to the port at Hull by cheap water transport. It also promised the Halifax manufacturers much greater control over their own business, because before the canal was built, much of Halifax's cloth and raw material was handled by merchants in Leeds or Wakefield, who had access to cheap water transport.[35]

After abortive discussions in 1741 and 1751, the first move toward the successful canal began with a series of meetings held at the Talbot

---

33. Christopher Hodgson, *An Account of Queen Anne's Bounty* (London, 1884). Five benefactions were made to Halifax chapelries after 1718 and before 1730, all for £200: J. Wilkinson gave to Illingworth, Sir John Armitage Bart. and John Bedford esq. gave to Rastrick, Mrs. M. Horton gave to Ripponden, Elkhana Horton gave to Sowerby, and J. Taylor gave to Sowerby Bridge.

34. See, e.g., CDA/HAS/297 (323) and CDA/HTB/1 on the Halifax-Burnley Turnpike, and CDA/HAS/250 (55) on the Halifax-Rochdale Turnpike.

35. Both Leeds and Wakefield were on the original Aire and Calder Navigation, which was opened in 1699.

Inn in Halifax in the spring and summer of 1756.[36] The meetings, advertised in the local press, were well attended, and in September a committee was established to begin the process of getting the necessary act of Parliament. The committee continued to meet throughout the rest of 1756 and into 1757, and in June, at a general meeting of the Halifax Union Club, it was decided to announce the intention of building a canal formally by advertising it in the Leeds, York, and Manchester papers and in one London paper. The meeting also decided to secure the services of John Smeaton, one of the foremost waterworks engineers of the day, to design the canal.[37] The committee's application to Parliament was successful; the act was passed in 1758, and work was begun in 1759.[38]

The survival of a full set of committee meeting minutes and subscription accounts makes it possible to identify the group responsible for building the canal. The members of both the committee established to organize the petition for the act and the larger group of subscribers who paid for it were drawn from the commercial and professional elite of the parish. Of thirty-six committee members, only three—Sir George Saville, Sir John Armitage, and John Smeaton, the engineer—were nonresidents; the remainder were merchants, manufacturers, and professionals. Most were residents of Halifax township and members of the Church of England—naturally enough, for the town was the marketing center for the parish and Anglicanism was its dominant religion. But a significant minority of the committee members were either residents of other townships or Dissenters or both. The same pattern is found among the men who subscribed money to secure the act.[39]

The local gentry are conspicuously absent from these records; no local gentleman served on the committee, and only one, Joshua Horton of Howroyd, subscribed money for the project. We should not imagine that the local gentry were unwelcome in such institutions. Rather, the assumed equality of all the members created an atmosphere that they

---

36. The *Leeds Mercury* of 29 September 1741 ran an advertisement for a meeting on making the Calder navigable from Wakefield to Halifax, and a firm was engaged to make a survey of the canal, but the Leeds merchants strongly opposed the scheme and it failed. Another attempt was made in 1751: Charles Clegg, "Our Local Canals," *THAS*, 1922, 207–15. For the beginning of the successful attempt, see CDA/CN/99/1.

37. CDA/MIC 2/1, Calder Navigation, minutes and accounts.

38. Clegg, "Our Local Canals." The act was 31 George II, c. 72. The canal was destroyed by flood in 1768 and had to be refinanced and reconstructed after the trustees got a second act of Parliament in 1769. The work was finally completed in 1774: 9 George III c. 71.

39. CDA/MIC 2/1, Calder Navigation, minutes and accounts; subscription list, 1757.

found uncongenial. The active participation of Sir George Saville and Sir John Armitage is the exception that proves the rule, for both were important figures whose regional and national influence was being courted by the committee.

The contrast between the membership of this group and, for example, those involved in the rebuilding of Sowerby's new chapel provides some sense of how different associations appealed to different audiences within the commercial and professional elite of the parish as a whole. With the obvious exception of Dissenters, the association that built Sowerby's chapel included almost all merchants and manufacturers in the township regardless of the size of their operations. Smaller worsted manufacturers such as Michael Normanton, John Riley, and Luke Greenwood had, by virtue of a minimum subscription of £5, equal votes with John Priestly and George Stansfield.[40] In the association formed to build the canal, however, such smaller manufacturers were much less in evidence. Only five residents of Sowerby appear on the navigation subscription list: two wealthy men, George Stansfield and John Lea; and three smaller manufacturers, Luke Greenwood, Elkhana Holroyd, and William Starkey. Both of the wealthy men subscribed over £5, the three smaller manufacturers each subscribed only a guinea—the lowest possible subscription. A project that appealed to the parish as a whole, then, was predominantly an affair for the mercantile and professional elites. Smaller manufacturers might appear at the fringes, but they were much more in evidence in smaller associations closer to home.

Although the canal promised the tangible benefits of access to cloth markets and cheap supplies of raw materials, it would be shortsighted to assume that the subscribers and the committee they appointed were acting solely out of self-interest. The association's format and the way the canal was discussed suggest that this group understood their activities as being appropriate to their roles as the leaders of their community. This attitude is clearest in the explicitly public orientation of the association, for while it is possible to argue that this was the only framework within which such a wide body of support could be mobilized, the fact that this association worked in the public sphere indicates the members' understanding of their new social role.

That this was a "public" institution is unquestionable, at least in eighteenth-century England, where the "public" was limited to the

---

40. CDA/Sowerby register microfilm, subscription list.

well-to-do. Besides advertising the meetings in the local and regional press, the committee printed and distributed 1,000 copies of the proposals for the canal. This document—four pages of closely spaced text—exhaustively catalogs the case for building the canal and refutes the objections raised against the project point by point. It is a classic example of the characteristic format of arguments in the public sphere, for reason reigns supreme in its presentation of the evidence. The committee answered objections about water levels and the like through carefully argued proofs, citing the appropriate manuals on hydraulics and engineering in case any readers were inclined to check the answers. There was also an implicit claim for political authority in the assertion that work of a more complex nature had "been carried to execution in France." To make such a statement in the darkest years of the Seven Years' War was to criticize obviously ineffectual government policy and assert the ability of tradesmen to get the job done.[41]

It is also significant that the men involved in the project frequently referred to it as a "public good." George Stansfield wrote to Robert Hargreaves, the curate of Todmorden, who had invested £500, that "the navigation succeeds surprisingly" and promised that there would be boats on the canal within the year. "This public good delights every one and must be an additional satisfaction to those who contributed so [generously?] towards it."[42] Similarly, when David Stansfield was sued for breach of contract after he reneged on an agreement to purchase lands affected by the canal, he defended himself on the grounds that he had acted in the public interest and not in his capacity as a private person.[43]

As a panegyric that appeared in the *Halifax Union Journal* on 27 February 1759 suggests, the "public good" of the project was associated in

---

41. WYAS/Bradford, SpSt/13/2/2, *Reasons for Extending the Navigation of the River Calder*. For the political context, see Nicholas Rogers, *Whigs and Cities: Popular Politics in the Age of Walpole and Pitt* (Oxford, 1989), chap. 3.

42. CDA/FH/375, Stansfield letters, n.d., probably August 1758.

43. The case was complicated. Early in the proceedings, to fend off a threat to obstruct their plans, Stansfield had agreed to buy the riverside mills of William Banks of Leeds if the canal affected them adversely. When the route of the canal was changed and the organizers decided to obtain an act providing for a public commission instead of a private body of proprietors, Stansfield did not complete the purchase, and Banks sued him. The case hinged on the basis on which Stansfield had entered into the negotiations with Banks. Banks claimed that it was as a private person and hence he was liable for damages for breach of contract. Stansfield claimed that he had agreed with Banks as the representative of a public body, particularly after the intent became to get a public act for the canal: PRO/C.12/424/12; C.12/57/28, and C.12/61/22, Chancery, Banks v. Stansfield et al.

Constructing the Public Sphere

6. A share certificate of the Calder Navigation, 1765, detail. (Reproduced by permission of the Calderdale District Archives, Halifax.)

the minds of the subscribers with the social benefits that would result from an expansion of industry. Written by one of the parish's curates, the poem describes Neptune's visit to the shores of Albion:

> Far o'er yon distant hills remain,
> A race who my affection gain:
> For with a right industrious hand,
> They strengthen, and enrich the land.
>
> A charming river these enjoy,
> Which yet runs almost useless by:
> This were it navigable made,
> Wou'd much extend their useful trade.

A similar message is conveyed by the engraving that graced the top left corner of the navigation's share certificates (photo 6). In the foreground, well-dressed merchants watch bales of wool or cloth being unloaded from a boat as another boat approaches. To their right are some beehives, the symbol of industry, and on the opposite bank Fortune, holding a horn of plenty, casts her blessings upon the land.

The merchants, manufacturers, and professionals who linked the "public good" and industry in this way were reinforcing an emerging middle-class consciousness by redefining their relations with the people above and below them in the social hierarchy. As the group that was providing this benefit to society, they announced their leadership of the community in a context and discourse that challenged any claims the local gentry might make for leadership in the parish's affairs. Yet they occupied this moral and political high ground as employers (the engraving has the merchants watching and the boatmen working). They were the ones earning substantial profits in the textile industry; what "industry" offered to the rest of the parish's inhabitants was merely useful employment.

Similar to the Calder Navigation in its parish-wide appeal was the association formed to build the Halifax Piece Hall. This magnificent building (photo 7), designed to provide a regular market for woolen and worsted cloth, had its gala opening on 1 January 1779, almost five years after the first advertisement appeared in the *Leeds Mercury*. The form that this association took was entirely typical of such broad-based organizations. It began its life when a group of interested men, in this case those who met at the weekly cloth market, decided to print up handbills advertising a public meeting to look into the possibility of a cloth hall. Those who attended this meeting decided to continue the process, and they advertised their intentions in the local press. At the second meeting a procedure was set up to solicit and collect subscriptions from interested persons, and these subscribers were to select the members of a committee to direct the project's affairs. The story of the Halifax Piece Hall, however, is a good reminder that these associations were not all about unity. Very soon after the project's inception, a dispute arose over where to build the new cloth hall. The matter was to be decided by a ballot of the subscribers, but when the supporters of the site that was not selected discovered the narrowness of their defeat, they threatened to build a cloth hall of their own. Though the disputants disagreed about the site of the hall, they agreed on more fundamental issues. The men on both sides had no doubts about their right to have a say in such an important decision, and the basis for this authority came from their identity as a group, for both sides were struc-

7. The central courtyard of the Halifax Piece Hall, 1779. (Author's photograph.)

tured as associations, and the dispute was carried out in the public sphere.⁴⁴

The creation of a circulating library in 1768 shows that purely economic motives were not required to unite Halifax's merchants, manufacturers, and professionals in pursuit of a common goal. Circulating libraries were uncommon before the mid–eighteenth century, but they began to appear throughout England in increasing numbers after 1750, at least in the more important regional centers. These libraries were signs of a developing market for refined leisure activities, a market that was a direct consequence of the financial success of the merchants, tradesmen, and professionals in places such as Halifax.⁴⁵ A library was first proposed in Halifax in 1768; as a pamphlet printed to secure support for the project explained, the intent was to provide "lovers of reading" access to books at moderate expense.⁴⁶

Like the canal, Halifax's circulating library was supported by a large proportion of the parish's commercial and professional elite. The committee that was chosen to run the library was headed by the two most prominent clergymen of Halifax, Dr. George Legh, the vicar, and the Reverend John Ralph, the minister at the Northgate End Presbyterian Chapel. The other eleven members of the committee were prominent merchants and manufacturers in the town, again a mix of Anglicans and Nonconformists. On the Church of England side were men such as John Roydes Jr. and Robert Alexander, and on the Nonconformist side were men such as Benjamin Cooke and his nephew John Kershaw, partners in trade and trustees of the Northgate Chapel. The subscribers to the library show a similar range, but they also included people outside the township of Halifax. John Edwards, for instance, was a large manufacturer in Skircoat, and Thomas Murgatroyd was another important figure in that township. Richard Hill, Samuel Hill's son, and John Howarth, the attorney, were among the members from Soyland and Sowerby.⁴⁷

Also like the canal, the library was very much an embodiment of the civic pride of this group. The proposals for the library made numerous

---

44. Ling Roth, *The Yorkshire Coiners* (Halifax, 1906), 207–12.
45. J. H. Plumb, "Commercialization and Society," in McKendrick, Brewer, and Plumb, *Birth of a Consumer Society*, 268, 270; Peter Borsay, *The English Urban Renaissance: Culture and Society in the Provincial Town, 1660–1770* (Oxford, 1989), 135.
46. CDA/MISC:5/96a/79, printed proposal for a circulating library, 1768.
47. Ibid. These are only a few of the more recognizable names. Most subscribers cannot be positively identified.

references to the circulating libraries that had been started in Manchester, Liverpool, and Leeds, implying that the residents of Halifax also deserved an institution of learning, refinement, and social grace. Like the libraries in these other towns, Halifax's project was an attempt to give institutional form to the emerging social power of a commercial and professional elite.[48] The library also allowed this group to define, explicitly, their perceptions of where the lower boundaries of their social group should be drawn. By setting the subscription fee at a guinea and charging an annual fee of 5 shillings, the organizers of the library intentionally put membership out of the reach of most of the parish's population.[49]

The profile of the library's trustees and subscribers suggests the emergence of a middle-class consciousness in the commercial and professional elite of the parish. Following a pull stronger than the ties of religion or neighborhood, the men and women who joined the library made explicit their developing class identity. Insulated from the common workers by literacy, leisure, and of course the membership fee, the readers in the library could interact with others who shared their perceptions of the world and their interests, goals, and expectations. In organizing the library, then, the members of this new class made a statement to the world about their arrival, and they did so in terms of a new political culture epitomized by the voluntary association. These associations provided this group with a new basis on which to exert local influence, but the fact that they exerted this influence *as a group* helped to make explicit a common class identity that was increasingly implicit in their shared experience. Indeed, the library shows with particular clarity the importance of group action to the social consciousness of Halifax's elite. Personal account books reveal that members of Halifax's elites collected books.[50] Unlike the canal or a new chapel, then, creating a personal library was within the means of these well-to-do families; in this instance, their choice of collective action was not conditioned by financial necessity.

48. Arnold Thackray, "Natural Knowledge in Cultural Context: The Manchester Model," *American Historical Review* 79 (1974): 678; John Seed, "Unitarianism, Political Economy, and the Antinomies of Liberal Culture in Manchester, 1830–1850," *Social History* 7 (1982): 1–25; and Morris, *Class, Sect, and Party*, 170–71.

49. CDA/MISC/49/1, Halifax library accounts, 1768–1790s. Fees rose rapidly in the latter part of the eighteenth century. In 1786 the membership fee was 1½ guineas, in 1787 it was 2 guineas, and by 1790 it was 3 guineas: CDA/HAS/MAC/88/2, Halifax library minute books (a twentieth-century copy).

50. See, e.g., CDA/SH:3/B/1/1, Lister account books.

Of course, not every merchant or lawyer participated in every associations. Each association had its own aim and attracted its own membership, and as the cases of Sowerby's chapel and the canal suggest, the geographical scope of different associations attracted members from different layers of the middle-class community.[51] Rather than a single group, Halifax's middle-class community should be conceived as a series of overlapping circles each defined by a particular association. Every association had some members who were not active elsewhere, but every association always shared many members with other associations. Thus though no single association defined the group that shared this middle-class culture, the memberships overlapped enough to justify the description of these merchants, manufacturers, and professionals as a single group, conscious of their place in the social order and sharing a common political discourse.

DISPUTES

As the founding of the Halifax Piece Hall suggests, the relations within Halifax's elite were not always as amicable as those that made possible the circulating library, the canal, and the new chapels. The same drive for power and prestige that led men to form associations and to become aware of themselves as a class turned them against each other as they vied for that power and that prestige. The resulting disputes helped to create a middle-class consciousness not through cooperative action but by identifying their participants as the dominant social group in the parish, united by the political culture in which the disputes were conducted.

The significance of these disputes, like that of the associations, lies in their timing and nature. In sixteen years, between 1748 and 1764, there were five major disputes in the parish, all of them revolving around the balance of power between the out-townships and the township of Halifax, and yet another dispute, the tail end of this burst of activity, erupted in 1776. This outburst has to be seen in the context

---

51. Morris argues that it was precisely this aspect of the voluntary association that made it so appropriate for the assertion of middle-class identity. Because one could choose among a range of activities, the middle class did not have to have a unity of purpose in order to achieve class identity: *Class, Sect, and Party*, 4–5, 161–68.

of the previous century, which was punctuated by only the occasional quarrel. It is hard to argue that this conflagration was coincidental, for all of the disputes shared issues and participants, and the connections between them were obvious to the participants. Moreover, at the root of these disputes were the economic and social developments that had created a group of powerful and wealthy manufacturers in the out-townships, who resented being dominated by the residents of Halifax township.

The disputes also took a distinctive form. In the first place, whereas earlier disputes had tended to be between individuals, these were struggles between self-constituted groups. They were characteristically voluble affairs. This is not to say that the earlier disputes were not heated; they probably were. What has survived of them, however, as in the case of a church-rate dispute of 1685, was often simply a laconic statement that there were differences between the two parties.[52] In contrast to these quiet whisperings, the disputes of the 1750s and 1760s seem to have been shouted out on the street corners—if not literally, then figuratively, with printed handbills and pamphlets. Thus the emerging middle-class consciousness engendered through these disputes was articulated within a new, public political world.

Of the five disputes that occurred between 1748 and 1764, four were challenges by the out-townships to Halifax's power. In 1748 (and again in 1759) a dispute arose over the church rate paid by all townships to the parish church in Halifax but administered by churchwardens in the township of Halifax, the charge being that the Halifax churchwardens had spent money on "their" church without the approval of the other townships. In 1748 the problem was repairs on the bells. The chapel-wardens for Midgley, Sowerby, and Warley did not dispute their obligation to contribute to the upkeep of the parish church, or indeed the necessity of most of the repairs; they simply refused to pay for the work done on the bells on the grounds that they had not been consulted before the repairs were ordered. The Halifax churchwardens took them to court for nonpayment of the church rate, and the suit was finally decided in 1754 in favor of the out-townships.[53]

---

52. CDA/MIC/8, Halifax churchwardens' accounts, 11 May 1685. The absence of records left by the earlier disputes is, as far as I can tell, not due to some accident of historical survival, but represents the different style in which those disputes were carried out.

53. The case was not actually brought to the consistory court at York until 1751–52. Each of the three townships fought a separate case but the papers in their files are identical: BIY/CP,

In 1749 another dispute arose over the administration of the Halifax workhouse, a charitable institution founded by Nathaniel Waterhouse in the seventeenth century and administered by governors from Halifax township. The governors had aroused the suspicions of the out-townships when they used funds from the workhouse to contribute to a new house for the lecturer at the parish church. Suspecting the worst, men from the out-townships looked into the original charter for the workhouse and into Nathaniel Waterhouse's will, where they found proof that the benefits of the workhouse were intended for the nine townships nearest to Halifax. Once again the dispute was resolved in favor of the out-townships: the old governors, all residents of Halifax township, were censured, and men from the out-townships were appointed to make up the full complement of governors stipulated in the charter.[54]

Finally, in 1764 a dispute arose as a consequence of the plan formed to install an organ in the parish church in Halifax. On hearing of the plan, the churchwardens of Sowerby quickly filed a suit in the consistory court claiming that the Halifax churchwardens had not properly consulted the other townships before proceeding, and expressing their concerns that with repairs and the organist's salary the project would become a financial burden on the parish as a whole.[55]

The participants in all four disputes were acting as members of a larger group and not as individuals. In Sowerby, for instance, the legal costs of the church-rate dispute were paid out of a subscription fund whose contributors were to be repaid, with interest, out of the rates.[56] This subscription list is nearly identical to the subscription list for the rebuilding of Sowerby Chapel except that the amounts involved were smaller and the names of one or two prominent Dissenters were included. Moreover, the "association" that was formed to carry out the dispute probably began its life as a public meeting.[57] The men of Hal-

---

I/1369 (Midgley), I/1370 (Sowerby), and I/1371 (Warley). A synopsis of this dispute and that of 1759 appears in CDA/STA/215/1, Sowerby's reply to Halifax, n.d. (probably after June 1764).

54. CDA/HAS/668/72/16, pamphlet on the disputes, 1764; CDA/FH/325/6, Commission of Pious Uses judgment concerning the Waterhouse workhouse, 1749.

55. BIY/CP, I/1449, Halifax organ dispute; CDA/HAS/B:8/4, documents prepared for the hearing of the organ dispute in King's Bench.

56. CDA/FH/279/1, subscription for the Sowerby debt, 1755.

57. By chance, the process by which such disputes were organized has survived. A public meeting was held to pursue a structurally similar dispute over the costs of maintaining the parish's highways: CDA/HAS/374 (577), Erringden Highway dispute, 1757.

ifax also constituted themselves as a group. When their plan for installing an organ in the parish church was challenged in the courts, the members of that association, having just collected £1,150, turned around and subscribed a further £1,000 for the town's defense against the suit.[58]

The groups on both sides of these disputes were concerned primarily with power and prestige. Indeed, if the ostensible issues of these disputes were all that was at stake, it is hard to imagine why they were taken so seriously. The sum involved in the church-rate dispute, for instance, was laughably small. Sowerby's portion of the parish church rate for 1748 came to £15/7/1 of which they were willing to pay £11/-/8; thus the unpaid portion, for which Halifax took them to court, was only £4/6/5.[59] The financial issue seems all the more trivial when one realizes that the annual bills for the land tax and poor rate in the township of Sowerby in this period often exceeded £200 each.[60]

What was at stake was power—the power that the town of Halifax was to have over the out-townships. The interrogatories that Sowerby directed at John Baldwin, the Halifax lawyer carrying out the suit for his township, attempted to discredit his evidence by proving that he was an interested party not only because he was a rate payer in Halifax township but also because a victory for Halifax would increase the "power or influence [of Halifax] over the rest of the parish or chapelwardens within the parish."[61] Financial issues were also of minimal importance in the workhouse dispute of 1749. The out-townships might expect to receive a small amount of money from the charity, but more important was the prestige that came with appointment as a governor of a venerable institution. Finally, the organ dispute had no substantive issues at all. Against the claim that the organ would become a financial burden on the parish as a whole the organizers in Halifax could point to the generous endowment raised by subscription to provide for repairs and the organist's salary.

Fundamental to the way these contending groups of merchants,

---

58. CDA/HAS/668/72/16, pamphlet on the disputes, 1764.
59. BIY/CP, I/1370; Midgley's and Warley's proportions of the church rate were much smaller than Sowerby's.
60. For the land tax see CDA/SPL/150/1–2, Sowerby land tax assessment, 1761, and the testimony of John Eagle of Bradford Gent. in the consistory court case: BIY/CP, I/1370. For the poor rates see CDA/SPL/31, Sowerby overseers' accounts.
61. BIY/CP, I/1370, interrogatory administered to John Baldwin of Halifax.

manufacturers, and professionals expressed their demands for power and prestige was the developing political discourse of the public sphere. Drawing on the rhetoric of the opposition to ministerial rule, the out-townships challenged what they painted as the arbitrary and excessive power that Halifax township exerted over parish affairs. In the church-rate dispute of 1759, one of the contested charges was a sum of £28/19/11 that the Halifax churchwardens had paid out for whitewashing the church. In this instance Sowerby did not deny that the church needed whitewashing, but they did claim that they had found someone who would have done it for £10. Halifax considered this man incompetent and rejected Sowerby's suggestion that a trial be held to determine which of the two was the better whitewasher. Sowerby's proposal of a trial was an assertion of one of the primary features of political discourse in the public sphere: the principle that critical judgment should be achieved through the examination of evidence and the use of reason. A similar conclusion can be drawn from the argument that Sowerby's case would be much strengthened if Halifax refused to present their account books at the trial, the relevant principle here being the right of public access to information about public finances.[62]

A comparison of the workhouse dispute of 1749 with an earlier dispute in 1719 shows how a public arena for local politics had developed. Like the 1749 dispute, the dispute of 1719 took the form of a suit filed before the Commission of Pious Uses, in this case charging that the governors of the Waterhouse workhouse had misused the building and appropriated £641 to their own benefit.[63] Though the two disputes were similar in form, the conceptual arenas in which they were fought were different. The 1719 dispute was an essentially private issue contested by individuals. The only issues in the case were the financial details of the governors' administration of the workhouse, and the dispute did not enter the public domain, for neither party appealed to public opinion or attempted to make political capital out of the issue.[64] The 1749

62. CDA/FH/284, Watson to Stansfield, September 1760.
63. WYAS/Wakefield, D53, Waterhouse workhouse case, 1719. The commission found for the plaintiffs, and they were appointed as the new governors. They did not take up their positions until 1723, however, because the former governors filed an unsuccessful countersuit in Chancery.
64. The dispute is mentioned in a pamphlet of 1764 (CDA/HAS/668/72/16), but the facts of the case are so distorted as to make the connection a sign of the author's attempt to make a long tradition out of more current issues.

dispute did take place in the public sphere. Organized groups replaced individuals as the antagonists, and unlike the judgment of the commission in 1719, which detailed and corrected the specific fiscal abuses of the former governors, the text of the 1749 decree concentrated on the *rights* of townships other than Halifax to benefit from the workhouse.[65] Like the earlier case, the dispute of 1749 also had a "judicial" solution, but its similarity with the dispute of 1719 ends there, for the impact of this judicial solution was political. Copies of the judgment were printed and the issues very quickly moved into the public domain to become part of a continuing controversy over the domination of the parish as a whole by the town of Halifax.

The role of the public sphere is also evident in Sowerby's objections to the Halifax organ. Given the weakness of their fiscal concerns, the only valid objection to the organ was the claim that most of the parish did not want it: essentially a claim about the rights of the out-townships not to be subjected to Halifax's domination. In support of this position Sowerby presented petitions signed by the men who paid "scot and lot" in the parish.[66] The scope of this petition was much broader than the typical subscription list. Five hundred and eight men signed the petition, 28 percent of whom could only make a mark. The large number of signatures resulted not from a public outcry against the organ, however, but from an extensive canvassing operation paid for by Stansfield.[67] The strategy followed in the fight against the organ suggests a developing view of the role of public opinion in politics. By canvassing for signatures, the elites were creating a political world in which power and prestige were increasingly measured by the public opinion they could harness. The more traditional articulations of power, the "interest" a gentleman could mobilize from his tenantry and dependents, were far from gone; one of Stansfield's weavers was unlikely to have refused to put his name to the petition. The emerging middle-class culture, however, was transforming that private political arena into a public one. Sowerby's elite thought it wise to obtain those signatures instead of simply claiming the right to speak for the township, and they

---

65. CDA/FH:325/6, judgment of the Commission of Pious Uses, 1749.

66. BIY/CP, I/1449, Halifax organ dispute. It is not possible to trace the residence of everyone who signed the petition, but while many signers lived in Sowerby, some are recognizable as men who lived in such townships as Warley and Skircoat.

67. CDA/STA/215/1/12, bill of William Whitworth to Stansfield for canvassing for votes against the organ, 1764.

assumed further that this display of public opinion would sway the court.

The fifth dispute in this series differs from the others in that the residents of the township of Halifax were the aggrieved party. The dispute arose in 1763 when the residents of Sowerby, having just completed their new chapel, decided that they would like to separate from Halifax and become a parish in their own right. George Stansfield, John Priestly, and John Welsh, the curate, petitioned the archbishop of York on behalf of the township's inhabitants to be allowed to become a separate parish.[68] They argued that the parish church in Halifax was too small and too far away, and that banns were subject to abuse because of this distance; they pointed with pride to their new commodious chapel. They also intimated that making Sowerby into a parish would solve the problem of Dissent. Sowerby's reasons for becoming a parish, however, derived from the long-standing grievances against domination by Halifax township. The elites of Halifax were furious; they matched Sowerby's petitions one for one and even enlisted the aid of the Earl of Sandwich, then secretary of state, who promised to oppose any bill, not only as a favor but as part of his duty to preserve the king's interest in the advowson. In the end, Sowerby's petition failed, for in the face of such strong opposition the archbishop, whose support was vital to the cause, lost heart.[69]

This dispute has three interesting features. First, it would be inappropriate to think of it in terms of interest politics. Even more than the construction of the chapel, Sowerby's attempt to gain parochial status appears to have been George Stansfield's project: he paid a surveyor to measure the exact distance from Sowerby to the Halifax parish church, and he also paid for an exhaustive census of the township to show how many upstanding members of the Church of England would go to the new parish church. Despite his leading role, however, Stansfield was dependent on the willing consent of other merchants and manufacturers in the township. In February 1764 John Priestly expressed doubts about the legality of trying to make a parish out of a chapelry and asked to have his name removed from the petition to the archbishop. He indi-

---

68. Stansfield and Priestly were the two top contributors to the Sowerby debt and to the new chapel.

69. CDA/STA/215/1/1, petition to the archbishop for parochial status, 1763; STA/215/1/6, petition to the archbishop by the curate, churchwardens, and principle inhabitants, n.d. (probably 1763); STA/215/1/8, Bates to residents of Halifax, 1764; STA/215/1/9, archbishop to Stansfield, 1764.

cated, however, that if the vestry (that is, the township's elite as a whole) continued to support the scheme, he would do so as well.[70]

Second, Halifax, in opposing parochial status for Sowerby, adopted the same kind of arguments that the out-townships had used against them with such effect in the church-rate and workhouse disputes. While presenting themselves as the aggrieved party with modest and eminently reasonable claims, they went to some lengths to portray their antagonists as status-hungry autocrats in pursuit of excessive power. Commenting on the new chapel that Sowerby's residents had built for themselves, they remarked that the old chapel was in good condition and in fact was larger than the new one. They continued: The men of Sowerby "say [that their new chapel] is in a more convenient situation, but in that we beg leave to differ from them, unless by convenient they mean *ostentatious* only."[71]

Third and most striking was the publicity that both sides gave to their positions. In a document printed in response to Halifax's objections to their petition, Sowerby cataloged Halifax's abuses of the out-townships and refuted each of their specific objections to parochial status. The wording of these refutations suggests that Halifax had already published their side of the story and that readers were expected to be familiar with it.[72] The dispute was being conducted in an explicitly public arena. Although the ability to mobilize influence played a vital and ultimately determining role, both sides were constructing their arguments in the public sphere and attempting to prove, by reason, the justice of their claims. The public they were trying to convince, of course, was an entirely artificial one—no vote was going to decide this debate. Yet members of the parish's commercial and professional elite, whether involved or not, no doubt followed the affair closely. Indeed, it is possible to argue that perhaps the most important point established by the debate over Sowerby's parochial status was this group's right to contend for political power and social prestige.

WHAT did this series of disputes mean? Since so little was actually achieved by a victory in any of these disputes, it is difficult to explain the intensity of the struggles without looking below the surface for

70. CDA/STA/215/1/12, bills of William Whitworth to Stansfield, February 1764 and June 1765; STA/215/1/10, Priestly to Stansfield and Welsh, February 1764.
71. CDA/FH/282/9, Halifax's answers to Sowerby's petition, 1764; emphasis in original.
72. CDA/STA/215/1, Sowerby's reply to Halifax, n.d. (probably after June 1764); CDA/FH/282/9, Halifax's answers to Sowerby's petition, 1764.

deeper meanings. The participants themselves recognized that the common theme of a struggle for power between Halifax and the out-townships was more important than the particular issue at stake in each event. A pamphlet titled *Memorandum, 1764,* though partisan to Sowerby's point of view, captures something of the disputants' picture of these struggles. Written in an ironic mode, it is full of such phrases as: "But the Organists suppose all power to be vested in themselves" and "it was boasted [by 'some persons in Halifax'] that the two Churchwardens for the township of Halifax had all the power; and that the ten Churchwardens of the *tributary* townships had only to raise and pay the money demanded of them."[73]

It is not, then, the victory of one group over another that makes these disputes useful for an analysis of class formation. By winning the church-rates disputes, the elites of the out-townships did not create their middle-class consciousness in opposition to the merchants, manufacturers, and professionals of Halifax town. Indeed, despite their apparent virulence, these disputes seem to have had little lasting impact on relations within the parish elite. Far from bearing a grudge, men such as John Caygill, John Waterhouse, Valentine Stead, and Nathaniel Holden, who had championed Halifax town's cause against Sowerby, Midgley, and Warley in the church-rate and organ disputes, were able to work with George Stansfield, Luke Greenwood, and John Lea to get the canal project under way in 1758.

The disputes are of interest because of what they show about the nature of local politics and, by implication, class relations. What was at stake in all of these events was a group's pursuit of political power and social prestige. Prestige was vital to the emerging commercial and professional elite because the political and social structures of mid-eighteenth-century society did not give them sufficient scope to parade their superior social and economic status. As the string of improvements carried out in the parish during these decades shows, this group went to great lengths to create institutions that would formalize their dominant position in the social order. What was worth organizing for was worth fighting over, and these disputes between Halifax and the out-townships, Sowerby in particular, gave voice to this group's quest for social prestige. At the same time, the conflicts gave form to their emerging class identity in two ways. First, their participation in these disputes identified the members of the parish's elite, both to themselves

---

73. CDA/HAS/668/72/16, pamphlet on the disputes, 1764; emphasis in original.

Constructing the Public Sphere 155

and to their neighbors, as a group that had the right to dispute such issues. Second, the use of the political discourse of the public sphere by men on both sides identified members of the commercial and professional elites to one another and identified them all as a distinct group in the social order.

"REAL" POLITICS: HALIFAX'S ELITE IN THE REGION AND THE NATION

The political discourse of the public sphere, like the elite's new fashions and accounting methods, was at once adopted and appropriated from sources outside the parish. Known by a host of names, the critique of arbitrary power based on a concept of "the public" and their right to representation and free discussion was an essential feature of eighteenth-century politics, particularly in shaping opposition to the oligarchic governments of the Hanoverian era.[74] Of course the critique was not used in quite this form; the emerging commercial and professional elites appropriated its essential message in order to make sense of their social and political circumstances, for it allowed these people to claim as a group political power that was not available to them as individuals. The parish's elite adopted this political discourse because it worked, and as the 1776 Waterhouse workhouse dispute shows, it had to work at the national level if it was to be effective at the local level.

This second workhouse dispute arose when many of the leading manufacturers of the out-townships proposed that the two institutions founded by Nathaniel Waterhouse—the workhouse and a charity—be joined by an act of Parliament. A central workhouse was no longer needed, they argued, and since the estate now yielded far more than the bequests stipulated in the will, the joint fund established by the merger would have a surplus to distribute to the townships for poor relief. The plan was opposed in Halifax, not only by the workhouse governors but by other men as well, most of them prominent manufacturers and merchants.[75]

---

74. See, among others, J. G. A. Pocock, *The Machiavellian Moment: Florentine Political Thought and the Atlantic Republican Tradition* (Princeton, 1975), and his *Virtue, Commerce, and History* (Cambridge, 1985), esp. pt. III; Rogers, *Whigs and Cities*; Istvan Hont and Michael Ignatieff, ed., *Wealth and Virtue: The Shaping of Political Economy in the Scottish Enlightenment* (Cambridge, 1983).

75. CDA/HAS/616/18, a printed "State of the Case," n.d., and HAS/616/23, petition to

The disputants drew heavily on the critique of arbitrary power expressed in the discourse of the public sphere. The meetings on both sides were public, and a positive flurry of handbills and pamphlets was produced to inform and persuade the public. They carried such ringing endorsements as "The plan of this intended Act was the result of many public meetings held at Halifax by the inhabitants of the town and parish, . . . copies whereof were printed and dispersed throughout the town and parish and public notice given long ago of this application of Parliament. . . ." The principles of the public sphere were even to be enshrined in the new trust that would be set up if the act was passed. The act stipulated that the trust properties be let on twenty-one-year leases, with public notice "given in some two newspapers printed in or nearest to the town of Halifax, and by hand bills."[76] This provision was designed to prevent the trustees from abusing their power and renting properties to each other at less than market value.

The strategy of founding the proposal on a critique of arbitrary power had implications at the national level, too, for it gave Parliament justification to abrogate existing property rights.[77] After a fairly extensive period of public meetings, advertisements, and a subscription, Robert Parker, the chief attorney for the new act, was dispatched to London to manage the passage of the bill. One of his first tasks was to discuss the merits of the case with experts so that he could present it to the best advantage. On the whole, Parker received a favorable response; none other than Sir George Saville, the influential MP for Yorkshire, told Parker that he did not think that "an opposition from trustees occupying part of the trust estate at an under-value can avail much." Though they were reasonably sure that justice was on their side, the bill's promoters left nothing to chance. They showered members of the House of Lords, where the bill was to begin, with abstracts and synopses

---

Parliament, n.d. (both probably 1776). The opponents of the plan were William Alexander (son of a doctor), John Alexander (son of a doctor), John Baldwin (attorney), John Bellamy, Richard Bracken, John Bramley (merchant), John Ferguson (merchant), Henry Hamer, Thomas Hudson (lecturer), John Lees (merchant), Thomas Ramsden, John Ramsden, John Royds (merchant), John Schofield, George Smith (merchant), William Smith (merchant), John Swire, Samuel Waterhouse (merchant), John Waterhouse (merchant), James Wetherherd (merchant), William Winn (merchant), Henry Wood (vicar), and William Wright. (I suspect that the Ramsdens, Henry Hamer, and John Swire were merchants but cannot be sure.)

76. CDA/HAS/616/16, Heads of a Proposed Bill for the Waterhouse Charities, n.d. (probably 1776).

77. Paul Langford, *Public Life and Propertied Englishmen, 1689–1798* (Oxford, 1991).

of the case, all of which played up the existing trustees' abuse of their power.[78] With both justice and organization on their side, the bill passed in short order.

A version of the same process was required in the case of the Calder Navigation and the Halifax Waterworks, both of which required parliamentary approval.[79] In all of these instances, the use of the political discourse of the public sphere has to be understood as the Halifax elite's appropriation of a set of ideas that helped them to make sense of their world and as their adoption of a particular rhetoric because of its efficacy.

The carefully crafted operation that Robert Parker set up to get the workhouse bill through Parliament shows that the residents of Halifax were well acquainted with the machinery of national government. Indeed, Halifax residents had petitioned Parliament for privileges or protection in the seventeenth and even sixteenth centuries.[80] Yet Halifax's relationship with national government underwent changes in the mid-eighteenth century that were associated with the emergence of middle-class consciousness. The nature of the transformation is suggested by the differences between the forms these appeals took—earlier a petition, now a bill. The two forms reflect the difference between the narrowly defined politics of interest and politics based on class identity. The purpose behind the petition—common participation in a particular trade—was essentially external to the group. The members of the group, often spread over a wide geographical area, were acting together in an ad hoc way because of their common interest in the issue at hand; nothing in this organization implies any durable form of group identity. The purpose of the charity bill, in contrast, was internal to the group. Moreover, procuring a bill was a much more complex process than

---

78. CDA/RP/3/144, 145, Parker to Howarth, 22 and 23 January 1777; CDA/HAS/171 (616)/48, materials relating to the charity bill, 1777.

79. The project to supply Halifax town with piped water was undertaken by yet another association organized through public meetings and advertisements. After getting the act in 1760, the trustees raised over £3,000 through mortgages secured by the rates. The act was extended in 1768 to give more authority to the trustees and to include street lighting and paving in their brief: H. Armitage, "Halifax Township's Early Water Supply," *THAS*, 1969, 89, 93, and CDA/MISC:5/96a/37, water works mortgage deed.

80. In 1699 the towns of Tetbury, Cirencester, Leeds, Halifax, Wakefield, Reading, and Coventry sent a petition concerning the cloth trade: Leo Francis Stock, ed., *Proceedings and Debates in the British Parliament Respecting North America* (Washington, D.C., 1927), 2:278. In the sixteenth century the townships secured the Halifax Wool Act of 1555.

sending in a petition, and the strategy shows a more sophisticated grasp of the political process as well as the existence of the common purpose necessary to produce the organization and wherewithal to achieve it.

Of course, interest politics did not disappear in the eighteenth century. On several occasions the textile interest in the West Riding industry as a whole, often speaking through the semi-official voice of the Quarter Sessions bench, presented petitions to Parliament. Stamping and measuring cloth, an issue of perennial interest, produced petitions in 1729 and 1765.[81] The crisis over the Stamp Act in 1766 produced a petition from the tradesmen and manufacturers of Halifax, the merchants of Leeds, and the broadcloth manufacturers in the West Riding in favor of repeal, and they sent a deputation of three witnesses to give evidence at Parliament's inquiry into the matter.[82] This kind of petitioning suggests that the emergence of a middle-class consciousness in Halifax was related to a less well defined "commercial identity" that was developing within the region as a whole and perhaps even, in a very hesitant way, in the nation.[83] These petitions increasingly adopted the language of the public sphere. That language is most evident in the opposition to the Stamp Act, where a direct critique of government policy was intended, for, as Linda Colley has agued, people engaged in trade increasingly came to feel that the government was not acting in their interests after the Seven Years' War.[84]

If these political actions suggest the development of a wider middle-class consciousness in the region as a whole, they also provide evidence of the limits of the identity that could be constructed simply on the basis of interest. The petition in 1765 calling for a repeal of the legislation on cloth searching was rebutted almost immediately by a petition from the broadcloth merchants of Leeds. Four more petitions were submitted over the next few months, those from the mixed cloth manufacturers and white cloth manufacturers supporting repeal and those from the Leeds cloth dressers and the broadcloth makers and manufacturers opposing it; both sides also sent witnesses to testify in Parlia-

81. WYAS/Wakefield, QS/10/16, Quarter Sessions order books, 15 January 1728/29; *Commons Journals* 30:91.

82. R. C. Simmons and P. D. G. Thomas, eds., *Proceedings and Debates of the British Parliaments Respecting North America, 1754–1783* (Millwood, N.Y., 1983), 2:95–96, 215–18.

83. On this issue see John Money, *Experience and Identity: Birmingham and the West Midlands, 1760–1800* (Manchester, 1977).

84. Colley, *Britons*, 100. Nicholas Rogers also detects an increasing criticism of government policy by London's tradesmen from the treaty ending the Seven Years' War because it was not in their interests: *Whigs and Cities*.

ment.[85] Joined on one issue and split on another, the multitude of groups that existed even within the West Riding woolen industry were not the basis for the emergence of a class identity. That development required issues that could transcend a narrowly defined economic interest.

Developments in the mid–eighteenth century helped to overcome the multitude of particular interests and to create the perception among Halifax's elites and others in the region that Halifax's merchants, manufacturers, and professionals were indeed behaving with a single purpose. Consider the responses to Halifax's plans to build a canal. In 1741 and again in 1751, plans to make the Calder navigable were abandoned in the face of strong resistance from the Leeds merchants, who stood to lose their monopoly over the large-scale export of the cloth sold at Halifax's markets. That opposition was not dropped in 1757 when a successful bid was made; it was simply overcome by the single-mindedness of the Halifax promoters. William Banks, the Leeds merchant who was persuaded to sell his mills to members of the committee in 1757 in return for dropping his objections to the canal, compared himself to Admiral John Byng, who was court-martialed and shot for neglect of duty in 1757, because of the feeling in Leeds that he had "sold [his] town and country" by coming to terms with the Halifax men.[86]

Regional relations, of course, were not always so antagonistic, but when groups cooperated, they were usually groups that identified first with their own communities. In 1780, for instance, West Riding merchants and manufacturers attempted to get the Treasury to negotiate a reduction in the duty on kersey cloth imported into Flanders. Writing to his cousin George Stansfield of Sowerby, David Stansfield of Leeds implied that though the merchants of Leeds and Halifax did not see eye to eye on the matter, there were substantial areas of agreement between them. He referred to the "merchants of Leeds" and the "merchants of Halifax" as if they were coherent groups, and as if the success of this project depended on each community's unity.[87]

From a regional perspective, what was happening can best be described in terms of ownership. Through their activities on the regional and national stages, Halifax's merchants, manufacturers, and profes-

85. *Commons Journals* 30: 143, 155, 158, 167, 207, 262–64.
86. PRO/C.12/61/22/g, Banks to David Stansfield, 13 March 1758.
87. CDA/FH/414, 1780. Whereas a fine broadcloth might incur a duty of between 5 and 10 percent of its value, a cheap kersey might be subject to a duty of nearly 25 percent.

sionals asserted, as a group, their ownership of the parish. Consider one final voluntary association. In December 1758 Sir George Saville wrote to the "Gentlemen of Halifax" to request that 150 to 200 of the freeholders in the parish be prepared to attend the election at York. This man was the lord of the manor to over half of the parish's townships and an important regional figure even before his election to Parliament. In response to his letter, a very exclusive group of merchants and manufacturers met and agreed to allocate the townships among themselves, assigning one or more of their number to "apply to the gentlemen of [the township] to request their attendance at York."[88] Yet Saville made his request for support not to individuals but to the "gentlemen" (read "elite") of Halifax as a whole. It was as a group that these merchants and manufacturers divided up the townships within the parish according to the influence each man had in his own township. Saville, while evidently acknowledging the social preeminence of the new elite, also approached them in a different fashion; this was not a letter to an individual gentleman asking him to secure the voters in "his" parish. For their part, the "gentlemen" approached by Saville were willing to assume the kind of "ownership" of the parish that this request implied, but it was as a group that they did so.

Sir George Saville's request that a contingent of Halifax voters be prepared to support him in a potential election raises a final issue: that of elections and party politics. Like most of the manufacturing towns of the Midlands and the North that grew so dramatically in the eighteenth century, Halifax was without parliamentary representation of its own. The relatively large number of freehold voters, however, made the parish important in the Yorkshire county elections, particularly because West Riding freeholders were long accustomed to exercise their right to vote.[89] We can assess the voting patterns of Halifax's freeholders by two poll books, one from the general election of 1734 and one from a by-election in 1741, and by the returns of two canvasses for the eventually uncontested election of 1784.[90]

88. CDA/FH/378, election agreement, 1758. The men who drew up the agreement were, with the exception of the vicar, all members of Halifax's middle class: William Greame, David Stansfield, Samuel Lees, Jeremiah Royds, Valentine Stead (all merchants and manufacturers), and Dr. Cyril Jackson. Most of the men they selected to canvass the townships were members of the middle class like themselves.

89. The tradition of voting stretched back to the late sixteenth century: Richard Cust, "Politics and the Electorate in the 1620s," in *Conflict in Early Stuart England*, ed. Richard Cust and Ann Hughes (New York, 1989), 134–67.

90. WYAS/Bradford, SpSt/11/5/3/14, poll book for the Yorkshire election, 1734; *The Poll*

The poll books of 1734 and 1741 show that, by and large, Halifax supported the Tories. In 1741 the vote was 346 for the Tory candidate, George Fox, and 143 for the Whig candidate, Chomley Turner.[91] Support for the two parties among the parish's elites split on fairly predictable lines. Most of the leading Anglicans voted Tory, while most of the leading Dissenters supported the Whigs. A few Anglicans voted Whig, most prominently the vicar, Dr. George Legh; but inasmuch as his place was in the gift of the crown, it is hardly surprising that he supported the ministerial interest. Indeed, Legh had been specially chosen as the incumbent for what the archbishop of York described as "a most disaffected corner of my diocese."[92]

The canvass returns from 1784 present a more complex picture. One important change was the decline of traditional Whig/Tory divisions that had occurred since the accession of George III.[93] More immediate were the effects of Christopher Wyvill's Yorkshire Association. This movement had collapsed shortly before the election, but the demand for parliamentary reform of some kind was still very much in the air, and the government candidates were opposed by men representing the association. In this "election" the government interest seems to have centered on the vicar and a substantial proportion of the parish's leading merchants and manufacturers. Other influential merchants and manufacturers—John and Samuel Waterhouse, George Stansfield, John Edwards, and most of the leading Dissenters, including Dr. Joseph Hulme and John Kershaw—supported the two association candidates, William Wilberforce and Henry Duncombe.[94]

Although there is clear evidence that Halifax's residents had a very well developed national political consciousness, it was central to their individual or group identity only insofar as trade or economic policy

---

Book for the County of York, 1741 (York, 1742); Sheffield City Library, 181/Z1/1, microfilm of a partial canvass for the election of 1784 and Wentworth Woodhouse Muniments/E/1, 2, canvass for the election of 1784.

91. *Poll Book for the County of York*. Turner won, 8,000 to 7,000; see J. F. Quinn, "Yorkshiremen Go to the Polls: County Contests in the Early Eighteenth Century," *Northern History* 21 (1985): 137–74.

92. A letter from the archbishop to Walpole cited in G. Collyer, "The Yorkshire Election of 1734," *Proceedings of the Leeds Philosophical and Literary Society: Literature and History Section* 7 (1952–55): 59. Legh, a low churchman, was quite popular with Dissenters.

93. James E. Bradley, *Religion, Revolution, and English Radicalism: Nonconformity in Eighteenth-Century Politics and Society* (Cambridge, 1990).

94. Sheffield City Library, 181/Z1/1, microfilm of a partial canvass for the election of 1784 and Wentworth Woodhouse Muniments/E/1, 2, canvass for the election of 1784.

was the primary issue. Preserved in George Stansfield's papers, for instance, is a copy of *Mother Shipton's Prophecy*. Supposedly written "above a hundred years ago and found under the tombstone of a Knight Templar," it is obviously a piece of political propaganda, contrasting the sacrifice in 1641 of "a minion that sits next the throne / who is both just and wise" (Strafford) with the fall in 1741 of "a minion perch'd above the throne / who is quite otherwise" (Walpole). Informing this political choice was concern over Britain's commercial policies. The prophecy continues:

> Britannia raise they drooping head!
> Deliverance is come.
> Thy Senate will revive thy trade
> And seal thy foes their doom.[95]

Exclusive of the issue of trade and commercial policy, there is little to suggest that an identity based on party politics was particularly meaningful in its own right; as much historiography on eighteenth-century politics suggests, analysis must focus on the intersection of local and national issues.[96] Members of groups on both sides of the church-rate dispute of 1748, for instance, had voted Tory in 1741. Similarly, some residents of Halifax township who had resisted the attempt to restructure the Waterhouse workhouse in 1776 split when they delared their intentions to the canvassers in 1784. This behavior is not particularly surprising. For many provincials, national politics was more a means to an end than an end in itself. Consider the almost universal support that Sir George Saville, an independent Whig, was able to muster among Halifax's commercial and professional elite in 1758. This support came from men who had supported both Whig and Tory candidates in 1741. In view of the fact that the bill for the Calder Navigation was on its way through Parliament when Saville's call came, such shifts are not difficult to explain. Nor, after their support of Saville in 1758, is John Roydes's and William Walker's reversion to their traditional support for the Tory party. In the early 1760s, with the party's revival in the reign of George III, both had petitioned John Stanhope to be allowed to collect the

---

95. CDA/FH/377.
96. Rogers, *Whigs and Cities*; Bradley, *Religion, Revolution, and English Radicalism*, 18–31.

West Riding land tax in the area immediately around Halifax, a very lucrative post.[97]

The way electoral politics worked in mid-eighteenth-century Halifax tends to confirm the view that local and national politics gave shape to the emerging class consciousness of Halifax's merchants, manufacturers, and professionals—a middle-class consciousness because this group was defining itself in opposition to the parish's yeomen and artisans and to the landed elites in ways that drew on their experiences as manufacturers and merchants.

97. WYAS/Bradford, SpSt/11/5/6/15, Roydes and Walker to Stanhope, 14 March 1765 and 6 March 1763. For more context see R. G. Wilson, "Three Brothers: A Study of the Fortunes of a Landed Family in the Mid–Eighteenth Century," *Journal of the Bradford Textile Society*, 1964–65, 111–21.

Chapter 6

Constructing the Private Sphere: The Family and Sociability

The emergence of a private sphere, defined by shared values and new forms of sociability, did as much as public political struggles to shape the emerging middle-class identity in Halifax. The scope and nature of this private sphere is not well defined. As historians have shown, there was no simple public/private division in seventeenth-, eighteenth-, and perhaps even nineteenth-century society, certainly not one that corresponds to clearly defined gender roles.[1] It is useful to define the public sphere as consisting of politics, for there is a coherence to those activities. But "public" here must not be used with the intent to contrast it to "private," for some aspects of politics always took place in private settings, as often as not ones in which women played some role. The

---

1. Dena Goodman, "Public Sphere and Private Life: Toward a Synthesis of Current Historiographical Approaches to the Old Regime," *History and Theory* 31 (1992): 1–20; Sara Maza, "Women, the Bourgeoisie, and the Public Sphere: Response to Daniel Gordon and David Bell," *French Historical Studies* 17 (1992): 935–50. For a sampling of some work on the subject see M. J. Daunton, "Public Place and Private Space: The Victorian City and the Working-Class Household," in *The Pursuit of Urban History*, ed. Derek Fraser and Anthony Sutcliffe (London, 1983), 212–33; Bill Bramwell, "Public Space and Local Communities: The Example of Birmingham, 1840–1880," in *Urbanizing Britain: Essays on Class and Community in the Nineteenth Century*, ed. Gerry Kearns and Charles W. J. Withers (Cambridge, 1991), 31–54; Peter Williams, "Constituting Class and Gender: A Social History of the Home, 1700–1901," in *Class and Space: The Making of Urban Society*, ed. Nigel Thrift and Peter Williams (London, 1987), 154–204; Janet Wolff, "The Culture of Separate Spheres: The Role of Culture in Nineteenth-Century Public and Private Life," in *The Culture of Capital: Art, Power, and the Nineteenth-Century Middle Class* (Manchester, 1988), 117–34.

same can be said for most activities outside the public sphere so defined, for much of what people did seems to have had both public and private aspects. Many of the forms of sociability found in seventeenth- and eighteenth-century Halifax, from gatherings at an alehouse to club meetings and balls, were private in the sense that they were not open to all comers, but they were public in the sense that they involved groups of individuals gathering together. Even the family, which one might think of as belonging exclusively to the private sphere, had a public aspect, for almost everyone in seventeenth- and eighteenth-century Halifax made a living in the context of the household economy and received visitors at home.

The "construction" of a private sphere, then, was less a definitive separation into two distinct worlds than the beginnings of differentiation between them. This differentiation is evident in two areas. First, Halifax's merchant, manufacturing, and professional families adopted new values and expectations that emphasized the difference between the public and private aspects of the family, most obviously in the separation of the family business from the rest of family life. Second, they developed new forms of sociability. Obviously, people socialize on the boundaries between the public and the private, but these new activities were differentiated between those concerned with public affairs, such as government and business, and those that had nothing to do with the public sphere so defined.

No mere expressions of a common economic or political interest, these values, expectations, and practices were expressions of the increasingly coherent sense that Halifax's merchant, manufacturing, and professional families had of their own identity as distinct from that of other social groups. Most important, the private sphere served to differentiate this group from those below them: a couple's expectation that the wife would not work, the building of a house suited to private entertaining, membership in a circulating library whose subscription fee was a guinea or in a club whose members dined with the county's MP helped to distinguish the elite from artisans and yeomen. The implications of these values and practices for the relations of this group with those above them are less clear; as we shall see, however, there was an implicit criticism of aristocratic license in the sober respectability that this group cultivated.

As the work of scholars such as Peter Borsay, Paul Langford, Neil McKendrick, and John Brewer has shown, the means by which such social distinctions could be made were proliferating throughout England during the eighteenth century.[2] These means included both material possessions and behaviors: the goods that fueled the consumer boom of the eighteenth century and the clubs, assemblies, and other practices that formed what Borsay has described as an "urban renaissance." London led the way in these developments, and from there they spread to the provinces. The appropriation of these values and practices and the meanings they acquired in the economic, social, and cultural context of the parish allowed Halifax's commercial and professional elite to construct a private sphere in which their new cultural identity was created and maintained.

Central to this cultural identity—and thus central to the emerging distinction between public and private spheres—was a new set of gender relations. The expectation that the woman of the family would not work suggests the differentiation between a male sphere that included business, politics, and local affairs and a female sphere that encompassed other activities. The new forms of sociability were also differentiated by gender. Associations such as the circulating library, which were intended to be apolitical, were open to both men and women, but those such as the Union Club, which had an avowed concern with politics and public affairs, were for men only. These gender relations, of course, were not unique to Halifax; a host of eighteenth-century publications described the behaviors, roles, and feelings that were proper for women of the middling ranks.[3] Yet as they were appropriated by the parish's elite, these gender relations helped to create and maintain an emerging middle-class identity in Halifax because they served to distinguish this emerging elite from their social inferiors, for the differentiation between public and private spheres was not so marked in the culture of the middling sort.

---

2. Peter Borsay, *The English Urban Renaissance: Culture and Society in the Provincial Town, 1660–1770* (Oxford, 1989), and "The Rise of the Promenade: The Social and Cultural Use of Space in the English Provincial Town, c. 1660–1800," *British Journal for Eighteenth-Century Studies* 9 (1986): 125–40; Paul Langford, *A Polite and Commercial People: England, 1727–1783* (Oxford, 1992); Neil McKendrick, "Commercialization and the Economy," and John Brewer, "Commercialization and Politics," both in McKendrick, Brewer, and J. H. Plumb, *The Birth of a Consumer Society* (London, 1983).

3. For but two examples see Dr. Gregory, *A Father's Legacy to His Daughters* (London, 1784), and James Fordyce, *Sermons to Young Women* (London, 1766).

FAMILY

In many respects, attitudes toward the family remained largely unchanged throughout the period. The desire to see one's sons established and one's daughters well married was common to the rich and the poor and to the seventeenth and eighteenth centuries. Even some of the more particular characteristics of Halifax's families remained. Most testators, for example, made an effort to provide all of their children with roughly equivalent portions. A preference for sons over daughters is evident, and sometimes assets were concentrated in the hands of one son, but equality rather than discrimination was the rule. Most people's economic activities were closely associated with the family. The domestic clothier of the 1690s and the merchant of the 1760s made a living in the context of familial relations: the members of the clothier family worked together in their own home; the merchant worked in partnership with brother, father, or brother-in-law.

The removal of women from the workforce was a major change. In the artisan's or yeoman's household, work and living were conceptually as well as physically inseparable. The family's productive activities, whether agricultural or craft, were carried out by all its members. To be sure, the sexual division of labor in the households of the middling sort was strongly marked; it was one household, however, not the two separate spheres of workplace and home. By the mid-eighteenth century, in contrast, women in the households of Halifax's elite had shifted their activities to a more clearly defined private sphere. This development was made possible, in part, by the financial success of their husbands and by the changing nature of the work they did. A successful manufacturer could afford to dispense with his wife's contribution at the spinning wheel, and since he no longer made cloth himself, that contribution would have been inappropriate.

The strongest and clearest argument for this aspect of middle-class culture is made by Leonore Davidoff and Catherine Hall in *Family Fortunes*.[4] They show that this demarcation between a male public sphere and a female private sphere became a distinctive feature of the emerging identity of the English middle class from the late eighteenth century. The evidence for the culture and practice of separate spheres in

---

4. Leonore Davidoff and Catherine Hall, *Family Fortunes: Men and Women of the English Middle Class, 1780–1850* (London, 1987). See also their "Architecture of Public and Private Life: English Middle Class Society in a Provincial Town, 1780–1850," in Fraser and Sutcliffe, *Pursuit of Urban History*, 328–29.

Halifax, a generation before Davidoff and Hall take up the story, supports the work of Margaret Hunt, who has argued that the roots of these separate spheres can be traced as far back as the late seventeenth century, to the distinctive response of trading folk to the perils of the new commercial world of the eighteenth century.[5] To argue that separate spheres had a much earlier origin than Davidoff and Hall suggest is not to diminish their contribution. Rather it is to suggest that the first emergence of a set of values and conceptions, in places like Halifax or contexts like those discussed by Hunt, must be distinguished from its later articulation as a coherent, structured ideology.[6]

Although culture is difficult to quantify, it is possible to measure this change through an analysis of the role that widows played in the management of the estates left to their underage children. Since a guardian had to be appointed to bring up underage children and manage their inheritances, the provisions that a testator made for them provide an explicit statement of his expectations about his widow's ability to manage the family's financial affairs and the desirability of her doing so.[7]

The provisions made in such cases fall into three categories, depending on the role the widow was to play in her children's upbringing. Some widows were given total responsibility; they were the sole executor of the will and had complete charge of their children. In 1696 John Jackson, an innkeeper of Halifax, instructed that his wife, Sara, was to have all of his copyhold and freehold land and his personal estate to pay his debts and funeral expenses, raise their son and daughter "according to their degree and quality," and give them the part of the estate she thought fit.[8] Similarly, Jeffrey Lodge's will (1709) gave his wife, Elizabeth, the power (and duty) of selling all of his real estate to pay off his debts; this done, she was to lay out £220 on a freehold estate for their son Jeffrey, give their other children £300 each, and put each of them out "as apprentice to be instructed in any lawful trade or employment."[9]

    5. Margaret R. Hunt, *The Middling Sort: Commerce, Gender, and the Family in Eighteenth-Century England* (Berkeley, forthcoming).
    6. This relationship is discussed in Chapter 8.
    7. I have not distinguished between male and female children or between families in which all children were underage and those in which only some of the children were underage.
    8. BIY/OW, John Jackson, Halifax, June 1696; Jackson had land in three townships and was probably reasonably well off.
    9. BIY/OW, Jeffrey Lodge, Halifax, July 1709. Elizabeth Lodge carried out her responsibilities with evident success, for when she died, she left behind a personal estate worth over £2,500 and all of the land she was supposed to have sold: BIY/OW, March 1714/15.

Other widows were given shared responsibility. In many of these instances the intentions of the testator are ambiguous. Some intended to limit the role their widow was to play, as in the case of a wealthy yeoman clothier of the township of Stansfield who named his wife and nephew as executors but gave the tuition of his sons to the nephew alone, presumably leaving the care of his young daughters in the hands of both executors. Other testators may simply have intended to relieve their wives of some of the executor's burden. Thomas Kitson left all of his goods and lands to his wife "in the hope that she will bring up my children;" she was the sole executor, but he wanted her to be "assisted" by Richard Walker and Jonathan Rawson, his "loving brothers in law."[10]

Some widows were given no responsibility for the tuition or estates of their children. In 1780 Richard Ashworth, a Wadsworth stuffmaker, appointed his four brothers as the executors of his estate. They were to sell all of his personal goods and put the money raised out at interest. The income was to go to the children's needs and education, and his widow, Mary, was to get the interest on £60 for her maintenance. Undoubtedly there were exceptions, but most men did not exclude their widows from the management of the estate out of malice. Indeed, if they had the means, they often left their widows a handsome portion. William Greame, a very wealthy merchant, left his wife £100 as pocket money until her jointure started, but he gave control of the entire estate to his brother and brother-in-law.[11] The fact that male members of the wife's family were often named as trustees shows that gender, and not some desire to keep the husband's patrimony in his family, was the important consideration in these cases.

Table 6 shows the numbers of sample wills that fell into each of these three categories from 1690 to 1785. We see that between the later seventeenth and mid-eighteenth centuries, widows were increasingly less likely to be given sole responsibility for their underage children. The change began in the 1730s and 1740s and was firmly established by the 1770s and 1780s. A testator might have any number of reasons to exclude his wife from the management of his children's estate. He might fear for the children's portions if she remarried, or he might be concerned that she would be unable to perform the necessary duties: one

10. BIY/OW, John Barker, Stansfield, May 1706; Thomas Kitson, Lightcliffe, October 1715. Kitson's estate consisted of one messuage and £100 worth of goods.

11. BIY/OW, Richard Ashworth, Wadsworth, January 1780; William Greame, Skircoat, September 1747.

TABLE 6. Widows' responsibilities in management of estates of their underage children under wills in a sample of all Halifax wills, 1690–1785

Period	Sole	Shared	None	Total
1690–1709	14	9	2	25
1710–1729	8	8	3	19
1730–1749	3	7	7	17
1750–1769	3	4	4	11
1770–1785	3	11	9	23
All periods	31	39	25	95

Source: Probate Records at the Borthwick Institute of Historical Research, Pontefract Deanery and Prerogative Court.

wealthy yeoman clothier explained that "my wife has been much indisposed and has nearly lost her eyesight."[12] No such reasons, however, can explain the aggregate shift toward the widow's exclusion from involvement in managing the estate. That shift represents the growing cultural perception that it was not suitable for women to be managing money, let alone running a business.

This conclusion seems even more valid in light of evidence that this behavior was more common in Halifax's elite families and, more generally, in families of relative wealth. When we compare Table 7 with Table 6, we see that less than a third as many women in these families as in the general population were left in sole charge throughout the period; even in the later seventeenth century, it was more common for women to share responsibility for bringing up their children with other executors. Yet the shift toward total exclusion of women from the management of estates is especially strong in this group: after 1750, very few elite women were included in the management of their children's estates in any capacity.

The implication of the figures in Table 7 is reinforced by an examination of the wealth of the testators in the sample shown in Table 6. Before 1729, the men who left their wives in sole control were spread across the spectrum from rich to poor. Of particular interest are relatively wealthy men such as Luke Crossley, a stapler of Halifax. He died in 1696, leaving a fortune of almost £800 to his wife and instructing her to bring up the children and manage the estate. John Jackson and Jeffrey Lodge were also men of fairly substantial fortune who left their

12. BIY/OW, Henry Dyson, Rishworth, March 1742/43. When a testator specified that his wife was to lose her control over the children if she remarried, I counted the will in the "shared responsibility" category.

Constructing the Private Sphere

TABLE 7. Widow's responsibilities in management of estates of their underage children under wills in a sample of wills of Halifax's elites, 1690–1785

Period	Sole	Shared	None	Total
1690–1790	1	7	4	12
1710–1729	3	11	3	17
1730–1749	4	12	5	21
1750–1769	1	4	8	13
1770–1785	–	2	7	9
All periods	9	36	27	72

Source: Probate Records at the Borthwick Institute of Historical Research, Pontefract Deanery and Prerogative Court.

affairs in the hands of their widows. In contrast, all but one of the six men who left their wives in complete control after 1750 were either poor or only moderately well off; a Halifax joiner, for instance, left his wife a small cottage and a personal estate of only £32 with which to bring up their son.[13]

The men who excluded their wives from the management of the estate show an opposite trend. In the period after 1750, the two poor men who excluded their wives had ample reason to do so. One had two grown sons, nearly grown daughters, and a wife who was probably quite old; the other wished to divide his estate between a child by an earlier marriage, a bastard daughter, and his wife's unborn child.[14] The exclusion of women from the management of their children's estates, then, was strongly associated with social status. These status differences were expressed through changing expectations of women's ability to function in what was being defined as the public sphere of business and beliefs about the desirability of their doing so.

Other evidence suggests that the exclusion of these well-to-do women from the management of their underage children's estates was only symptomatic of their more general exclusion from the household's productive process.

A few testators of the late seventeenth and early eighteenth centuries explicitly spelled out what they meant when they left their wives in complete control of their estates and their children's futures. The first part of Joshua Lea's will was concerned with making arrangements to divide the land and rather substantial personal estate that this wealthy

13. BIY/OW, Luke Crossley, Halifax, June 1696; Thomas Bradley, Halifax, October 1780.
14. BIY/OW, William Horsfall, Wadsworth, September 1751 (Horsfall left bequests of only £40 and a personal estate of only £50); Bramham Hudson, Halifax, July 1755.

clothier had accumulated in his lifetime. Two of his sons were underage, and to provide for them he desired that his wife, Susannah, should carry on the "trade of a white clothier in such manner as I now do ... and that she shall take in my said sons John and Thomas, their minority not withstanding, into partnership and trade with her." To that end she was to have the use and profit of £300 to invest in the trade as well as the legacies of her sons, which amounted to a further £920. In sum, Lea expected his wife to carry on his business, and he thought her perfectly capable of instructing her sons in the intricacies of the trade as well. Edward Ferguson made a similar bequest in his will of February 1735/36. His wife was to have £120 to "enable her to carry on the linen drapery trade which I now follow"; she could take that money either in cash or from his stock in trade.[15]

More often than not, of course, the testator did not explicitly state his expectation that his wife would carry on the business. When Luke Greenwood, a moderately well off clothier, made his will in 1691, he left his wife the customary one-third that was her dower; the rest of his estate was to go to his children when they reached the age of twenty-one. Since Elizabeth, his wife, was his sole executor, she had the responsibility of raising those children and control over their portion of the estate. In all likelihood she carried on the household weaving operation, perhaps hiring an extra apprentice or journeyman to replace the labor of her husband.[16] This, of course, can only be speculation, for Elizabeth Greenwood may not have been able or willing to carry on her husband's trade. In most households, however, the woman's involvement in the day-to-day production process would have given her the necessary experience and financial necessity would have supplied the motivation.

Some widows carried on trade on a spectacular scale. Susannah Lea certainly looked well placed to do so, for with a capital of £1,220 she had quite a head start. Susanna Riley of Soyland, a widow who made her will in February 1706/7, was heavily involved in the woolen industry; indeed, she was one of the most substantial early manufacturers in the parish, one of the few who sent goods directly to Holland.[17] Like Susanna Lea and Elizabeth Greenwood, Riley probably inherited her business from her husband. All three widows demonstrate the role that

15. BIY/OW, Joshua Lea, Sowerby, September 1737; Edward Ferguson, Halifax, June 1738.
16. BIY/OW, Luke Greenwood, Erringden, June 1691.
17. BIY/OW, Susanna Riley, Soyland, November 1707.

women played in the society of the middling sort. Active participants in the household economy, they could, at least as widows, be direct participants in trade.

In the mid–eighteenth century, women's role in the household economy of the commercial and professional elites was changing. Some merchants and wealthy tradesmen left their wives in control of the household business, but this practice became less and less common.[18] Many a testator made explicit his intention that even though his wife was to bring up the children, she was not to continue in his trade. The will of Thomas Metcalf, a Halifax grocer, probated in 1746, instructed the executors to collect all of his debts, sell his stock in trade, and pay the interest on the sum so raised to his wife and children. Hannah Metcalf, then, was to bring up the children on the interest, but she was not intended to carry on in her husband's trade. Indeed, in a codicil Thomas bequeathed the tools he used to "roll, cut, and press tobacco" to his nephew rather than to his wife; since the sale of his goods could provide her with a comfortable annuity, he saw no reason to leave her the means to carry on his business.[19]

The provisions that Samuel Lees made for his widow, Susanna, in his will of 1760 show a similar set of assumptions. Lees, the giant manufacturer in Skircoat encountered earlier in connection with his partnerships and his perception of his business as an investment, left a very complex will in which he disposed of his land, fortune, and business to his wife and underage sons and daughters. The unique feature of Samuel's will was his provision that his trustees should employ his estate "in the way of trade or business which I now follow" as long as it yielded above 4 percent per year. Susanna's role in these affairs was that of a passive bystander. She was allowed a generous annuity of £40 a year, and could live in Willowhall as long as she was his widow, but she was to have nothing to do with the continuation of Samuel's manufacturing business except that the trade was, as he put it, "to be carried on in the name of my widow."[20]

---

18. BIY/OW, Joshua Hudson, Halifax, January 1765. Hudson was an ironmonger of some substance. He left his wife in charge of his business, with the suggestion that she take their son into partnership with her if she thought it proper to do so.

19. BIY/OW, Thomas Metcalf, Halifax, February 1745/46.

20. BIY/OW, Samuel Lees, Skircoat, Prerogative Court, July 1761. In a codicil to this will Lees did name his wife as one of the trustees. It does not appear that her role changed, however, for the trade was carried on by his partner and son-in-law, John Edwards; Susanna was simply a sleeping partner: CDA/RP/2110, 2111, Lees and Edwards partnership articles, 1772, 1773.

Compare, then, Susanna Lees with Susanna Riley, the widow who died in 1707 with nearly £450 of cloth in Holland "safe arrived." Both women were members of the very top layer of the society of their day, of families that were making a fortune in the rapidly expanding textile industry. Despite her "advanced" economic activities, Riley was culturally one of the middling sort. She participated directly in her household's productive activities, and after her husband's death she became a substantial manufacturer in her own right. Lees had quite a different experience. The closest she got to the cloth trade that had made her husband's fortune was having the business carried on in her name by her husband's partner. The contrast between these two women suggests that the change was fundamentally a cultural one, for the economic practice (large-scale putting out for foreign trade) was essentially the same in each household. The difference was that Lees and her husband shared cultural assumptions that excluded women from the productive life of the household.

The exclusion of women from the productive process was in part simply a luxury that only wealthy families could afford. Women's labor was crucial in the households of the midding sort, and this continued to be the case among yeoman and artisan families in the eighteenth century. The wealthy manufacturer, though, could easily afford to keep an idle wife to testify to his financial success, and if she did not work, she was not going to be thought capable of managing the estate. Again, it is significant that the status distinction was expressed in gender roles and became evident only in the mid–eighteenth century.

There is no evidence to suggest that women resented their exclusion from the household's productive enterprise. Leisure was a valued commodity in the eighteenth century, and many women were no doubt pleased to be relieved of the drudgery of spinning and carding wool, perhaps even of keeping up the house, if the family could afford to dispense with her labor and hire the necessary servants. And after all, women had as great an interest as men in establishing the status differences that separated this commercial and professional elite from the common folk. Inasmuch as highly gendered expectations concerning the family were one way to establish that difference, women should be thought of as willing partners in the creation of the values that constructed the private sphere by distinguishing it from the public.

By describing the change solely in terms of women's role in the household economy, of course, one gives the false impression that the emergence of the private sphere was simply a decline of traditional patterns; rather, this cultural change must be understood as the emergence of alternative values, expectations, and practices. In the mid-eighteenth century, as the wives of Halifax's merchants, manufacturers, and professionals became less active in the public sphere of business, they shifted their energies and attentions to an increasingly distinct private sphere. This private sphere was constructed around the home and the family and the cultivation of domestic virtues. The ideology of separate spheres did not blossom into full maturity until the nineteenth century, but it was implicit in the values and practices of Halifax's elite women from the middle of the eighteenth century.

To say that the emerging distinction between the public and private spheres excluded women from direct participation in the household economy is not to say that these two spheres were in different universes. Elite women did have a role in promoting the family business, but the evidence suggests that it was one that emphasized the distinctiveness of the private sphere. Perceptions of a man's character played a far greater role in his economic success or failure in this new commercial world than it ever had played in the family economy of the middling sort.[21] Merchants and manufacturers could make a sale only if their buyers believed that goods of the quality promised would show up at the time they were promised. Creditworthiness, of course, depended in large part on past performance, but the image put forward by the merchant or manufacturer and his family was also relevant. Women had an important role to play in the creation of this image of respectability and reliability. Caroline Walker's memoirs, for instance, contain several biting comments about the imprudent and extravagant way Mrs. Sharp ran her household, and these criticisms were intimately linked with her perceptions of the financial instability of Mr. Sharp's business.[22] Thus it seems that in their dealings with men in the immediate neighborhood of the parish, merchants and manufacturers took into account the impressions formed in the round of visits among their families.

Connections with more distant business associates were less likely to involve frequent personal contact, but here too evidence suggests that women had a role to play. Halifax's merchants and manufacturers sometimes appended a postscript to their letters to inquire about the health and welfare of their correspondents' families, and if they could not invite their London or Amsterdam associates to tea, they tried to

---

21. Brewer, "Commercialization and Politics," 214–15.
22. CDA/SH:3/AB/20, Walker memoir, ff. 64, 79, 97.

extend what hospitality they could through the mail. The letters of a family of Leeds merchants, for instance, show that some customers might be sent a cheese or a ham to help cement a special relationship.[23] Of particular interesting are the letters of Samuel Hill, which suggest that it could be the woman's responsibility to maintain this side of the business relationship. In 1739 he remarked to his London banker that "my wife has sent [you] a ham which with other humble services desire may be acceptable to Madam Gaussens." Another family received a ham and half a dozen tongues, which Hill's wife had sent as thanks for the oysters they had sent the Hills.[24] Hill's wife was not acting as a general promoter for his business, for this kind of treatment was reserved for only a few of Hill's most special customers and associates. Yet that practice is in keeping with the character of the emerging private sphere that such activities helped to construct. It was the closer, personal ties that Hill's wife helped to cultivate, not the more anonymous relations with other customers.

Changes in domestic architecture created the physical setting in which the private sphere could exist. Domestic architecture in the parish in the sixteenth, seventeenth, and even early eighteenth centuries suggests that the public and private spheres were not differentiated. Obviously this was the case in the one- or two-room cottages of poor clothiers and weavers, but even the houses of wealthy clothiers had multiple uses. The workshop attached to most yeoman clothiers' houses, though often divided from the other rooms by a passageway, was an integral part of the house.[25] Inventory evidence shows that no clear distinction was made between the uses of the various rooms. Goods associated with production might be concentrated in the shop, if there was one, but they frequently appeared in other rooms as well. The inventory of Paul Greenwood, a clothier of Northowram, is typical in this respect. The rooms in his house consisted of the housebody (great room), sun parlor, north parlor, kitchen, cellar, shop, shop chamber, buttery chamber, kitchen chamber, and sun chamber, and at

---

23. WYAS/Huddersfield, DD/TO/11, Tolson family letters, 5 August and 4 October 1780.

24. CDA/MISC/8/117/2, Hill letter book, Hill to Peter Gaussens, 10 February 1739, to William Radcliffe, 14 February 1739; and to John Yeo, 7 February 1739. Evidence of this practice also appears in the letter books of 1749 and 1750 (CDA/FH/441): on 28 January 1749 John Bowden thanked Hill for the tongues and beef he had received.

25. Colum Giles, *Rural Houses of West Yorkshire, 1400–1800* (London, 1986), 152–55. This "hearth passage" plan was very common in the houses built in the Pennine uplands in the sixteenth and seventeenth centuries.

Constructing the Private Sphere

8. Whitewindows, the house of John Priestly, a Sowerby manufacturer/merchant, 1768. (Photo by Andrew Caveney.)

the back somewhere, but probably not attached to the house, was the barn. Most of the £20 in textile goods that Greenwood owned were in the shop, but there were also six pieces of cloth in the north parlor, a spinning wheel in the kitchen, some wool in the shop chamber, and a packing sheet in the buttery chamber.[26] In a house such as this, Mary Greenwood, his wife, could not have avoided involvement in the family business, whether as an active participant, spinning or carding wool, or as an oversser of the apprentices while Paul was at the market.

The new architectural style of the grandiose mansions that many merchants and manufacturers built for themselves removed the shop from the house. In the township of Sowerby alone, four such mansions were built in the third quarter of the eighteenth century, all of them by members of the township's commercial elite: George Stansfield built Fieldhouse (photo 3) in 1749; Samuel Hill rebuilt Making Place shortly before his death in 1759; John Priestly built Whitewindows (photo 8) in 1768; and the Lea family rebuilt Haughend in the 1770s. All of these

26. BIY/OW, Paul Greenwood, Northowram, March 1699/1700.

houses were designed in the so-called classical style, a symmetrical arrangement of bays bracketing the front door. Other such mansions appeared elsewhere in the parish, especially in the town of Halifax. Among them were John Caygill's Square, a direct model of a London square; David Stansfield's Hope Hall; and the Roydes family's mansion (photo 9, p. 198).[27]

These mansions were undoubtedly intended to impress upon the visitor the status and wealth of the families that lived in them, for they were on a different scale than the dwelling of even the wealthiest yeoman family. These houses served physically to separate this new elite from the artisanal community. At the same time, the new architectural style embodied the new gender relations of the emerging elite. Workshops had no place in these mansions; the production of the household was removed to an outbuilding or to a water-driven mill some distance from the house. The houses themselves were designed to reflect the greater importance attached to the private sphere. Separate entrances and separate staircases defined a boundary between the servants and the polite society of the master and mistress and their guests, and the internal layout of these mansions gave pride of place to refined dining rooms, drawing rooms, and parlors, rooms well suited to the cultivation of domestic virtues.[28] Such rooms, of course, were used for visiting and therefore had to be furnished and equipped with the appropriate panoply of consumer goods. Although men no doubt took an interest in these matters, the setting and paraphernalia associated with visiting were within women's domain. As we saw in Chapter 4, for instance, it was women who received bequests of tea services and other such goods.

Finally, the construction of a distinct private sphere is suggested by testators' changing expectations for their sons and for their daughters. In the late seventeenth and early eighteenth centuries, it was not uncommon for testators to make similar provisions for the future training of their children of both sexes. William Scott left the maintenance of

27. Giles, *Rural Houses*, 168–69, 216; T.W. Hanson, *The Story of Old Halifax* (1920; Otley, Yorks., 1985), 210–11, and "The Roydes of George Street, Halifax, and Bucklersbury, London," *THAS*, 1941, 76; R. Bretton, "The Square and the Piece Hall, Halifax," *THAS*, 1961, 69–76; Derek Linstrum, *West Yorkshire Architects and Architecture* (London, 1978), 99; W. B. Trigg, "Northowram Hall," *THAS*, 1932, 144. The "classical" house plan is also referred to as "double pile."

28. Giles, *Rural Houses*, 99–101. For the direction in which these trends went, see Davidoff and Hall, "Architecture of Public and Private Life," 332–33.

his underage children to his wife "until such time or times as they shall be severally and respectively fit to be put forth or go to be servants or apprentices."[29] Scott's expectations were of course gendered, for his sons were destined for apprenticeship while his daughters were going to be household servants. But Scott could speak of sons and daughters in the same breath, and he saw apprenticeship and service as roughly equivalent elements in the life cycle of his children—as indeed they were.

The elite of the eighteenth century had different expectations for boys and girls. Like men of the middling sort, many merchants, manufacturers, and professionals with underage sons provided for their entrance into apprenticeships. But there was a world of difference between the ordinary apprenticeships of artisanal families with a fee of at most £10, and apprenticeships to merchants or manufacturers, whose fees could be as much as £100. When Joshua Hudson instructed that his sons be put out as apprentices to some "art, trade, science, or mystery" for at least five years, he specified that the apprentice fee should not be above £100. The daughters of such families were certainly never expected to enter into household service; Hudson's daughters were to be brought up "in a manner suitable to my degree."[30] What did such a manner involve? The account books of John Howarth give some clues as to what other members of this elite perceived their daughters' futures to be. The girls were expected to be literate; among the payments for shoulders of lamb, for clerk's wages, and for the tea and coffee that were served in his parlor, Howarth records payments to Jeremy Rothera for teaching his children to read and write. They were also taught the finer social graces, for he sent them regularly to dancing school in Halifax.[31] Thus, while the boys were learning to be merchants and manufacturers, the girls were being trained to be gracious hostesses. These expectations for boys and girls reflected a profound transformation in perceptions concerning the family. The elite family's status was now to be expressed through the creation of a separate private sphere for women.

29. BIY/OW, William Scott, Halifax, December 1689.
30. John Senior of Halifax left £5 to his daughter to put her son out as an apprentice to a joiner: BIY/OW, December 1773; Joshua Hudson, Halifax, January 1765.
31. CDA/HAS/346 (15), Howarth cashbook, 1762–63; J. H. Priestly, "John Howarth at Home," *THAS*, 1947, 9. The accounts of the Lister family show that on top of the charges for room and board, they paid for dancing, music, drawing, and French lessons for their daughter in 1764: CDA/SH:3/B/1, bill for Miss Lister's schooling, 1764.

SOCIABILITY

The values and practices that served to create a distinct private sphere had repercussions outside the home. Drawing rooms, china tea sets, and dancing lessons were regular features of elite life, and it was in such public or semipublic settings, as well as in the home, that the meanings attached to these values and practices were articulated. Consider the banquet that George Stansfield and his sisters held in 1758 to celebrate the opening of the Calder Navigation, at which they were able to show off the glass punchbowl specially engraved for the occasion. Consider the reception held at Walterclough to celebrate the christening of Mr. Sharp's daughter, at which two tables had to be laid in the dining room to accommodate the numerous and distinguished guests.[32] Such occasions suggest that the new patterns of sociability that emerged in the mid–eighteenth century had a part in the creation of the private sphere. Indeed, in comparison with the gradual change in women's role in the family, distinctively gendered forms of sociability emerged swiftly in the decades after 1750.

The elite's new patterns of sociability stand in marked contrast to the social world of the middling sort, which was determined largely by work and residence. The depositions taken in 1720 in the dispute over Jonathan Baumforth's will show that this early manufacturer socialized with people he met in the course of his day-to-day affairs—his neighbors of both sexes and the people who worked with or for him. Baumforth "clubbed his two pence" for ale with Jonathan Hargreaves the collier and his penny for tobacco with his neighbor Judith Wood.[33]

Obviously, a social world whose interactions were largely or even partly determined by the priorities of neighborhood and work was at odds with the evolving sense that Halifax's merchant, manufacturing, and professional families had of their distinct social status, and a social world without strong gender differences was at odds with the emerging ideology of public and private spheres. As that identity crystallized in the mid–eighteenth century, new forms of sociability emerged which were increasingly determined by the priority of status and the specificity of gender. Simultaneously, of course, these new forms of sociability were making a class identity by creating a distinctive social space for

32. H. P. Kendall, "Antiquarians at Sowerby," *THAS*, 1902 (unpaginated); CDA/SH:3/AB/20, Walker memoir, f. 63.
33. BIY/CP, I/498, testamentary, Stead v. Baumforth.

Halifax's commercial and professional elite.[34] The new sociability took two forms: organizations in the public sphere, concerned with business and government, were exclusively male, while activities in the private sphere were open to both men and women.

Among the new forms of sociability unique to the parish's commercial and professional elite were the meetings of the parish's voluntary associations. The trustees of most of these institutions held regular meetings, so prominent figures in the community were involved in a cycle of gatherings that often crossed religious and residential lines. These gatherings, of course, were as much social as official functions, for they were usually held in one of Halifax's many inns and therefore involved drinking and eating as well as business.[35]

The role of such meetings in the emergence of middle-class consciousness was limited, for after an intense period at the beginning of an association's life, meetings became relatively infrequent. As John Brewer argues, however, the voluntary association was closely related to another distinctive feature of eighteenth-century English society, the club. As he points out, the word "club" was used more often as a verb than as a noun. Thus what was important about joining a club or participating in an association was the act of coming together in pursuit of a common goal. Associations and clubs offered both material and social benefits. Many clubs, offered their members some security in the fragile eighteenth-century economy, perhaps by backing up a member whose creditors were pressing for payment. Nor were they purely defensive. Through his club a manufacturer might meet new trade contacts or men with capital to lend. And a club, like an association, could give its members a certain amount of independence with respect to the traditional authorities.[36]

The close connection between the club and the association is seen

---

34. For two accounts that suggest how sociability could be used to create and maintain social boundaries see Borsay, "Rise of the Promenade," and Leonore Davidoff, *The Best Circles: Society, Etiquette, and the Season* (London, 1973).

35. The Calder Navigation meetings, for instance, were held at the Talbot Inn in Halifax: CDA/MIC/2/1.

36. Brewer, "Commercialization and Politics," 217, 219–24. Brewer is careful to point out that the eighteenth-century club was not unique to the commercial and professional elites. There were aristocratic and gentlemen's clubs, clubs of artisans and small tradesmen, even clubs that mixed men of different social, economic, and religious backgrounds. Brewer argues that tradesmen's and manufacturer's clubs, unlike the more hedonistic upper-class clubs or the middling sort's friendly societies, exhibited a strong sense of this dual purpose of protection and advancement through sociability.

in the Halifax Union Club, which was founded in 1756, just after the beginning of the Seven Years' War. As a correspondent explained to the readers of the *Halifax Union Journal*, the Union Club is "so called, as it is a congress of parties, in order to sacrifice all their differences to the good of the state, and to all other social advantages as well private as public."[37] The tone of this letter, like that of a poem extolling the virtues of the Union Club printed in the *Journal* two weeks earlier, was nationalistic. The club, whose nominal leader was Sir George Saville, was an attempt to unite Whigs and Tories in common cause against the French. Despite this apparent concern with affairs national and international, the club was deeply rooted in Halifax, providing an organization that could encompass divergent local interests. The Calder Navigation began its life in the Union Club, as did the association formed to build the Halifax Piece Hall.[38]

To its members (and to those excluded) the social meaning of the Union Club was clear, for it was very exclusive. Consider the advertisement that appeared in the *Union Journal* on 27 May 1760 to announce the next meeting of the club:

UNION CLUB

The members of the Union Club are desired to meet Sir George Saville their President at the house of Mr. John Mellin, the sign of the Talbot, in Halifax on Wednesday the fifteenth of June next.

Dinner will be upon the table at two o'clock.

A dinner at the Talbot Inn was certainly beyond the means of a domestic clothier and probably would have been a luxury for even a yeoman clothier; rubbing shoulders with Sir George Saville was well beyond the social reach of either of them.

Scattered references to clubs in Halifax reveal that this new feature of eighteenth-century society arrived in the parish at midcentury. The first recorded instance of a club is the Masonic lodge founded in 1738 by John Senior, a Halifax wool stapler/comber. His lodge, the Lodge of Probity no. 61, was small at first, but by 1750 it was becoming a prominent feature of life in the parish and in 1764 it subscribed toward the defense of Halifax against Sowerby in the organ dispute. Most of

37. *Halifax Union Journal*, 27 March 1759.
38. CDA/MIC/2/1, Calder Navigation, minutes; Ling Roth, *The Yorkshire Coiners* (Halifax, 1906), 207–8.

the clubs were organized after 1750s. In general, these clubs were socially exclusive, though perhaps less so than such associations as the Calder Navigation committee. The members of John Senior's Masonic lodge, like those of the order as a whole, were merchants and manufacturers as well as the whole gamut of professionals, from lawyers to schoolmasters. There were also a few shopkeepers and even one or two craftsmen, all from the more skilled and respectable end of the spectrum: a printer, a bookseller, a clockmaker, and a linen draper.[39]

Clubs and boards of trustees, concerned as they were with the public sphere—with politics, local affairs, and business—were the exclusive preserve of men. Other new forms of sociability connected with associations, however, were explicitly apolitical and included women. The trustees of the Halifax Circulating Library, the people charged with the management of this public institution, were all men, but the library's subscribers, the people who actually used it, included a number of women. They were members in their own right, and no doubt many more women enjoyed its privileges by virtue of their husband's membership. A rather tantalizing organization is the Halifax Music Club, formed in 1767 by the musician hired to play the parish church's new organ.[40] No details have survived concerning this club's membership or activities, but it is likely that both women and men were involved.

The existence of such clubs helps to put the social and cultural implications of their respective associations into perspective. These improvements were not simply moments of effervescence but rather were signs of a much more durable class consciousness that emerged out of and persisted in new forms of sociability. These new forms of sociability were differentiated on the basis of gender in a way that echoed the emergence of the private sphere in the home.

This same pattern is seen in other new social activities that were not so explicitly connected with voluntary associations. Perhaps the most important of these new institutions of sociability, the visiting that went on between the parish's elite families, is almost completely hidden from

39. A. Porritt, "Eighteenth and Nineteenth Century Clubs and Societies in Halifax," *THAS*, 1964, 65–68, 84–86. At least one other Masonic lodge, no. 39, was started in the same period: T. W. Hanson, *The Lodge of Probity No. 61, 1738–1938* (Halifax, 1939), 17–20, 48, 352–54; J. W. Houseman, "The History of the Halifax Parish Church Organ," *THAS*, 1928, 81–82. Brewer describes the members of the order as a whole as "solid burghers and respectable tradesmen": "Commercialization and Politics," 220.

40. CDA/MISC/49/1; Porritt, "Eighteenth and Nineteenth Century Clubs," 85. One of the surviving copies of the proposals for the library is endorsed to "Mrs Cooke": CDA/MISC:5/96a/79.

view. Caroline Walker's memoirs reveal that her mother, Elizabeth, went on a round of visits after her wedding in 1772 and received visitors at her own house. Elizabeth's participation in these rounds of visits seems to have diminished with time, but the memoir suggests that this had more to do with the isolated location of her house than with either her desires or established practices among the commercial and professional families in the parish.[41]

The mid–eighteenth century also saw a proliferation of social events held at Halifax's inns.[42] Inns were particularly important to the developing middle-class social world because the town was not of a size to warrant an assembly room or the theater.[43] In 1766, for instance, plans were made for a celebration to mark the official installation of the new organ in the parish church. The event was well publicized in the regional press, and, in addition to the two performances of Handel's *Messiah* which were to be given on 26 and 27 August with full chorus, the advertisements also made much of the assemblies that were to be held each evening at the Talbot Inn. Theatrical troupes also relied on inns. Traveling companies performed in a special room at the Talbot, and also in the yards of the Old Cock and the White Lion.[44]

Although there is no way of identifying the people who attended these assemblies and theater performances, it is hard to imagine any but Halifax's more prominent citizens taking a significant part. The price of admission ticket alone would have excluded most of the parish's population. The advertisement in the *Union Journal* for a ball to be held at the Talbot to celebrate the twenty-first birthday of the Prince of Wales indicated that tickets were available for 3s each—between a

41. CDA/SH:3/AB/20, Walker memoir. This material is discussed in more detail in Chapter 7.

42. In 1735 Halifax township had twelve inns with a rental value of over 10 a year, and half of those were worth more than £20 a year: P. W. Robinson, "The Emergence of the Common Brewer in the Halifax District," *THAS*, 1981, 70–107. The importance of the development of respectable inns to middle-class sociability is noted in Davidoff and Hall, "Architecture of Public and Private Life," 341.

43. As Peter Borsay has shown, the assembly rooms at Bath were merely among the most famous of what was in fact a host of provincial assembly rooms built in the eighteenth century: "English Urban Renaissance," *Social History* 5 (1977): 582. The citizens of York, for instance, raised a subscription and built an assembly room in 1731: Brewer, "Commercialization and Politics," 225n.

44. Houseman, "History of the Halifax Parish Church Organ," 84; A. Porritt, "The Old Halifax Theater, 1789–1904," *THAS*, 1956, 17. Advertisements for theatrical performances appeared in the *Halifax Union Journal* during its short existence. On 8 January 1760, for example, an ad announced a performance of *The Siege of Damascus and a farce called High Life Below Stairs*.

quarter and a half of the weekly wage of a skilled artisan.[45] And only a merchant, manufacturer, or professionals could have afforded the suit of fine cloth and the fashionable dress that were necessary to make a good showing at such an affair.

Some occasions of this sort, of course, were open to the population at large. One was the celebration held to mark the opening of the Halifax Piece Hall on New Year's Day in 1779. Though this event was more inclusive, the social boundaries that identified a distinct private sphere were evident. According to a nineteenth-century account, "the workmen of the various trades [were to] assemble, accompanied by their masters, in the Piece Hall in the forenoon; and the ambulatories of the pile were filled with ladies and gentlemen, for whom seats had been prepared, whence they could witness the arrival of the various bodies of workers with their badges and such uniforms as they might assume." The evening before, "Signor Petro, an Italian artist," gave an exhibition of fireworks in the large central courtyard of the hall; admission was by ticket only.[46] Although open to the whole community, the celebration for the Piece Hall divided the "gentlemen and ladies" (of the middle class) from the "workmen" and "their masters" (journeymen and independent craftsmen).

Other forms of social activity, though not new to the mid-eighteenth century, came to have new meanings. The diary of Oliver Heywood, a prominent Dissenting minister of the later seventeenth century, records many horse races and cockfights, but his description of these events makes it clear that these were rough-and-tumble affairs. Everyone from the gentry to the poor mingled, as in the brawl that broke out between some "gentlemen" and the "poorer sort" at a cockfight, when Thomas Thornhill, Esquire, lord of the manor of Fixby, opined that "beggars" ought not "to fight their cocks among gentlemen."[47] Thornhill may have been asserting a social distance between the local gentry and the Halifax cocksmen, but he had to prove his point with his fists.

Horse races and cockfights continued to be popular activities in the eighteenth century, but efforts were made to improve the tone of these

---

45. *Halifax Union Journal*, 19 May 1759. On wage rates, see CDA/FH/461a, 31 January 1775, where a wage of 12s a week was mentioned, and an advertisement in the *Union Journal* of 25 March 1760 for a man to oversee the finishing of shalloons at a wage of 6s a week. These were skilled positions; weavers would have earned even less.

46. Roth, *Yorkshire Coiners*, 215–16.

47. Oliver Heywood, *Autobiography, Diaries, Anecdotes, and Event Books*, ed. J. Horsfall Turner (Brighouse, Yorks., 1882), 2:272.

events. In 1736 the principal innkeepers of Halifax, joined by the vicar, a couple of gentlemen, and several prominent manufacturers, entered into an agreement to collect a subscription to provide a purse for a regular horse race on Skircoat Moor. According to Peter Borsay, the 1730s saw a peak in horse racing throughout the country, but there was increasing concern over its potentially disruptive character, and the Halifax initiative should be interpreted in this context. Legislation of 1740 dramatically curbed the proliferation of races, and the number of meetings being held each year declined. Yet the sport survived in Halifax in this more respectable form. On 25 September 1759, for instance, "the gentlemen of Halifax" saw fit to announce in the *Halifax Union Journal* that anyone running in or organizing a horse race for a prize of less than £50 would be prosecuted and fined £200. Although it is unlikely that the races on Skircoat Moor provided the kind of seating available in York, where a seat in the stands cost a guinea, horse racing in Halifax had become a more exclusive social event.[48]

THE emergence of a distinct private sphere, then, was associated with the emergence of new forms of sociability. It is only a slight exaggeration to say that the sociability of the middling sort can be summed up in the image of the local alehouse, a place where the men and women who lived in the area could congregate. Indeed, although he was too sick to leave the house, Jonathan Baumforth, with his constant sending out for beer, was simply replicating in his own home the social world of the alehouse. It was a social world in which neither status nor gender was a particularly strong social marker. For Halifax's commercial and professional elites in the mid–eighteenth century, sociability was more orderly and exclusive, and it had been differentiated into public and private spheres. Thus the middling sort's alehouse was replaced by two parallel institutions, the male club and the mixed assembly. The emergence of these forms of sociability suggests that social status and gender were becoming fundamental to the ways in which Halifax's elites constructed and perceived their world. Participation in the associations, clubs, assemblies, and theater performances contributed to the sense that Halifax's elite had of their middle-class identity because it provided a yardstick against which social difference could be measured. The

---

48. CDA/MISC/325/4, horse race agreement, 1736; Borsay, *English Urban Renaissance*, 180–96. Borsay's survey indicates that while racing experienced a revival from 1760, the legislation of 1740 had made the sport much more organized and more exclusive. In these circumstances, it is noteworthy that a meeting survived in Halifax.

middle-class consciousness engendered through the creation of the distinct private sphere, moreover, was a yardstick that complemented the class consciousness that was developing in the public sphere of local politics, for clubs and assemblies were more durable forms of the same cultural attitudes that were evident in the more episodic improvements and disputes described in Chapter 5.

Conclusion

Chapter 7

The Middle Class and Their World

In constructing the public and private spheres, Halifax's merchant, manufacturing, and professional families created the basis for a class culture by defining a common identity that was distinct from that of other social groups. Crucial to that identity was gentility. As the work of historians such as Peter Borsay and Paul Langford has demonstrated, this pervasive concept encompassed matters of dress, manners, taste, and pastimes.[1] There was no fixed standard of gentility, for perceptions of what was genteel depended on the observer, yet gentility was pervasive precisely because it provided a means for expressing social differences in a world where traditional social categories were less and less relevant. As Halifax's merchants, manufacturers, and professionals construed a social identity for themselves in the mid–eighteenth century, they appropriated the culture of gentility, shaping it to fit their own experience.

LOOKING DOWN: THE LOWER ORDERS

Gentility, above all, was what divided them from the lower orders, yet by and large, the question of how middle-class culture constructed its

---

1. Peter Borsay, *The English Urban Renaissance: Culture and Society in the Provincial Town, 1660–1770* (Oxford, 1989); Paul Langford, *A Polite and Commercial People: England, 1727–1783* (Oxford, 1992).

lower boundary has not been seriously addressed in the historical literature. Theodore Koditschek's excellent study of the emerging bourgeoisie of Bradford, for instance, describes the social order of proto-industrial Bradford in terms which suggest that the social gulf between domestic workers and the "gentleman-capitalist elite" was a natural and permanent feature of the social landscape, and hence does not need to be examined or explained. Leonore Davidoff and Catherine Hall's *Family Fortunes* is somewhat better on this score. They address the issue of how the middle classes differentiated themselves from the lower orders by discussing how a concept such as "respectability" could be used to divide groups from one another. In other respects, however, their discussion is problematic, partly because the boundaries of respectability were too fuzzy to be mapped clearly on different patterns of economic practice.[2]

The lack of attention that this aspect of the history of the middle class has received is not particularly surprising. Most studies of the middle class focus on the period after 1780, or even after 1820. Therefore they are exploring middle-class identity in a period when the economic and social changes associated with the Industrial Revolution were already much in evidence. Factory hands, impoverished urban artisans, and exploited rural outworkers were so far removed from the manufacturers, merchants, professionals, and tradesmen who made up the middle class that the social gulf between them hardly needs explanation. Moreover, the fundamentally hierarchical nature of English society throughout the early modern period seems to suggest that it was relatively easy for a group with superior wealth and influence to construct themselves as different from those below them. Indeed, the work of such scholars as David Underdown, William Hunt, Keith Wrightson, and David Levine has shown that the boundaries between respectable folk and the poor became stronger in the seventeenth century than they had been earlier, apparently creating in advance the social gulf between the laboring population and local merchant capitalists to which Koditschek refers.[3]

---

2. Theodore Koditschek, *Class Formation and Urban-Industrial Society: Bradford, 1750–1850* (New York, 1990), chap. 1; Leonore Davidoff and Catherine Hall, *Family Fortunes: Men and Women of the English Middle Class, 1750–1850* (London, 1987), 22–24.

3. David Underdown, *Revel, Riot, and Rebellion: Popular Politics and Culture in England, 1603–1660* (Oxford, 1985); William Hunt, *The Puritan Moment: The Coming of Revolution to an English County* (Cambridge, Mass., 1983); Keith Wrightson and David Levine, *Poverty and Piety in an English Village: Terling, 1525–1700* (New York, 1979).

Of course the poor have always been different from the well-to-do, but for the middle class in Halifax this lower social boundary was not at all what it had been for the middling sort. The crux of the difference was a shift in the position of the independent artisan in the textile industry. In the late seventeenth and early eighteenth centuries, an artisanal family whose members worked with their own hands, their own tools, and their own materials would undoubtedly have been classified, by themselves and by their social superiors, as belonging to the middling sort. They might have occupied a position toward the bottom of this rather amorphous social grouping, but their economic independence would have separated them from the laboring poor and the destitute. By the middle of the century, that same artisanal family would have appeared in the eyes of the parish's merchant, manufacturing, and professional familiess, as belonging to the laboring classes. As this new elite constructed their class identity, then, they made artisans into workers.

These changing social relations had their roots in the new modes of economic practice that emerged during the first half of the eighteenth century. The rise of large-scale manufacturing in the parish's textile industry emphasized differences between the roles of capital and labor that had never been very significant in the artisanal mode of production of the middling sort. Manufacturers, and merchants too of course, were increasingly less likely to do any manual work themselves. They paid workers to do it for them, workers who no longer owned the material on which they worked. Even highly skilled artisans were treated in a paternalistic manner that emphasized the different social positions of master and worker.[4]

This social and cultural transformation of economic relations was part of a broader process that created two distinct social worlds where there had been but one, and these two worlds were differentiated on the basis of gentility. In the late seventeenth and early eighteenth centuries, even individuals as apparently different as the manufacturer and the artisan occupied essentially the same social world. Thomas Pollard was a dyer employed by Jonathan Baumforth, and his depositions show that Baumforth treated him with the respect that was due to an independent craftsman and offered him the companionship that was due

---

4. For two examples, both discussed at greater length in Chapter 3, see CDA/RP/107c, defense brief for Thomas Walton, 1755, and CDA/FH/461a, Hill to Stansfield, 31 January 1775, from Boulogne.

to a neighbor. Similarly, depositions in a defamation case of the 1680s reveal that the son of a well-to-do wool stapler, Abraham Mitchell, spent time in an alehouse in the company of artisans.[5]

In some respects very little seems to have changed by the mid–eighteenth century. A quarter sessions case of 1783, for examle, tells of a series of petty thefts perpetrated by Isaac Schofield and some of his mates over the space of several months: stealing a few rabbits and ducks here, four fleeces of wool there, several bags of shot, some coal. Generally they sold what they took, pocketing a few pence or spending it on beer. Schofield and his companions were not indigent paupers. He was a weaver and four of the others were wool combers, and the deposition suggests that they were employed at the time of these exploits. One expedition to steal chickens was decided upon while they were all having a drink at Mr. Wilkinson's combshop, where some of their number were working. The same kind of workshop culture is depicted in a defamation case that was tried in 1769. One of the witnesses, William Taylor, a cordwainer, told the court that on Saturday night, "having had a hard day's work, he and his shopmates agreed to have a little ale and sent for some from Absalom Wilkinson's house." Wilkinson apparently came along and wanted to "be his penny with them," and while they were all drinking, Elizabeth Hitcheon came in and had some words with Wilkinson which Taylor did not hear. (This was the occasion of the suit, for she claimed that Wilkinson had called her a "whore and a brimstone whore.") Another member of the company, James Radcliffe, a stuff weaver, told much the same story.[6] The petty theft and sexual slander that brought these two cases to the attention of the courts is less important than the contexts in which they were set. Like the glimpses we have into late-seventeenth-century Halifax, these episodes reveal a social world built around the workshop and the alehouse. The significant difference is that in the eighteenth century this social world belonged only to the artisans. The commercial and professional elite—the employers of artisanal laborers such as Schofield, Taylor, and Radcliffe—had abandoned these two locales in their quest for gentility.

Obviously the worlds of the artisan and the manufacturer were not completely separate, if only because some groups occupied a marginal position between the wealthy merchants, large-scale manufacturers, and

---

5. BIY/CP, I/498, testamentary, Stead v. Baumforth, and H/3489, defamation, Lister v. Barraclough, 1682.

6. WYAS; Wakefield, QS1/122/2, West Riding Quarter Sessions, Indictments, Wakefield sessions, January 1783; BIY/CP, I/1545, defamation, Hitcheon v. Wilkinson, 1769.

highly trained professionals on the one hand and working artisans on the other. These people included bookkeepers, schoolteachers, and other lesser professionals; independent craftsmen such as clockmakers, tanners, and joiners; and finally shopkeepers and victualers of various types. In addition, since the transition from household to large-scale production was far from complete, there were no doubt still a fair number of independent craftsmen in the textile industry, a group that might have included the smallest of the new worsted manufacturers.

One could, simply for convenience, call these groups the "lower middle class," but by applying this label one merely evades the problem of specifying the precise place such groups had in the developing social and cultural context of mid-eighteenth-century Halifax. One possibility is to argue, as do Davidoff and Hall, that the "lower middle class" shared aspects of middle-class ideology and practice but in somewhat "diluted" forms. They present a "table of correspondences" which is suggestive of the different forms that ideologies and practices took in what they refer to as the upper and lower ranks of the middle class.[7]

Certainly the case for a similar sort of slippage between the upper and lower ranks of the middle class can be made for Halifax. Many of its institutions encompassed individuals of divergent social backgrounds. The masonic lodges, for instance, were to some extent conceived of as places where men of a variety of social backgrounds could mix, though Halifax's lodges were probably not as socially diverse as those in some more cosmopolitan centers.[8] Similarly, many of the people who subscribed the minimum £5 to Sowerby's new chapel were modest landowners who employed outworkers in the textile business. They were, in short, the smaller manufacturers who were common figures in the parish's worsted trade.[9] Active in township affairs, such men were unlikely to be players in the parish as a whole.

It would be unwise, however, to see the boundary between the commercial and professional elite and any group one might be tempted to call a "lower middle class" as being infinitely permeable. The organizations that included members of both groups were under the elite's control. The Presbyterian chapel built at Northgate End is a case in point. Individuals of a variety of backgrounds contributed what they

---

7. Davidoff and Hall, *Family Fortunes*, 24.
8. T. W. Hanson, *The Lodge of Probity No. 61: 1738–1938* (Halifax, 1939), 352–55.
9. Pat Hudson, "Landholding and the Organization of Textile Manufacture in Yorkshire Rural Townships, c. 1660–1810," in *Markets and Manufacture in Early Industrial Europe*, ed. Maxine Berg (London, 1991), 261–91; CDA/Sowerby register microfilm, subscription list.

could toward the new edifice, but the bulk of the contributions came from a narrow elite, and this elite ended up in control of the congregation. As I have argued, this sense of ownership, evident in everything from township government to institutions to elections, was crucial to the emerging class consciousness. It separated the elites from intermediate groups no less sharply than from the "workers."

It must also be noted that in the latter part of the eighteenth century, the social differences between the middle class and the "lower middle class" became more marked. Consider the Loyal Georgian Society, founded in 1779. At first glance this appears to be yet another voluntary association, but the Loyal Georgian Society was in fact a friendly society. Its charter begins:

> Whereas in consideration of the many afflictions which men are subject to, who are not in affluent circumstances to support themselves ... we therefore severally and mutually have proposed and agreed to the following articles for our relief and support when we shall be so rendered incapable of earning our livelihoods through lameness, sickness or old age....

The "following articles" set out rules for a monthly meeting, the election of stewards, and the amount of benefit members were eligible to claim. Unfortunately, the list of members does not mention occupations, but since the monthly contribution was fixed at a shilling, with an additional tuppence to be spent on beer, its members lived well above the poverty line; indeed, the fifth article stated that only "established master workmen" could join.[10] This was not the world of working artisans, but neither was it the world of merchants and manufacturers.

The existence of voluntary associations geared to intermediate groups more interested in mutual benefit than in the public good suggests one aspect of the boundary between the commercial and professional elite and these peripheral groups. Equally important were the boundaries constructed with aspects of the culture of gentility, particularly the set of values, expectations, and practices concerning the family and sociability that separated Halifax's elites from these peripheral groups.

Nowhere was the boundary of gentility more evident than in the new mansions built by the parish's elite. Here was the domestic space where

---

10. CDA/LG/1, Loyal Georgian Society articles, 1779.

a common standard of gentility could find expression. The Square, built for John Caygill in the late 1750s by the renowned York architect John Carr, was actually a block of houses with a common facade built around an extensive central garden and approached through a single entrance for security and privacy. Each house had three large entertaining rooms downstairs, five bedrooms upstairs with dressing rooms and a drawing room, and solid mahogany doors throughout. With stables, one of these residences rented for £50 a year. More spectacular still was John Roydes's new house, also designed by Carr (photo 9). It was built facing "pleasure grounds tastefully arranged and secluded from observation by a high wall." The house itself had seventeen bays in seven sections, including the rooms that Royds used for his bank and for a warehouse. The interior was very lavish, its most prominent feature being the rococo plasterwork that depicted Aesop's fables and a great set piece in which Roydes, his wife, and his four daughters appeared in a patriotic group. Carr designed several other houses in the parish, all of them in the fashionable Palladian or neoclassical style. Even the new chapels built by these elites followed this fashion; the new chapel at Sowerby and the Square Chapel (photo 5), for instance, had Venetian windows.[11] The grand style and the distinctive architecture of these new houses created an exclusive social world, one that would not, as a rule, have been open to any but the uppermost ranks of parish society.

In sum, the view that Halifax's elite saw as they looked downward from their niche in the social hierarchy was relatively unambiguous. The boundary that separated them from lesser professionals, shopkeepers, and independent craftsmen was not precise, for the two groups belonged to some of the same institutions and shared common values and practices, but a boundary there was. Much more obvious were the markers—local political power, social practices, taste—that distinguished them from artisans and of course the laboring poor. Yet, clear though it was, this boundary was relatively new. Traditional articulations of the social order in Halifax had not separated the parish's elites and the independent artisans into different social species, nor

---

11. R. Bretton, "The Square and the Piece Hall, Halifax," *THAS*, 1961, 67–77; *Union Journal*, 5 June 1759; Derek Linstrum, *West Yorkshire Architects and Architecture* (London, 1978), 98–99, 186–87, 200; W. B. Trigg, "Northowram Hall," *THAS*, 1932, 144. John Wesley commented that the Square Chapel was "very refined," although some of the Londoners who contributed toward it thought that it was "too grand": *The Complete Works of John Wesley* (London, 1872), 3: 475; and James Miall, *Congregationalism in Yorkshire* (London, 1868), 267.

9. Somerset House, Halifax, John Roydes's mansion, mid-eighteenth century. (Reproduced from an early twentieth-century slide by kind permission of Dr. J. A. Hargreaves, Hon. Secretary of the Halifax Antiquarian Society.)

could these merchants and manufacturers adopt the social position of the landed gentry. Thus this lower social bound was not only a recent construction but a new type; unlike older articulations of social difference, it was founded on new forms of economic practice, particularly the increasing ubiquity of the wage relationship. This fact suggests that the earliest articulation of this middle-class culture was as concerned to maintain its lower bound as it was to challenge the social and political hegemony of England's traditional elites.

LOOKING UP: THE LANDED ELITE

Given the much more nuanced picture of the political, economic, and social terrain of the eighteenth century that we now have, it is no longer possible to assume that the middle class's relationship with the landed elites were inevitably antagonistic. As Linda Colley has shown, land and trade were assumed to enjoy a mutually beneficial relationship until the latter part of the eighteenth century, and as Peter Borsay and Paul Langford have shown, the patrician or aristocratic element in English society was not the monolith it was once thought to be. They argue that the eighteenth-century culture of gentility, although it drew its inspiration from the aristocracy and greater gentry, was not simply a phenomenon of landed society. This being the case, there can hardly have been a monolithic landed element against which a potential middle class could struggle, since the two putative contestants seem to have been playing on the same side. Amanda Vickery makes this point in a very concrete fashion with her analysis of the social world of a Lancashire gentlewoman, a world shared by women and men of mercantile and landed backgrounds. Dror Wahrman has taken this evidence one step further and argued that the latter eighteenth century saw the emergence of two opposing elite cultures, one "provincial" and the other "cosmopolitan," neither of which was particularly associated with either land or trade.[12]

---

12. Linda Colley, *Britons: Forging the Nation, 1707–1837* (New Haven, 1992), 100; Borsay, *English Urban Renaissance*; Langford, *Polite and Commercial People*; Amanda Vickery, "Women and the World of Goods: A Lancashire Consumer and Her Possessions, 1751–81," in *Consumption and the World of Goods*, ed. John Brewer and Roy Porter (London, 1993), 274–301, and "Women of the Local Elite in Lancashire, 1750–1825" (Ph.D. dissertation, London University, 1991); Dror Wahrman, "National Society, Communal Culture: An Argument about the Recent Historiography of Eighteenth-Century Britain," *Social History* 17 (1992): 43–72.

The evidence from Halifax amply confirms that the boundary between the commercial and professional elites and landed society was not very clear. Giving evidence in a court case, Richard Townley of Rochdale, Esquire, testified that Richard Hill, son of the great manufacturer Samuel Hill and himself a manufacturer and merchant until his bankruptcy, visited at the houses of "several of the first families of fortune and repute in that neighborhood."[13] Moreover, though the practice was not common, marriages between Halifax's elite and landed families did take place.

When they could afford to do so, Halifax's commercial elite adopted some of the trappings of landed society. The wealthy merchant William Greame, for instance, was the captain of the local militia in 1757, and with his purchase of the submanor of Southowram he joined the hunting fraternity. Others adopted the gentry's practice of distributing their landed estate by primogeniture, though usually in a somewhat modified form. Finally, the absence of a hard-and-fast boundary between trade and land in mid-eighteenth century Halifax is evident in the absence of a vocabulary that distinguished the parish's commercial and professional elite from the gentry or the aristocracy.[14]

This evidence for a degree of slippage between Halifax's commercial and professional elite and landed society suggests that middle-class culture did not originate in a simple contest between land and trade. Yet there is no reason to expect it to be so. As William Reddy has remarked with reference to the emergence of a working-class culture in nineteenth-century France, class consciousness, or more generally the discourse within which class consciousness could be expressed, requires a huge investment; it must be laboriously constructed by individuals and groups as they lead their lives.[15] Middle-class culture had

---

13. PRO/C.12/451/14, Chancery, Vincent v. Stansfield and Habergham, 1785; J. H. Priestly, "Old Ripponden," *THAS*, 1932, 196.

14. CDA/HAS/378 (425)/70, Sowerby militia case; CDA/RP/2031, gamekeeper's appointment. In my sample of Halifax wills I found only two instances of strict primogeniture: BIY/OW William Greame, May 1766, and James Lister, October 1766. The will of John Roydes (ibid., Prerogative Court, July 1781) exemplifies this modified version, whereby the eldest son's portion, usually the largest, was entailed to descend to his sons in strict order of birth but then passed to the daughters of the first son before going to the heirs of the younger sons. For a discussion of the issues concerning class vocabulary see Asa Briggs, "The Languages of Class," in *Essays in Labour History*, ed. Briggs and John Saville (London, 1967), and P. J. Corfield, "Class by Name and Number in Eighteenth-Century Britain," *History* 72 (1987): 38–61.

15. William Reddy, *The Rise of Market Culture: The Textile Trade and French Society, 1750–1900* (Cambridge, 1984), 17.

to be constructed in the same way. Thus we should expect that at this early stage, some of its elements would be borrowed from systems that had different implications. What requires analysis is the distinctive way in which elements were appropriated and then articulated.[16]

Just such a process is evident in the way Halifax's commercial and professional elite differentiated themselves from the lower orders by appropriating notions of gentility. It was natural for them to do so, for concepts of social difference that distinguished between manual and nonmanual work had a deep resonance in English society. Yet the particular location of the boundary that was drawn on the basis of gentility is significant, as was the close relationship between that lower boundary and changing economic practices, particularly the spread of wage labor.

The same sort of process also allowed Halifax's commercial and professional elite to differentiate themselves from those above them. Here the story begins not with the culture of gentility but with the eighteenth-century critique of aristocratic privilege and corruption. Although its roots stretch back to the late seventeenth century, this critique was familiar to the characters in this story as the Tory and "Old Whig" critique of Walpole's regime, and especially of the corruption thought to result from the government's close connections to the "money interest." This "Country" critique was obviously not a critique of "land" by "trade," but by appropriating it, Halifax's merchants, manufacturers, and professionals could establish the legitimacy of their political authority, and in doing so they began to articulate the superiority of their virtuous way of life as against the vices of the idle rich.[17]

Evidence that Halifax's elites adopted this perspective emerges from a variety of sources. During its existence from 1759 to 1760, the *Halifax Union Journal* published a number of letters that drew on this "Country" critique. One of these letters, published in the issue of 13 February 1759, began as a complaint about the disruption caused by an argu-

16. William Sewell makes a very similar argument about the emergence of working class consciousness in his reworking of Thompson's theory of class formation: "How Classes Are Made: Critical Reflections on E. P. Thompson's Theory of Working-Class Formation," in *E. P. Thompson: Critical Perspectives*, ed. Harvey Kaye and Keith McClelland (Cambridge, 1990), 70.

17. This issue is very complex; one survey of the various strands of thought is J. G. A. Pocock, "The Varieties of Whiggism from Exclusion to Reform: A History of Ideology and Discourse," in *Virtue, Commerce, and History* (Cambridge, 1985), 215–310, esp. sec. II. Also see Istvan Hont and Michael Ignatieff, ed., *Wealth and Virtue: The Shaping of Political Economy in the Scottish Enlightenment* (Cambridge, 1983); W. D. Rubinstein, "The End of 'Old Corruption' in Britain, 1780–1860," *Past and Present* 101 (1983): 55–86; and Gerald Newman, *The Rise of English Nationalism: A Cultural History, 1740–1830* (New York, 1987).

ment over a card game at an inn. The writer, who signed himself "Rebus," went on to charge that the reason that laws against gaming were not enforced was that "gaming is become the favorite business of high life." A letter in the *Union Journal* of 6 February 1759 pointed out the danger of meddling in politics. Since corruption in government stemmed from corruption in moral character, the writer argued that the best course was "promoting as far as our sphere reaches, the virtue of individuals." He concluded:

> instead of descanting therefore upon public measures, and which few that do understand, instead of unfolding the mysteries of state and teaching mechanics to dictate to majesty or his ministers, it becomes us better to look at home....To promote sentiments of love and peace of truth and universal integrity to cherish a spirit of economy, temperance and industry in opposition to idleness, luxury and extravagance, is the way to make the constitution we live under as lasting as it is good.

Other writers were not so diffident about meddling in politics, but they, too, based their critique of government policy on the virtues of commercial people. A little from "Funnibus" appeared in the *Union Journal* 19 May of 1759:

> Sir, it being customary for tradesmen to settle their accounts and strike a balance once a year, princes, we hope, will not take it amiss if we advise them to settle theirs once in a century; and as in looking over the ledger of England, I find we have a demand upon a great house in Germany of many years standing, we shall take leave to send in her bill.

There followed a parody of a ledger entry listing "Maria Therisa and Co." as debtors to "George Rex and Co." for items such as these:

– to dying the Danube with the best French blood at battle of Blenheim:	2M
– to beating Louis the Grand at Ramilles:	1M
– to ditto at Oudenard:	1M
– to spades and shovels etc. for burying 20,000 heros at Fontenoy:	1M
– to British blood spilled at Val, 10s the gallon:	1M

The total debit came to £96 million, against which "Maria Therisa" had made no payments to date. It was, then, the virtue of the ledger, not that of the country estate, that Halifax's residents upheld when they criticized vice in government and in the people who ran it.

It is always difficult to evaluate the cultural significance of the printed word, since it is impossible to determine how widely the message was received or even if it was received at all. Therefore it is reassuring to find that individual members of Halifax's commercial and professional elite expressed similar sentiments. This evidence shows that their perceptions of the social world clearly differentiated between "us" (the nascent middle class) and "them" (the landed elite). Moreover, while the basis of this differentiation had its roots in the critique of the corrupt court aristocracy by the virtuous country gentry, they adopted and elaborated these ideas in ways that made them more meaningful in light of their experience.

Consider the text of a draft arbitration bond prepared in 1748 by the attorney Robert Parker or one of his clerks. The bond itself was a prepared form with gaps left for the names and other details. Instead of choosing culturally neutral names—the eighteenth-century equivalents of John Doe and Richard Roe—Parker and his clerk indulged in a revealing joke. The relevant portions of the bond appear below with the text inserted in the blanks in italics:

> KNOW all men by these presents that *I Timothy Thrifty of Halifax in the county of York Shalloon maker am* held and firmly bound to *Thomas Saveall of the same place yeoman in one hundred pounds*. . . .
>
> THE CONDITION of this obligation is such that if the above bounden *Timothy Thrifty his* heirs, executors, and administrators . . . shall . . . obey, abide, perform, fulfil and keep the award, order, arbitrament final and determination of *William Curious of Halifax aforesaid Gent. and Samuel Pry of the same place Gent.* arbitrators indifferently elected and named as well on the part and behalf of the above bounden *Timothy Thrifty* as of the above named *Thomas Saveall* to arbitrate, award, judge, and determine. . . . [18]

Obviously the contrast between the virtuous shalloon maker Thrifty and the hardworking yeoman Saveall, on one hand, and the gentlemen

---

18. CDA/RP/106i, draft arbitration bond, 1748. For a truly generic template, see the sample pin-money agreement reproduced in Susan Staves, *Married Women's Separate Property in England, 1660–1833* (Cambridge, Mass., 1990), 137–39.

Curious and Pry, on the other, is intentional. It is unfavorable to the gentlemen, for the implication is that their status as gentlemen merely gave them an excuse to indulge in the "feminine" pursuit of gossip.[19] The supposed effeminacy of the idle rich, of course, was a standard part of the eighteenth-century critique of vice; Parker, however, used it to differentiate virtuous, because productive, trading folk from the idle rich. The choice of names is all the more significant bcause the arbitrators could as easily have been a merchant and a manufacturer—as indeed they often were.[20]

Jonathan Hall, the upholsterer whose accounts were examined in Chapter 4, also shows us how these commercial folk perceived the boundary separating them from those above. The notebooks he kept after he retired from his successful career in London to his home in Halifax are peppered with declarations such as the following: "A rule to walk by . . . : Sir Peter Port and Sir John and Admiral Punch are good in moderation but many have been ruined by it. . . . Temperance [is] the best physic and a good conscience the best estate; let a man . . . take the air and exercise as much as he can and take Mr. Moor and Mr. Green for his companions as much as he can."[21] Fortunately, Jonathan Hall's predilection for inserting such comments in accounts of his activities permits us to explore just how he understood the contrast between excess and prudence, between vice and virtue, embodied in the figures of "Sir Peter Port" and "Mr. Moor." In the summer of 1749 he railed against the treatment he had received on a visit to the spa at Buxton:

> I did not come to Buxton in fine gay clothing as some people might do to make their fortunes; perhaps I look upon [a] man's character before clothing; perhaps you that are my neighbors know something of my character to give me either a good one or a bad one. A man ought not to be despised that has not land for the same God rules over the poor as well as the rich landed men.

It appears that Hall had been the butt of some kind of practical joke about his unfashionable clothing. The insult that he felt, and felt

---

19. The femininity of the aristocracy is discussed in Newman, *Rise of English Nationalism*, 81.

20. In the partnership agreement between Sam Lees and John Edwards, for instance, the arbitrators were to be chosen by the two parties, with no assumption that they would be gentlemen: CDA/MISC/645/2, 1760.

21. CDA/SH:3/AB/13, Hall notebook.

deeply, was an insult to his gentility, and in reacting this way Hall implicitly acknowledged the inferiority he felt as a tradesman in a genteel world. His criticism of "rich landed men," however, was based on this same background in the world of trade, for their vices had commercial implications. As Hall explained, "people love to be well used where they spend their money." The people of Buxton, a town where there is but "little trade," ought not to discourage company by their actions; they ought, indeed, to "encourage company for the good of themselves and the good of the public of their town." To Jonathan Hall, virtue was at heart a matter of good business practices.

John Sutcliffe of Ovenden, a worsted manufacturer active in the second half of the eighteenth century, was also a keeper of notebooks. One item, sandwiched between cryptic notations about the dimensions of types of worsted cloth and above a recipe to cure gout, could be taken as an encapsulation of the worldview of the emerging middle class:

> As the world increases in years so the children of men multiply in wickedness. Wealth creates care, care brings luxury, luxury gives birth to extravagance, and extravagance is the parent of ruin. When the means are gone; methods are sought to recover them, and hence it is that guilt is not alone confined to inherent indigenous and birthright plebianism. The great as often err as the little; but gold conceals many a crime that poverty discovers.
>
> NB: [by] one who is going to suffer for forgery.[22]

In copying this item Sutcliffe placed himself in the middle of the social order, distinguishing himself from luxury and extravagance on one hand and "birthright plebianism" on the other. The identity of the group that is being criticized here, as in the other examples, is rather imprecise. The world against which these people were defining their own identities seems to be that of the landed elite, but only insofar as they saw luxury, idleness, and arbitrary power, as the particular characteristics of landed society. Thus it is more accurate to identify this group as the idle rich.

When members of Halifax's commercial and professional elite perceived the landed elite in this way, they appropriated the eighteenth-century critique of the corrupt aristocracy and modified it with a

22. CDA/HAS/449 (714), Sutcliffe memorandum book, 1768–77.

package of sentiments and values that I shall lump together under the umbrella term "thriftiness." Two other passages that Sutcliffe copied into his notebook suggest what "thrift" meant to him:

> —An Italian Proverb: Never do that by proxy which you can do yourself, never defer that till tomorrow which . . . you can do today. Never neglect small matters and expenses.
> —DeWitt, the great statesman of Holland, being asked how he went through such a multiplicity of business, answered that his whole art of doing business consisted in thinking of and doing but one thing at once.

Sutcliffe copied out these passages to inculcate these qualities in himself, for he was prone to both of the faults they specified. Yet he saw these qualities, which were so suitable, even necessary, for manufacturers like himself, as the very antitheses of the values of the idle rich who resorted to forgery to satisfy their unnatural appetites for luxury. In this sentiment he echoed Robert Parker's flattering caricature of a "thrifty" shalloon maker or Jonathan Hall's recommendation of tea as a "sober companion," one preferable to port and punch.[23]

Like the critique of extravagance and luxury, "thrift" had cultural roots of its own. Since the late seventeenth century, it had been part of a critique of the excesses of metropolitan society, yet men such as Sutcliffe also knew it as part of the culture of Halifax's middling sort. In his memorandum book of 1715, Japhet Issot wrote that "those riches that the gods freely bestow are lasting, but those which men pursue through injustice, as they are got together by unjust arts and labor, so miseries and inquietudes soon mingle with them."[24] Francis Parrat conveyed a similar message in the sermons he preached in the parish while he was a curate there during the first decade of the eighteenth century. In a sermon on the text "Abstain from all appearance of Evil," he warned his congregation not to equate worldly riches with salvation, and in another sermon he explicated the text "Be content with what you have."[25] A more practical statement of the middling sort's thriftiness can be found in a letter that Phoebe Lister wrote in 1661 instruct-

23. CDA/SH:3/AB/13, Hall notebook.
24. CDA/MISC/509/9, Issot commonplace book, 1715.
25. Sermons of Francis Parrat, lecturer at Halifax Parish Church, Dr. Williams Library, London, Ms. 24.193. I thank Michael MacDonald for bringing these sermons to my attention.

ing the recipient about what he or she should bring along on a visit to her in London: "When you come down I would wish you to be as sparing as you can in bringing any thing down. You have no friends, I think, [that] expect anything, except it be some toys for the children and in that be as thrifty as you can."[26]

The context in which these merchant, manufacturing, and professional families appropriated the concept of thrift altered the meanings it had had for the seventeenth-century middling sort. Halifax's mid-eighteenth-century middle class no longer saw thrift as the antithesis of gentility; rather the two values existed side by side. The emerging middle-class culture, then, was highly ambivalent. Halifax's commercial and professional elites used thriftness to distinguish themselves from the sybaritic world of the idle rich, a world that was often equated with, though it was certainly not the same as, that of landed society. At the same time, that world was at the apex of the culture of gentility that they so desperately sought as a way of distinguishing themselves from their social inferiors.

This ambivalence is evident in Parker's arbitration bond. The "Thrifty" and "Saveall" who appear there were engaged in a supposed dispute—perhaps a petty one—which they were not capable of solving themselves. Although the names "Pry" and "Curious" suggest little respect for "landed" society, the document implies that the possession of land conferred a degree of authority that was desirable in an arbitrator. The same ambivalence emerges in Jonathan Hall's notebooks. He acknowledges, for instance, that port and punch are good in moderation. The poor man who cannot afford such luxuries is not virtuous: virtue lies with those whose means give them the choice. His description of his ill treatment in Buxton is also riddled with ambiguity. Although Hall labeled his tormentors as "rich landed men" and held up the honest virtues of a tradesman in his own defense, the reality was much more complex. One of his tormentors was a "Lady Waxe Arse," a "fortune hunter" who was "not to be spoken with at all but by them that can make her a landed settlement to answer her fortune" of £1,000. It turned out, however, that "Lady Waxe Arse" was not from the landed elite that Hall blames for his maltreatment. She came from Liverpool and was probably a merchant's daughter. Hall's identification of himself in this story is no more accurate as a depiction of social

26. Quoted in Mark Pearson, *The History of Northowram* (Halifax, 1898), 242.

reality. The contrast to the "rich landed men" is "the poor"—hardly an appropriate label for a liveryman of a London company who spent his retirement visiting northern spas.²⁷

Hall's desire for gentle status at the same time that he criticizes aspects of the genteel world captures the essence of this ambivalence about gentility. Seen from our vantage point, his account suggests the beginnings of a process that constructed two different conceptions of gentility: a respectable gentility, associated with such virtues as good character and temperance; and a superficial gentility, associated with such vices as extravagance, spite, and idleness.

We can see this contrast in a variety of accounts. The memoir of Caroline Wyvill Walker, daughter of John and Elizabeth Walker of Walterclough in Southowram, relates episodes from her parents' life in the years shortly before and after their marriage in 1772. Here the ambivalence between gentility and thrift is highlighted by the clash of worlds that took place with the courtship and marriage of John Walker and Elizabeth Waddington. John Walker was the son of a wealthy wool stapler and a prominent member of Halifax's elite; his father was active in the organ and the Calder navigation associations. Like many of his contemporaries, the father trained one son for business and the other for the professions, so he sent Peter to a tradesman's school in London while John, who had shown an aptitude for learning, went to Cambridge. Elizabeth Waddington, for her part, was an heiress from Kent, living in Thirsk with her mother, who had married an apothecary.²⁸

Before her marriage, Elizabeth Waddington was a member of that national genteel culture which Borsay and Langford have described so well. Caroline describes her as having "superior manners, elegant dress, and [a] good person" (65), and shows her doing the round of visits and events that made up so much of genteel life. Her future husband, John Walker, for all of his Cambridge polish, was not part of

---

27. CDA/SH:3/AB/13, Hall notebook. As the notebooks make clear, Hall had visited the spa at Scarbrough on a number of occasions.

28. Obviously interpretive problems surround this evidence, for what Caroline wrote about her parents' life in the 1770s and 1780s she probably first heard as stories her mother told her, stories that were then filtered through her own perceptions of the world. The memoirs are undated so it is difficult to establish when Caroline Walker wrote them down, and thus how much time had passed between the events described and their inscription. I am surmising that Caroline's knowledge of her parents' life came largely from her mother because that is the point of view that is privileged until Caroline's own memories provide the information. The loose-leaf folios of the memoir (CDA/SH:3/AB/20) are numbered. Hereafter references to these will appear in the text.

this genteel world, or at least not entirely. His daughter recorded what must have been her mother's impressions of him when they first met: he had good manners but no grasp of "that fashionable kind of chit chat which renders a man's company amusing to ladies," and while "he dressed according to the fashions, . . . he did not get fresh coats often enough" (69).

John Walker's shortcomings, however, were not simply individual idiosyncrasies. In fact, if anything, his gentility was of a higher standard than that of many members of his community. When Elizabeth Waddington first visited Halifax she was appalled by its backwardness in matters of taste and quality. Her hostess took her to visit "Mr. Walker of Crownest, who then lived in a very parsimonious manner. Mrs. Walker was then living, [and] a maid waited at tea with a large hole in her apron" (61). This couple were not poor relations but among the wealthiest residents of the parish. Mrs. Walker was none other than Elizabeth Caygill, daughter of John Caygill, who had provided her with a marriage portion of £2,500 when she married William Walker in 1746. When Elizabeth Waddington moved to Walterclough as John Walker's wife in 1772, she was no more favorably impressed. They lived far from town, "where no pleasant society could even be obtained" (73), and the best dressed woman she encountered on her bridal visits was a woman from the chapel (76). The house itself was in need of "repairs and furniture." In fact, when she moved in, only two rooms were "sufficient to accommodate visitors": the "drawing room had been fitted up by an upholsterer from Wakefield and the dining room had been papered and painted" (75).

Of course, it was not as if Halifax's elite did not try to achieve gentility; they knew it when they saw it and did what they could to get it. Elizabeth's first visit to the parish was at the invitation of her stepfather's cousin, who explained that "it would make her so well thought of in the neighborhood if a young lady of Miss W's consequence was seen at her house" (60). Similarly, when Elizabeth and her husband returned to the parish after their wedding, "they were visited by all who thought themselves genteel in Halifax and the neighborhood," and "Elizabeth's dress and manners were so superior that the visitors all testified their admirations." When the couple "returned the bridal visits the neighborhood resounded with applause, no lady had ever been seen in Halifax so well dressed" (75–76). Of course, society in Halifax did not always fall short of Elizabeth's expectations; the christening party given by her father- in-law's partner, complete with a violinist playing in the passage, dancing in the drawing room after dinner, and good company, comes across in her daughter's memoirs as a successful occasion (63). Yet this was the exception rather than the rule.

Why was Halifax so backward in comparison to Thirsk? True, Thirsk, located near several aristocratic halls, the spa at Harrogate, and of course York, was closer to the hub of genteel society in the county; but Halifax, a significant trading center in its own right and less than a day's ride from Leeds and Wakefield, was not exactly isolated. Thus it is legitimate to speculate that part of the difference between the two communities was a result of an unwillingness on the part of Halifax's elite to totally immerse themselves completely in the culture that Elizabeth knew so well. Ultimately, Halifax measured virtue by the ability to balance the desire for gentility against the necessity of thrift. Many of those who failed in this balancing act did so because they succumbed to the extravagant side of gentility. Caroline Walker describes John Sharp, who had been her grandfather's partner, as living in "a house of riotous profusion" that was "conducted with little prudence," and his wife as being a woman of "vulgar extravagance" (64, 97, 79). Having spent too much time pursuing pleasure instead of profits, Sharpe went bankrupt, a fate that Caroline thought he deserved (97). Similarly, she describes her cousin Samuel Stead, the son of her father's sister by her first husband, as a lazy, contentious brat. At one point he was placed as an apprentice to an upstanding merchant, but he left after three weeks, declaring "to his mother that he could not bear to stay any longer [as] he was made to do such hard work" (96). He was then apprenticed to John Sharp, but spent his days in bad company and learned nothing (102). He, too, suffered an appropriate fate: he married a "girl who had neither fortune nor connections to be of use to him" and lived in (relative) penury in York (112, 116).

The ambivalence about gentility cut both ways. Although less disastrously, Caroline's father also failed to achieve this balancing act, for he was too "parsimonious in his habits" (73), an observation that tallies with her mother's complaint that he did not buy new coats often enough. The problem, of course, was that parsimony could be misinterpreted as a lack of gentility, and another story about him confirms this danger. After settling into Walterclough with his new wife, John Walker took a great interest in managing the farming of his estate, and Caroline blames an accident he suffered as he walked home on a dark evening on the fact that he kept all of his horses for husbandry, so he had to walk everywhere himself (77). Caroline makes it clear that such behavior was not becoming to a genteel person. It was fortunate that he was parsimonious, though, for he "never had the knack of doing business" (82), and Caroline criticizes him on numerous occasions for having "entered into no profession to improve his fortune" (73). The message is clear: one should work to improve one's fortune but in a genteel fashion.

Obviously Caroline Walker's memoirs present interpretive problems, not the least being the difficulty of knowing how much her version of events in the 1770s and 1780s was shaped by the expectations and values of the era in which she herself lived, when the vocabularies and culture of the middle class were much more highly developed. Another source, however—one that presents fewer interpretive problems—confirms the impression that Halifax's elite were deeply ambivalent about the issue of gentility because of their attachment to the concept of thrift.

This source is a series of five letters that Richard Hill wrote to George Stansfield Jr. from Europe in the mid-1770s.[29] At the time he wrote them, Hill's circumstances were not the happiest, for he was still suffering under a commission of bankruptcy, which Stansfield was helping him to resolve. In his day Hill had been a partner with his father, Samuel Hill, and later he was a manufacturer and merchant in his own right. Although he was dependent on Stansfield, he was also a social equal and was well acquainted with Stansfield's affairs, both personal and commercial. His letters contain candid comments that reveal something of the attitudes and lifestyle of one of the parish's preeminent manufacturers and a central character in this story about the emergence of middle-class culture in Halifax.

On 7 March 1774, before setting out on his journey from Boulogne, Hill tells Stansfield what he has discovered about the trade at Leghorn. One of his remarks concerns the importance of a good appearance, and he assumes he will have to convince Stansfield of its necessity:

> I am told that ostentation and show is no where more attended to than at Leghorn—is it not surprising that folly like this should be so very much countenanced in a commercial city? It is still more so in my opinion that Will Denison [a Leeds merchant] should have amassed the greatest part of his immense fortune [some £200,000]

---

29. CDA/FH/461a. Hereafter the letters will be cited in the text by date. Hill was in Europe acting as an agent for Stansfield: CDA/FH/462.

by placing his brother Robert in Italy, by directing him to assume the title of Count, and by encouraging him to live as an Eastern Prince.

To press home his point about the necessity of fancy clothes, Hill relates a story he had been told of a Quaker captain whose ship arrived at Leghorn with the first cargo of fish from Newfoundland. According to custom, the captain was entitled to the first choice of cargo for London, but although "he appeared regularly upon Change in his Quaker dress, nobody noticed him." His broker then told the captain that he would have to dress the part if he expected to get his cargo, and back in London, the captain billed the ship's owners for the cost of his fancy suit. No doubt Hill intended this story to amuse, and it probably did, but the pointed moral of the story leads one to suspect that Stansfield may have been inclined to dress more like the Quaker captain than like an "Eastern Prince." Certainly Hill, who follows this story with a fairly detailed description of his own wardrobe, goes to some pains to assure Stansfield that his clothes will "agree pretty well with the character of a private gentleman of economy and of moderate fortune."

Other letters in the series provide some sense of what Hill and Stansfield perceived as the antithesis of "the private gentleman of economy." In a letter of 20 February 1775, which begins with a promise to use the bank bills that Stansfield sent him with "frugality" and "prudence," Hill (a widower) comments on the upbringing of his daughter, Amelia. It is his ambition, he explains, that she should "be as good, as amiable, as virtuous, as discreet, as useful, as accomplished in household affairs as her Mamma." To this end he had sent her to live with her grandmother, under whose influence he expected her to be "a stranger to those fashionable vices and sentiments inculcated almost at every boarding school." One imagines that Jonathan Hall's nemesis, Lady Waxe Arse, was educated in one of those boarding schools, for her vices seem to have been just those that Hill wishes Amelia to avoid: the pretentious affectations and the dangerous extravagance of the idle rich.

The same impression is given by a letter of 22 December 1778, in which Hill relates some of the gossip about the English residents of Brussels, much of it directed specifically at dissolute noblemen. These reprobates include the impoverished Lord Torrington, a member of Parliament reduced to begging for his bread, and a Mr. Dillon, son of Lord Dillon, who reputedly owed £140,000 in gambling debts. As Hill ruefully remarks, the effect of all this dissipation is that while "thirty years ago an Englishman's word (though an utter stranger) was good for £1000, at present it will not pass for a single florin unless supported by letters of credit." Hill's analysis of the reasons for these changes in financial customs was probably not entirely accurate, but it suggests his perceptions of an antithesis between the sober and respectable world of trade and the extravagant and idle world of land. In a letter of 31 January 1775, Hill explains his surprise at being offered "letters of civility" and "even of a considerable credit" by the leading merchant house in Boulogne; he had not thought they even knew his name. The reason, he surmised, was that

> a set of wretches from England who assemble here, and lead a life the reverse of prudence, have placed my conduct at Boulogne in an amiable light.... Their faces have constantly, but mine has never, been seen at any masquerade, mask ball, opera, play, or other place of dissipation. I have indeed, occasionally, put myself to a moderate expense, in my own room, to some respectable married families here, in giving them a dish of coffee and liqueur after the French custom, not because I can afford it, but in hopes of some good coming from it, and this is all the extravagance I have fallen into (anywhere) since my arrival in France.

Hill's letter of 22 December 1778 cuts much closer to home and suggests the same set of sentiments:

> I hope the planting, not as I intimated but as you approve, is going to take place at Fieldhouse. In time you will find it equally commodious and beautiful. The warmth, the shelter such plantations will afford will be about complete when it ought to be so, that is, just when the distant tokens of old age are beginning to creep in upon your constitution, but which I am persuaded is a great way off unless brought on by your own too great assiduity and application; but besides this general attention to your own and to public concerns and benefits, there is another motive which may impair your vigour more than all the rest, I mean your too moderate mode of life in eatables and drinkables. Take my advice, for I give it you upon experience and from a heart warm with affection for your person—live well; have all good wholesome things about you, say of the very best [of] these blessings for yourself and Miss Stansfields. Those less genuine may do for company, for those who can GORGE at others expense, but who

will neither allow themselves the comforts of life at their own homes, nor give them to others. You told me Scarbrough had been of use to your health, so pray never neglect to visit that place yearly. To preserve life as long as we can is duty which we all owe to the SUPREME BEING, and early to begin to take care on it is the surest way to fulfill that duty. If I remember right you do in common drink malt liquor at dinner out of choice, let me prevail on you always to have by you for your own use, the very best London porter that can be procured. Pray believe my assurances, namely that it will have the kindest influence on your habit of body, and which you must allow is as essentially necessary to the enjoyment of perfect health as to keep off other diseases.

Here Hill portrays Stansfield as one of the "proprietors" of the parish, assiduously applying himself to "public concerns and benefits," yet all his good works were threatened by his "too moderate mode of life in eatables and drinkables." Recall that George Stansfield was one of the wealthiest men in the parish. Thus the gist of this advice—to avoid being seen as someone who gorges at others' expense while denying himself at home, to give up malt liquor in favor of the "very best London porter," and to visit Scarbrough—was advice about the incongruous conjunction of his public role and his miserly lifestyle.

Men such as Stansfield were caught in a bit of a trap. They disapproved of and feared the slippery slope that led from folly to imprudence to extravagance and eventually to ruin, and they used the talisman of thrift to protect themselves. At the same time they wanted gentility, in the shape of plantations, porter, and the pleasures of Scarbrough, and too much thrift would make the genteel image impossible to maintain. Stansfield's life was a bit of a balancing act as he, in company with others, tried to construct a social position that condemned extravagance and idleness but allowed a degree of necessary and respectable gentility.

Finally, the ambiguity surrounding gentility is evident in the role of women in the emerging middle-class culture. As the development of the new private sphere increasingly removed the wives of Halifax's merchants, manufacturers, and professionals from day-to-day involvement in the family's business, they and their daughters busied themselves in the construction of a distinct and exclusive social world revolving around visits, nonpolitical clubs, and assemblies. This private sphere, too, had its ambiguities.

"Rebus," the correspondent to the *Halifax Union Journal* who complained about the vices of gambling, was particularly critical of female card players. On 13 February 1759 he carped:

> Might not the fair sex who divide their winter evenings between cards and romances find entertainments more suitable as well as more beneficial? Anciently, the title of an unmarried woman was SPINSTER, I suppose, because their chief employment was the distaff, that employment has long been lost in the TOILET and the TEA-TABLE and yet I'm persuaded that the tea table with all the idle chat and scandal attending to it has not been so fatal to their charms as a pack of cards. Do but observe the attitude of a lady while the game is depending and you shall not find many charms in her countenance. Her thoughts are so wholly engaged and her mind so much upon tenters (for you must know that a lady seldom plays with indifference) that upon the least disappointment or success she flames out either in immoderate laughter or immoderate anger. I have seen so many instances of both kinds as convince me the way to improve the charms and attractions peculiar to the fair sex is not to spend too much of their time at cards.

The ambiguity of this passage is clear. Women, Rebus believes, ought to spend their time in some manner more useful than chatting around the tea table, let alone playing cards. At the same time, he still places women in a separate sphere, where they can remain as the objects of male attentions.

Other correspondents made their concerns about the potential extravagance and vice of the idle wife more explicit. Consider the plaintive letter written to the editor of the *Halifax Union Journal* by "Deborah Drive-About" and published there on 1 April 1760. Deborah, it seems, had been forced to marry "a citizen in the wholesale way of trade"; this was, as she put it, "a mighty falling off from expectation," for she had hoped for a much "higher life." Deborah's husband was positively cruel to her, denying her a coach and an extra servant after the birth of her second child (he had given in on her demands for a footman and an extra servant after the birth of the first child). This behavior Deborah found quite unreasonable. "What business, Sir, have men with wives and families which they cannot support in as much splendor as their neighborhood? All men, sure, ought to know how to get money, as it is well known all women do how to spend it." Obviously, the sympathies of the satirist responsible for this letter were with Deborah's husband, and she was an extreme case. When her husband pointed out to her that the income on her (small) portion of £300 would not even keep her in shoes and stockings, she was affronted at the "pitiful spirit ... of such odious calculations." But the problem she represented to the commercial and professional elites who read the *Unin Journal* was a real one. Were their wives, now increasingly removed from active participation in the family business, going to appreciate the value of the money they spent?

Another letter in the same issue of the *Union Journal* raises the same concern. A bachelor who wrote to explain why he had never married revealed that one match had been called off at the last minute because the intended bride demanded pin money "to the amount of half our computed yearly income." As he put it, he had wasted his time with "half a dozen females successively who seemed to think they were born only to *Tea and Quadrille.*" The bachelor's account is no more to be taken as a true story than Deborah's, but it too bears witness to the concern that the leisure of women in the emerging private sphere was at odds with the prudence necessary for commercial success. Of course, it is very difficult to gauge the reality of such concerns, for it is not possible to determine how extensive or how complete the retreat of women into the private sphere was. The extravagant woman was a stock character of eighteenth-century satire; but she does seem to have been sufficiently common to excite the concern of these correspondents, and of the testators whose practices we surveyed in Chapter 6.

Needless to say, not all members of Halifax's commercial and professional elite were prepared to have their wives and daughters retreat entirely into the private sphere. As Richard Hill explained to George Stansfield on 31 January 1775, he wanted to bring up his daughter with "useful knowledge," and he intended to teach her "to conduct a little business with as much propriety as myself." If Hill's expectations for his daughter were exceptional, they are the exception that proves the rule, for Hill's circumstances were unique. He sent these letters from Europe because he had fled there after his bankruptcy, which he could blame in part on his extravagant lifestyle. Hill, then, had suffered personally from the ambiguities inherent in the manufacturer's position in this society. By aiming too high in the game of gentility, he had ruined his own and his daughter's future. If he wanted to teach his daughter some "useful knowledge," it may well have been because he was all too well aware of the dangers inherent in a life that was given over to luxury, and, of course, because he could no longer afford to support her.

As Davidoff and Hall argue, the tensions created by the new private sphere were to some extent resolved by the emerging expectation that women, in the private sphere, were uniquely responsible for maintaining the values necessary for commercial success. That ideology took time to develop, but there is evidence of its emergence in Halifax in the mid-eighteenth century. Elizabeth Walker, for instance, was not directly involved in her husband's business affairs, but she was not extravagant, either. Indeed, according to her daughter, it was only Elizabeth's careful management of the money her husband allowed her that kept the family in a state of respectable solvency. A middle road between Amelia Hill and Deborah Drive-About could be found. Women such as Elizabeth Walker could remain in the private sphere without succumbing to the lures of luxury and extravagance.

The evidence provided by these glimpses into the emerging culture of Halifax's elite suggests that as members of the middle class scanned the social hierarchy, they saw a somewhat contradictory world. Gentility was crucial to all of them, for it was a primary component not only of local political power but of the boundary that separated them from the lower orders. The evidence we have examined suggests that members of Halifax's elite were constructing a distinct version of the culture of gentility. No doubt part of the impetus for such a project came from the inferiority that even wealthy men of trade felt, particularly if they were first-generation arrivistes in the world of gentility. But political and moral imperatives were also involved. The resultant version of gentility was constructed around a series of virtues—thrift, hard work, temperance, good character, and prudence—which were contrasted with the potential vices of gentility taken too far: idleness, extravagance, excess, and imprudence.

LOOKING AROUND: HALIFAX'S MIDDLE-CLASS CULTURE IN CONTEXT

To what extent were these developments unique to Halifax? Perhaps the virtuous version of gentility had nothing at all to do with the parish's particular circumstances. After all, many of these concerns—about corrupt politics, about thrift, and about extravagant women, even gentility itself—originated in late seventeenth- and early eighteenth-century London, suggesting that the ambivalence of Halifax's middle class was simply a reflection of more general developments.

On one level Halifax was obviously not unique, for this virtuous gentility was not the sole property of commercial and professional people. Extravagance, after all, is a relative term; it is the imprudence (to use a word much in the minds of Halifax's elites) of spending more than one can afford. Men such as Stansfield and Sutcliffe no doubt expected their MP, Sir George Saville, to live in a house much grander than theirs, and they praised his assiduous pursuit of Yorkshire's interest in Parliament. Once elected in 1759, Saville was as secure in his county seat as any member for a pocket borough, and no doubt one of the reasons was that both commercial and landed Yorkshire freeholders could see him as a shining example of virtuous gentility. In a similar vein, Halifax's commercial and professional elites no doubt joined provincial gentlemen and urban elites in reading with interest the report of a "distinguished nobleman's" advice to his son on the occasion of the trial of "the unhappy E——l" in the House of Lords, for the gist of the message was "that it is not mere title which constitutes the noble."[30]

Certainly it is not difficult to uncover criticism of the potential vices of gentility from across the social spectrum: contemporary plays and novels often showed aristocratic characters in an unfavorable light, as they did commercial people who discarded virtue in pursuit of excess and idleness.[31] More directly, we know that Elizabeth Shackleton, the eighteenth century Lancashire gentlewoman studied by Amanda Vickery, had a very clear sense of what level of luxury was appropriate for a given individual—a sentiment that would have been equally at home on the pages of Elizabeth Walker's journal if she had left one.[32]

Yet any investigation of cultural transformation must pay attention to the ways in which a group appropriates available cultural forms to construct a new identity.[33] The cultural forms available to Halifax's elite included gentility, even its virtuous version, but when these people justified and defined virtue, they appealed to a commercial ethic whose

30. *Union Journal,* 13 May 1760. The trial in question was almost certainly that of Lord Ferrers for murder, and this report from London would have been reprinted in other provincial papers as well.

31. See, for example, Newman, *Rise of English Nationalism,* 63–120.

32. Vickery, "Women and the World of Goods," 281–88.

33. Roger Chartier, *The Cultural Origins of the French Revolution,* trans. Lydia Cochrane (Durham, N.C., 1991).

roots lay in their own experience as manufacturers and merchants. On this level the answer to the question of Halifax's uniqueness is yes. After being insulted at Buxton, Jonathan Hall consoled himself by observing that such behavior would soon bankrupt the town. Similarly, Richard Hill was sure that the letters of civility and credit given him by a leading French firm had been prompted by his virtuous conduct, which thus had proved to be beneficial to Stansfield's business. While this group's relations with those above them in the social hierarchy were fraught with ambivalence and contradiction, a distinctive position was being constructed, a position founded on the economic and social experience of this commercial and professional elite.

A theme that pervades Caroline Walker's memoir, for example, is the shame of a lack of gentility. Again and again she criticizes members of the genteel world for failing to maintain their standards. She blames her aunt, her father's sister, at two points in the memoir for stripping her brother's home of all of the best linen. The occasion of this crime was an even more serious offense, her marriage to Mr. Dawson, an unbeneficed clergyman; as Caroline reminds herself on the basis of this and any number of similar incidents, "low marriages impoverish a family extremely" (75).

The imperative of maintaining a standard of gentility was even stronger with respect to the world of manual labor. When Caroline was a child, her father "accidentally met with a man . . . who had invented a machine for spinning worsted yarn," and he bought it with the intent of setting up a spinning mill on his estate. The idea horrified Caroline's mother; all of the other (real) manufacturers in the district had dismissed the gadget, and her husband was a man with no knack for business. Her concern grew as her husband began to sink money in the project, leaving her short of funds and subject "to many mortifications." Eventually the mill was completed and provided "employment for most of the poor people in the vicinity . . .[who] began to improve in their appearance by having better wages." Her father's relative success in the manufacturing world, however, was not without its drawbacks. He was still chronically unable to manage his money, always paying out whatever he had and never leaving anything for "contingencies." Perhaps more serious were the mill's social effects. The problem of the eternally declining standard of household service plagued Mrs. Walker, and she was always "being obliged to part with servants that did not suit her." These troubles were compounded by the fact "that our servants were rather injured from associating with the men employed in [the mill]." And not only the servants. "My brother, by going down to the mill with my father began now to associate a little with the common boys about, which hurt my mother very much" (119–24).

It was John Walker's manufacturering activities that elicited from his wife and daughter the greatest concern over gentility. Although he did hire an overseer, Walker was involved by necessity in a certain amount of hands-on management of the mill, and he exposed not only his servants but his son to the pernicious influence of the workers. This aspect of commercial life in the eighteenth century *was* unique to manufacturing communities such as Halifax. Most tradesmen, merchants, and landowners did not employ large numbers of laborers in this kind of wage relationship; and it was precisely in this context that the maintenance of gentility assumed such great importance. Notice, however, that it was a "useful" kind of gentility: Walker's new mill allowed the poor "to improve in their appearance by having better wages." This improvement would not have been possible without the input of even Walker's bumbling version of entrepreneurial spirit. Thus, insofar as men such as Walker were appropriating a discourse about virtuous gentility and making it their own, they were doing so in terms of a socioeconomic experience in which they construed themselves as improving the world through their thrift, hard work, and prudence—sentiments which bring to mind the iconographical message of the engraving of the Calder Navigation's share certificates (photo 6).

This example shows the necessity of viewing this account as a story about the *origins* of middle-class culture. Given the nature of eighteenth-century society, it is hardly surprising that of the two boundaries necessary for the emergence of a middle-class culture, the one that separated the elite from workers, artisans, and perhaps even shopkeepers and clerks was going to be more clearly conceived and articulated. Even the "engineer" hired to manage the worsted spinning mill was described in terms that show that he belonged on the workers' side of the fence (123–24). Despite the scant attention it has received in the historiography, this boundary was initially the more important of the two precisely because it stemmed directly from the experience these manufacturers and merchants had as employers.

Equally unsurprising is the fact that the upper boundary was not conceived or articulated particularly clearly. Halifax's commercial and professional elite sought to distinguish themselves from the world of idle luxury. They worked, albeit in genteel "occupations," and they were proud of doing so, and most of them expected at least some of their sons to follow them in the trade—even John Walker, who was intended for the ministry, ended up as a manufacturer. In the absence of a discourse in which this group could easily specify what made them different from the idle rich, however, and relying as they did on gentility to separate themselves from those below, they inevitably fell into ambiguity and even contradiction as they attempted to articulate this difference. We can conclude, however, that the discourse of virtue was the beginning of an articulation of the upper boundary that would define a middle-class culture, and that it developed in the specific socioeconomic context of a manufacturing parish.

Chapter 8

Implications and Speculations

I have argued that Halifax's history during the long century that separates the Restoration from the Industrial Revolution illuminates the origins of middle-class culture. In the latter part of the seventeenth century, the parish was a community of the middling sort: a relatively large and loosely defined congeries of independent rural artisans and small landowners which shaded up to a few substantial yeomen on one hand and down into the ranks of the simple clothiers on the other. This community was a relatively prosperous one; its extensive rural textile industry (usually supplemented by pastoral farming) provided many of the parish's inhabitants with a degree of modest independence, an independence they carried over to other aspects of their lives.

Between the late seventeenth and the mid-eighteenth centuries, economic changes in the parish's primary industry and associated changes in the entire English economy transformed this community. The increasing importance of large-scale manufacture of textiles gradually reduced the descendants of the parish's independent clothiers to the status of semi-independent wage laborers working for a new group of manufacturers and merchants. The cultural shifts that these economic developments caused—and that made them possible—emphasized the differences between this new elite group and the rest of the community. Although the effects were never absolute, this long-term process of economic and cultural change polarized the very broad and relatively undifferentiated social middle of the late seventeenth century and created a new commercial and professional elite who shared a common economic and social experience.

This long-term process of change was joined in the decades after 1750 by a more rapid and concentrated series of changes that made explicit the class relations implicit in the new economic and social practice. The community's new elite embarked on a series of projects that had the cumulative effect of establishing this group in a position of social dominance unlike that enjoyed by the middling sort. Their "ownership" of the parish was much more absolute, it was much more institutionalized, and it was concentrated in the hands of a much smaller and more uniform group. Parallel to these political changes—what I have called the making of the public sphere—and indeed one of the signs of this group's uniformity, was the making of a private sphere identified by a distinctive set of values, gender relations, and practices. The making of the public and private spheres transformed the culture of the group of merchants, manufacturers, and professionals into a class culture, for it provided them with the means to articulate their common identity vis-à-vis other social groups.

Reduced to a single sentence, my argument thus modifies and specifies Thompson's oft-cited formulation: Middle-class culture in Halifax emerged when a commercial and professional elite came, as a result of the way they had construed a common social and economic experience, to feel and articulate the identity of their interests as tradespeople against the interests of both workers and the idle rich. This identity of interests, their culture, was constructed in the political and social realms as well as the economic realm and ultimately supplied the terms in which they understood their world.

ALTHOUGH it focuses on the first half of the "long eighteenth century," this argument about the origins of middle-class culture in Halifax has implications for our understanding of the entire period from the late seventeenth to the early nineteenth centuries. Most important, it focuses on a social group—merchants, manufacturers, and professionals—central to the history of this period. Whether one does or does not hold with the term "Industrial Revolution," it is hard to deny that this century and a half saw a fundamental transformation of the British economy, and it is equally hard to deny the role that this group played in these developments. From the late seventeenth century, they were the ones behind the emergence of new modes of production and the new consumer economy that ultimately gave rise to large-scale production (mechanized and not) and an urbanized society. In addition, the same group played an important role in political and social developments during this period, such as parliamentary reform, evangelical religion, and new social institutions.

This book offers a framework for making sense of this group and their role in these transformations by using a cultural analysis to explore the local contexts of national phenomena. Both of these features of the analysis are important, for it is only as an argument about culture and about local history that this analysis of class formation works.

Cultural analysis is crucial because it has allowed me to explore class formation without getting trapped in the theoretical morass that surrounds this concept. On one hand, the problem with the traditional Marxist approach to class is the difficulty of identifying the common economic experience of the members of the putative middle class. An argument about "the middle class" will not hold water, particularly when it is extended to the national level, for the group's membership was too fluid.[1] As I suggested in the Introduction, this is especially the case in regard to the eighteenth century, but many historians would extend the argument to the nineteenth century.[2] On the other hand, the problem with the linguistic turn is that in rejecting the legitimacy of a class analysis, its partisans deny the existence of connections between the obvious fact of economic and social change during this period and the political rhetoric employed by the groups they examine.

It is possible to avoid the dilemma by arguing, as Patrick Joyce has done in *Visions of the People*, that socioeconomic and linguistic conceptions—"class" and "the people" respectively—exist side by side. There are even grounds for agreement between historians who take more partisan positions. Both a sophisticated Marxist account such as Theodore Koditschek's history of Bradford and a linguistic analysis such as Gareth Steadman Jones's account of Chartism grant to "common sense" important features of the opposing argument. Koditschek acknowledges that the language or discourse of class—I would use the term "culture" here—was to a degree independent of the material

---

1. See, for example, John Seed's critique of Theodore Koditschek's book on Bradford: "Class Formation in Early Industrial England," *Social History* 18 (1993): 17–30.

2. William Reddy has argued that we should all but abandon the concept of class: *Money and Liberty in Modern Europe: A Critique of Historical Understanding* (New York, 1987) and "The Concept of Class," in *Social Orders and Social Classes in Europe since 1500: Studies in Social Stratification*, ed. M. L. Bush (London, 1992), 13–25.

base. Jones is willing to grant that aspects of the socioeconomic experience of workers in the early nineteenth century made Chartist rhetoric appealing to them.[3]

I have argued for the need to bring what is granted to "common sense" in these two examples to the forefront of the analysis by conceiving of class formation as a process of cultural transformation. This cultural analysis makes explicit the insights of Marxism and the linguistic turn. Indeed, class makes sense *only* when it is conceived as a culture, a culture in which a group's attitudes, practices, and very conceptions of their world were shaped (but not determined) by their conscious understanding of their place in the relations of production (relations that were themselves embedded in a cultural context). So conceived, a class analysis focuses less on the diverse social and economic experiences of individuals than on the construction of the world that they, as a group, made on the basis of that experience, for it is the construction, not the particular group of people and their experiences, that persists. Yet in doing so, it brings the connections between experience and identity to the surface, assuming that they were both real and important.

Local history is crucial to this argument for the same reason; it too resolves some of the difficulties surrounding the concept of class. I have argued that class formation makes sense *only* at the local level, because only in that context is it possible to explore and explain the relations between the economic, social, and political practices of individuals and the class consciousness they constructed for themselves. The argument for the necessity of a local history is an argument about a *mode of analysis*. It is not, for instance, an argument about parochial peculiarities—mere antiquarianism—based on some misconceived notion of the essentially local outlook of eighteenth-century middling groups. Halifax's elites were in contact with regional and national developments, borrowing ideas, examples, and values from the wider world. Nor is it an argument that the origins of middle-class culture were unique to Halifax; this has not been a search for the one true source of the river Nile. Rather, the local context has allowed me to trace how a particular combination of attitudes and practices came together in a specific way to create a middle-class culture.

3. Patrick Joyce, *Visions of the People* (Cambridge, 1991); Theodore Koditschek, *Class Formation and Urban-Industrial Society: Bradford, 1750–1850* (New York, 1990); Gareth Steadman Jones, "Rethinking Chartism," in *Languages of Class: Studies in English Working-Class History, 1832–1982* (Cambridge, 1983), 90–179.

THE emergence of a middle-class culture in Halifax, then, suggests ways to analyze the disparate experiences of middling groups in the eighteenth and early nineteenth centuries and to discover features shared by the cultures they constructed on the basis of those experiences. A serious attempt at comparative analysis is hampered by the relative lack of local or even regional studies dealing with the eighteenth century. The evidence available, however, suggests that while the particular culture package that emerged in Halifax was different from those emerging in other commercial communities, they all shared key features related to economic, political, and social developments of the eighteenth century.

Not ten miles from Halifax, the town of Leeds presents such a combination of similarity and difference. R. G. Wilson's excellent history of the merchant community that was at the heart of the West Riding's textile district shows that the mercantile focus of Leeds, which existed from a very early stage, created a distinctive socioeconomic context in the town. It is not for nothing that Wilson's book is titled *Gentlemen Merchants*, for the Leeds merchants, particularly in the latter part of the eighteenth century, increasingly moved into landed society, either through marriage or through the purchase of an estate.[4] The dominance of merchants in Leeds highlights the importance of manufacturers in Halifax, for merchants did not employ large numbers of laborers. Contributing to the difference between a mercantile and manufacturing community was the difference in the types of cloth traded there. Leeds was at the center of the broadcloth region in the West Riding, which, as Pat Hudson has shown, continued to be dominated by the production of independent yeoman clothiers. The narrow cloth and worsted production in the area around Halifax, in contrast, was characterized by a more proletarianized workforce.[5]

There were other differences as well. One was Leeds's status as an incorporated town—though not a parliamentary borough. From a very

---

4. R. G. Wilson, *Gentlemen Merchants: The Merchant Community in Leeds, 1700–1830* (Manchester, 1971).

5. Pat Hudson, "Proto-industrialization: The Case of the West Riding Woollen Industry in the Eighteenth and Early Nineteenth Centuries," *History Workshop* 12 (1981): 34–61. Merchants were also the dominant economic group in Wakefield, the other major town in the West Riding woolen district. Trade in the town was controlled by a narrow elite of "merchant princes," who did all they could to limit the development of new mercantile houses or manufacturing concerns: J. W. Walker, *Wakefield: Its History and People* (1934; East Ardesley, Yorks., 1967), 397–401.

early stage, commercial people in Leeds had a political institution that reflected their ownership of the community. The same kinds of institutions had to be created in Halifax. They *were* the same kinds of institutions, however, so similarities existed alongside differences. Halifax's circulating library, for instance, was established in response to an identical library established in Leeds the previous year, and both libraries expressed their organizers' sense of corporate ownership of their communities.[6]

There were other commercial communities where large-scale manufacturing was important: Bradford with its worsted industry and the towns in Lancashire with their cotton industry. Here the story is again similar but different. One of the important differences is that the most rapid economic development came much earlier in Halifax than in either Bradford or Lancashire. As a result, the commercial community in Halifax achieved a critical mass at a much earlier date: the mid-eighteenth century instead of the late eighteenth century.

The timing of the emergence of a substantial commercial and professional elite perhaps did most to shape relations with the local gentry. Of course relations between manufacturers and local gentlemen were not necessarily antagonistic. Amanda Vickery's work on the Colne valley in the eighteenth century shows the extent to which the two groups socialized with each another, much as Halifax's commercial and professional elite socialized with the few gentry families who remained in the parish. Moreover, values and practices similar to the virtuous gentility of Halifax's elite were common among the provincial gentry.[7] Halifax's commercial and professional elite, however, had a distinctive social space in which to articulate their class identity, for they far outnumbered the local gentry. The sense of ownership that this group expressed through their many voluntary societies played an important part in the way they constructed their class identity, and these associations were essentially devoid of gentry participation. Both Bradford and the cotton districts in Lancashire had their share of such associations—canals, turnpikes, libraries, and so forth—but though manufac-

---

6. The founding of the Leeds Circulating Library in 1767 was cited as a reason for founding a library in Halifax in 1768: R. J. Morris, *Class, Sect, and Party: The Making of the British Middle Class, Leeds, 1820–1850* (Manchester, 1990), 171.

7. Amanda Vickery, "Women and the World of Goods: A Lancashire Consumer and Her Possessions, 1751–81," in *Consumption and the World of Goods*, ed. John Brewer and Roy Porter (London, 1993), 274–301; and "Women of the Local Elite in Lancashire, 1750–1825" (Ph.D. dissertation, London University, 1991).

turers, merchants, and professionals seem to have taken the lead, the local gentry were involved as well, subtly altering the character of the group identity that was constructed through such institutions.[8] One could also argue that the fact that a critical mass of wealthy merchants, manufacturers, and professionals in Bradford and in Lancashire did not develop until the late eighteenth century was reflected in the class tensions of the nineteenth century. According to Koditschek, for instance, Bradford's gentry retained enough influence during the eighteenth century to set the stage for an early nineteenth-century struggle between an increasingly vociferous manufacturing interest of Whigs and Dissenters and a landed, Anglican, Tory elite.[9]

Farther afield, Sheffield and Birmingham suggest another variant of the eighteenth-century commercial community. Like Bradford and Halifax, Sheffield and Birmingham were important manufacturing centers, but although they had large manufacturing and mercantile concerns, small masters remained much more prevalent there than they did in Halifax. Thus the employment of wage labor on a relatively large scale, which was an important element in Halifax's experience, was less prominent in these towns. Here, too, we find similarities that complement the differences. As John Money's study of the West Midlands has shown, the region had an associational culture similar to Halifax's; newspapers, theater, scientific societies, and political action all shaped the emerging commercial identity in the midlands.[10]

Finally, although London can legitimately be claimed as the fountain of the culture of gentility from the late seventeenth century, its economic, social, and cultural complexity makes any meaningful discussion of middle-class culture there somewhat suspect. The extraordinary pull that the aristocratic world exerted on London, not to mention the multiplicity of economic practices and the sheer size of the city, created a very particular "metropolitan" experience that bore little relation to

8. John Styles was kind enough to inform me about this aspect of Bradford's history. He has reached his conclusions through an extensive study of the region; the conclusions I have drawn from this information are, of course, my own.

9. Koditschek, *Class Formation*, esp. chap. 5. A a similar kind of story, obviously modified in important respects, emerges in John Seed's work on Manchester: "Gentlemen Dissenters: The Social and Political Meanings of Rational Dissent in the 1770 and 1780s," *Historical Journal* 28 (1985): 299–325; and "Unitarianism, Political Economy, and the Antinomies of Liberal Culture in Manchester, 1830–50," *Social History* 7 (1982): 1–25.

10. See, for example, John Money's discussion of his reluctance to use the term "middle class": *Experience and Identity: Birmingham and the West Midlands, 1760–1800* (Manchester, 1977), 141.

other contexts. Strictly speaking, it may not even be possible to compare Halifax with London in the way we can compare it with Birmingham.[11]

As brief as it is, this survey should make it clear that the experiences of eighteenth-century commercial communities hinged on the particular social, economic, and cultural forces at work in them. Halifax, then, is but one place where a middle-class culture developed.[12] This formulation of the problem raises the issue of the relationship between the middle-class cultures that emerged in places such as mid-eighteenth-century Halifax and the middle-class culture of the nineteenth century. Obviously, there is some relationship, for the cultural patterns that emerged among Halifax's merchant, manufacturing, and professional families clearly correspond to those associated with the middle class in the nineteenth century. The voluntary associations, domestic ideology, and entrepreneurial drive studied by Morris, Davidoff and Hall, Koditschek, and Seed all have precursors in the Halifax of the third quarter of the eighteenth century.[13]

In terms of a cultural theory of class formation, the question how *a* middle-class culture in Halifax became part of *the* English middle-class culture comes down to the question how a set of values, concepts, and practices articulated in a particular context was made relevant to individuals and groups in different though related contexts. To answer this question, it is helpful to think about the emergence of local and national class cultures in the temporal dimension.

In the beginning, as it originated in a specific socioeconomic context, class consciousness was expressed and comprehended in a practical form. Individuals knew that they shared a class culture because an interlocking network of social practices created self-fulfilling and consciously adopted divisions within the society. The class consciousness expressed in the building of the Halifax Piece Hall, for example, was

11. Peter Earle, *The Making of the English Middle Class: Business, Society, and Family Life in London, 1660–1730* (London, 1990).
12. Although I doubt that it is exactly what he had in mind when he wrote it, E. P. Thompson's assertion that "consciousness of class arises in the same way in different times and places, but never in *just* the same way" can be read as a call for the analysis of class formation in the local context: *The Making of the English Working Class* (Harmondsworth, 1968), 9.
13. Morris, *Class, Sect, and Party*, 6–7; Leonore Davidoff and Catherine Hall, *Family Fortunes: Men and Women of the English Middle Class: 1750–1850* (London, 1987), 18–35; Koditschek, *Class Formation*, 165; and John Seed, "From 'Middling Sort' to Middle Class in Late Eighteenth- and Early Nineteenth-Century England," in Bush, *Social Orders and Social Classes*, 130–33.

practical in the sense that this organization's members became conscious of their class identity simply by *doing* what was necessary to build the edifice. Subscribing toward its costs, voting on the choice of sites and plans, and sitting in the central square of the new hall while the "workmen" marched by in their ranks told this group about their class identity vis-à-vis those below them in the social order. Belonging to an association in the public sphere and choosing a design for the building that had "that elegant simplicity which should adorn the Manufacturer's hall" told this group about their class identity vis-à-vis those above them in the social order.[14]

Practice is particularly important as a vehicle for class identity in the early phases of the formation of a class culture because a coherent conceptualization of class identity was still being constructed. It took time, for instance, to develop a "vocabulary" of class identity that matched the practical reality. The terminology that differentiated members of the middle class from the gentry hardly even existed in the eighteenth century, and even simple terms such as "workman" and "maker" were only just becoming attached to a group that included highly skilled artisans in the decades after 1750. In time a coherent conceptualization of middle-class identity was constructed; the necessary vocabulary did emerge by the late eighteenth century. As the practical reality of class relations endured, those relations came to be conceived and expressed in a more abstract but also a more coherent form.

This temporal dimension to the articulation of a class identity, the shift from the practical to the abstract, also helps explain the transition from a local class culture to *the* national class culture. A coherent conceptualization of class identity was constructed not only in time but in space. Again what was involved was a certain abstraction and distance from the practical realities of class relationships in the locality. That distance was gained as local middle-class cultures were articulated in regional and eventually national contexts and as connections were made between them.

As an example of this process, consider the following reading of E. P. Thompson's *Making of the English Working Class*. In many ways, the history of the working class presents the same problems as the history of the middle class. One of the chief, and admittedly serious, objections raised against Thompson's argument is that the experiences of working

---

14. The quote is from Ling Roth, *The Yorkshire Coiners* (Halifax, 1906), 213.

people in the 1830s and 1840s, at a time when the factory was not yet universal, were too diffuse to permit them to be labeled the "English working class." Given this problem of the relationship between experience and identity, it is significant that one of the strongest sections of the book is the discussion of the Luddites, and particularly the Luddites of West Yorkshire. The reason is not just that it is a good yarn in which the forces of capitalism were held, however temporarily, in abeyance. Rather it is that Luddism was a local class culture, for the relationship between the particular socioeconomic experience of these croppers and their class identity is plain as day. Although Thompson does not develop his argument in terms of the transition from local to national class cultures, he is aware of the issues involved, for he takes pains to trace the similarities and differences between the various branches of Luddism—the distinct local class cultures that were then articulated in a wider arena. He shows, for instance, that spies could penetrate these organizations only as the Luddites left their immediate community and tried to make wider contacts; thus the organizations that emerged from this early, very practical form of working-class culture were vulnerable just at the point where the abstraction necessary for communication made impostors less detectable. In the last analysis, I am largely convinced by Thompson's argument about the making of a national working class, but the implicit assertion about the relationship between the practical and contextualized local class discourse and the more abstract national class discourse needs to be made more explicit.[15]

Some sense of how this process might have worked for middle-class culture is evident in the articulation of a common commercial identity. One aspect of this identity was the influence that the manufacturing interest, broadly conceived, could exert on the government over trade policy. Obviously, as in the agitation that led to repeal of the Stamp Act, pressure from this manufacturing interest could be very strong. Yet as Samuel Garbett's failed attempt to create a formal manufacturing lobby shows, there were limits, at least at this stage, to the unity of the "manufacturing class."[16] But England's commercial elite were much more successful at constructing a common commercial identity with

---

15. Thompson makes the same implicit contrast between the local and national elsewhere. His evocative "Eighteenth-Century Society: Class Struggle without Class" can be read as a history about the emerging antagonisms, in specific local contexts, of class struggle on terms that later would be articulated in much wider contexts: *Social History* 2 (1978): 133–65.

16. Money, *Experience and Identity*, 35–47.

respect to groups below them. In the West Riding, the success of the Worsted Committee and the prosecution of the Cragg Vale coiners suggests how effectively people of the many socioeconomic and cultural contexts in the region could construct a common identity vis-à-vis the workers they employed.[17] A similar process seems to have been at work when textile merchants and manufacturers in the West Riding and the West Country agitated for repeal of restrictive legislation that affected the woolen industry toward the very end of the eighteenth century.[18] Up to that time, employers in these two regions had related to their workers in very different ways, for the West Country workers had been proletarianized for a considerable period. The success of this joint project thus depended on the ability of Yorkshire and West Country merchants and manufacturers to articulate their local class cultures in more general terms, to find, as it were, a cultural common denominator.[19]

Implicit in this particular example is industrialization's role as an engine of class formation. This role is not to be denied or hidden, for the transition from *a* middle-class culture to *the* middle-class culture cannot be explained without reference to the Industrial Revolution. Indeed, among this book's implications is the need to embrace the Industrial Revolution as an "event" and to reconsider the way we think about that event.[20]

The importance of culture and of local history are hardly unknown to historians of the Industrial Revolution. Many scholars have already begun to pay greater attention to the local and regional variants in the pace and course of economic development; in the process they have been more willing to acknowledge that the cultural conditions necessary for industrial development need as much explanation as the eco-

17. John Styles, "'Our Traitorous Money Makers': The Yorkshire Coiners and the Law, 1760–83," in *An Ungovernable People*, ed. John Brewer and John Styles (London, 1980), 172–249; also his "Embezzlement, Industry and the Law in England, 1500–1800," in *Manufacture in Town and Country before the Factory*, ed. Maxine Berg, Pat Hudson, and Michael Sonenscher (Cambridge, 1983), 173–210.

18. John Smail, "New Languages for Labour and Capital: The Transformation of Discourse in the Early Years of the Industrial Revolution," *Social History* 12 (1987): 49–71; Adrian Randall, "New Languages or Old? Labour, Capital, and Discourse in the Industrial Revolution," *Social History* 15 (1990): 195–216, and *Before the Luddites: Custom, Community, and Machinery in the English Woollen Industry, 1776–1809* (Cambridge, 1991).

19. Although the terminology is different, Patrick Joyce makes a similar point in his discussion of the difference between "class" (narrowly defined as economic interest) and "people": *Visions of the People*, Introduction.

20. For an analysis of why this is a question, see Pat Hudson and Maxine Berg, "Rehabilitating the Industrial Revolution," *Economic History Review* 45 (1992): 24–50.

nomic conditions.²¹ Seen as part of the history of the Industrial Revolution, this account of the origins of middle-class culture offers an explanation for the origins of "industrial culture," for the worldview of Halifax's merchants, manufacturers, and professionals was one in which industrialization was possible. This middle-class culture valued thrift and hard work as ends in themselves; it had successfully reduced, in conceptual terms, independent artisans to wage-dependent laborers; and it contained an articulation of "rational" economic practice.

The distinct phases of class formation that I have called "process" and "crystallization" also help to make sense of the Industrial Revolution. This distinction allows us to incorporate the evidence for long-term economic growth throughout the eighteenth century (process) with the evidence that something fairly dramatic began to happen in the last part of the century (crystallization). It suggests that the gradual economic growth experienced in some regions and in some industries from the early eighteenth century gave rise to many of the assumptions, conceptions, and values that were necessary for the Industrial Revolution. Like the middle-class experience in Halifax, these assumptions and values developed as a result of shifting structures of economic and social practice. Yet the industrial culture created by this long-term process of change was largely implicit in practice. Thus we also have to analyze how—again in some regions and in some industries—this diverse set of values and practices was made explicit in the worldview of a new group of "industrialists." That development, in turn, made further industrialization possible, for it provided a broader social and cultural context in which such values and practices could be articulated. Thus while the Industrial Revolution was an "event," it was an event that incorporated both gradualism as well as revolution.

I am not suggesting for a moment that the Industrial Revolution, by itself, caused the formation of the middle class. For one thing, the outline sketched here suggests that industrialization was as much caused by class formation as it was a cause of class formation; should we not expect to find gradualism and revolution in the history of the Industrial Revolution, since the history of its middle-class perpetrators exhibits that pattern?

For another thing, the cultural theory of class formation developed here is largely compatible with the linguistic, political, and cultural ap-

---

21. See Maxine Berg, *The Age of Manufactures: Industry, Innovation, and Work in Britain, 1700–1820* (London, 1985); and Pat Hudson, *The Industrial Revolution* (London, 1992).

proaches to class in the nineteenth century. These approaches suggest, and I agree, that at the very least both the Napoleonic wars and the agitation for political reform were as instrumental as industrialization in the making of the middle class. Indeed, in the light of this work, it would be wrong to suggest that the national middle class that was created during the late eighteenth and early nineteenth centuries was a coherent, consistent, and cohesive group with a uniform social and economic experience. Rather, like its mid-eighteenth-century "ancestor," it was a culture, not a thing, a culture articulated through a wide variety of pathways, each with its own particular characteristics. In addition to the factory floor and the putting-out merchant's warehouse, art, literature, political reform, and Dissenting congregations and academies all provided means through which, over time, an increasingly coherent middle-class culture could be articulated on the basis of origins experienced in such places as Halifax and in ways that made sense in the light of the diverse experiences of the individuals and groups that adopted these new cultural forms.

But I part company with some of the work informed by the linguistic turn in asserting that this class culture was there, for to argue that this culture was no more than a political rhetoric is to miss the point. If I am right in suggesting that the transition from the local to the national was a process in which local class cultures were articulated in wider and wider arenas, then we should expect the developing class discourse gradually to lose its precise connection to a specific socioeconomic and cultural experience. In the shift from practical to more abstract expressions of class identity, the common elements that bound different local contexts together became increasingly salient. Thus any discourse or culture that works on a "national" level will necessarily be rather abstract, and it will emphasize generalized political or cultural rhetoric rather than a specific experience.

The abstractness of the national middle-class culture that emerged toward the end of the eighteenth century is beautifully delineated in Davidoff and Hall's description of the struggle that Isaac Taylor and his family had to maintain their middle-class identity among the "sleepy villagers" of Lavenham in Suffolk. Obviously, a middle-class culture could not have originated or been maintained in such a context. Davidoff and Hall show that the family brought their middle-class culture with them from London and that they refreshed it through letter writing, reading, and the occasional visit to the metropolis.[22] In a setting

---

22. Davidoff and Hall, *Family Fortunes*, 61.

where the practicalities of class relations were absent, the Taylors' middle-class identity was bound to be relatively abstract and apparently unattached to any socio-economic reality. This is not to say that in the nineteenth century the local context, or indeed a specific socioeconomic and cultural experience, became unimportant. Local studies of the middle class in the nineteenth century show that it is possible to specify the relation of an increasingly national middle-class consciousness to the local context; Koditschek's extensive study of Bradford is a case in point, for he shows how the specific nature of the economic and social developments in Bradford affected the "outcome" of the process of class formation.[23]

In the nineteenth century, then, middle-class culture existed on two levels. On the regional and national level it was an often abstract but nevertheless relatively coherent articulation of political, cultural, and economic ideas that appear most vividly when they inform political and social action. This national middle-class culture was also appropriated in specific local contexts because it allowed groups to make sense of the political implications of their socioeconomic experience, and these appropriations not only gave meaning to the national class culture but shaped its nature and development.

The history of class formation in the late eighteenth and early nineteenth centuries—the history that appears in the work of Davidoff and Hall, Koditschek, and others—is a history of the articulation, in both local and national contexts, of the values and conceptions that created a national middle-class culture. This articulation happened as a result of a series of political, social, and economic crises. These crises—the war with the American colonies and France, the pressure for political reform, the increasing economic tensions between labor and capital—provided the occasions on which local and national leaders, both political and intellectual, could construct a broader vision of their class identity and also the context in which the broader view would make sense to a much larger group.

The ideologies around which this national middle-class culture were constructed, however, came from somewhere; what is missing is an analysis of how this culture was originally fashioned. The Taylors did not *make* their middle- class identity in Lavenham; they brought it with them. Similarly, the bourgeois values of thrift, hard work, and temperance that Koditschek argues were the driving force behind the actions of his liberal, often Dissenting entrepreneurs did not have their origins

23. Koditschek, *Class Formation*, esp. chaps. 6 and 7.

in the period he studies; by 1820 the notion of the self-made man already existed. What is missing from both accounts is the origins of this middle-class culture, the point from which such a process of articulation could have begun.

I have argued that those origins lie in the process of economic development that transformed, most obviously, the social structure and relations of production in places such as Halifax. In conjunction with such national developments as the increasing sophistication of the economy and the spread of consumer goods, this transformation, which was as much cultural as economic, created a new commercial and professional elite with an increasingly distinct socioeconomic experience. When this group gave their common experience a coherent political and social expression, their culture can legitimately be described as middle class. The timing and character of the emergence of a middle-class culture varied from place to place. In Halifax that culture emerged in the decades after 1750, taking shape through the associations, disputes, and distinctive forms of sociability that have been discussed here. Elsewhere, different kinds of economic development—more merchants, more small masters—or different social contexts—an existing corporation or the presence of a substantial number of gentry families—created their own particular history. But these different histories make a common point, for it is in the specific context of commercial communities in the mid- to late eighteenth century that the origins of middle-class culture are to be found.

INDEX

Ackroyd, Jonathan, 125
Agriculture, 20, 23, 57
Alehouses, 41, 186, 194
Alexander, Robert, 144
Anglicans. *See* Church of England
Apprenticeship, 69, 92, 105, 107, 179
Armitage, Sir John, 138–39
Assemblies, 184, 186
Associations. *See* Voluntary associations

Baldwin, John, 149
Bancroft, Peter, 79–80
Banks, William, 159
Baumforth, Jonathan, 38–43, 68, 71, 75, 80, 107, 180, 186, 193
Bills of exchange, 85–87
Birmingham, 16, 228
Bookkeepers, 72–73, 94, 100, 126
Borsay, Peter, 13, 165, 186, 191, 199, 208
Bourdieu, Pierre, 7
Bradford, 9, 227–28
Brewer, John, 121, 165, 181
Buxton, 204–5, 207, 219
Byng, Admiral John, 159

Calder Navigation, 90, 110, 137, 157, 159, 162, 180, 182–83, 208, 220
Carr, James, 4
Carr, John, 197
Caygill, John, 69, 95, 136, 154, 178, 197, 209
Charlesworth, Robert, 125
Chartier, Roger, 15, 49, 82
Church of England, 136, 138, 152, 161
Church rates, 147, 149–50, 162
Circulating library, 144–45, 183

Class, 5–10, 45–48, 115–19, 122–24, 165–66, 224–25, 229–36
Clubs, 181–83, 186
Cockfight, 33–34, 41, 185
Coley, 4–5, 32, 35
Colley, Linda, 158, 199
Consumption:
    of goods, 94–101
    by middle class, 96–99
    by middling sort, 37–38, 95–96
    of services, 93–94, 181–86
Cooke, Richard and Benjamin, 125, 135–36, 144
Craftsmen, 95, 126, 183
Cragg Vale coiners, 87, 232
Crouzet, François, 84
Cultural theory, 5–10, 14, 46–48, 115–17
    applied to complex societies, 48–49
    and class formation, 5–10, 83–84, 224–25, 229–36

Davidoff, Leonore, 11, 16, 118, 167–68, 191, 195, 217, 229, 234–35
Defoe, Daniel, 19, 58
Disputes, 121, 146–55
Dissent/Dissenters:
    chapels of, 134–36
    among middling sort, 23–34, 36–37, 42, 126
    relations with Anglicans, 129, 138–39, 148, 152, 161
Domestic architecture, 107–13, 176–78, 196–97
Dorville, John and Peter, 63, 75, 77
Duncombe, Henry, 161

East Anglia, 51
East India Company, 67
Edwards, John, 3, 57, 66, 72–73, 126, 134, 144, 161
Elections, 160–63

Fairfax, Lord, 26, 31
Farrers of Midgley, 29
Fieldhouse, Sowerby, 110–13, 131, 177
Firth, John, 125
Fox, George, 161
Friendly societies, 196

Garbett, Samuel, 231
Geertz, Clifford, 7, 9
Gender relations:
  of middle class, 98–99, 166–87, 214–17
  of middling sort, 40, 167, 171–73, 180
Gentry:
  local, 29–30
  and middle class, 122–23, 131–32, 137–38, 199–200, 218
  and middling sort, 29–34
Geography, 19
Giddens, Anthony, 7
Greame, John and William, 4, 134, 169, 200
Greenwood, Elizabeth, 172
Greenwood, John, 33, 41
Greenwood, Luke, 125, 129, 133, 139, 154, 172
Greenwood, Paul, 176

Habermas, Jürgen, 123, 133
Halifax township, 32, 37, 102
  in parish politics, 134–36, 147, 149–54, 182
  relations with out-townships, 138, 144, 147–55
Hall, Catherine, 11, 16, 118, 167–68, 191, 195, 217, 229, 234–35
Hall, Jonathan, 99–100, 204–8, 212, 219
Hargreaves, John Sr. and Jr., 93
Hearth tax, 24–26, 37, 101–2
Heywood, Oliver, 32–37, 42, 134, 185
Hill, Christopher, 26
Hill, Richard, 64, 79–80, 126, 144, 200, 211–14, 216, 219
Hill, Samuel, 125, 144, 177, 200, 211
  textile business of, 57, 60–68, 71–72, 75–79, 85, 176

Himmelfarb, Gertrude, 104
Holden, Nathaniel, 4, 136, 154
Holroyd, Elkhana, 133, 139
Holroyd, Jeremiah, 3
Holroyd, Joseph, 60, 62, 65–68, 72, 74
Horse races, 33, 185–86
Horton, Joshua, 32, 138
Horton, Sir William, 131–32
Horton, William, of Howroid, 29, 33, 41
Howarth, John, 86, 97, 124, 144, 179
Howe, Anthony, 11, 117
Hudson, Joshua, 4, 179
Hudson, Pat, 84, 91, 105, 226
Hughes, Ann, 27
Hulme, Dr. Joseph, 125, 135, 161
Hunt, Margaret, 118, 168
Hunt, William, 103–4, 192

Industrial Revolution/industrialization, 11–13, 16, 68, 71, 192, 223–24, 232–33
Inns, 184
Issot, Japhet, 206

Jackson, Dr. Cyril, 4, 125
Jackson, John, 168, 170
Jones, Gareth Steadman, 117, 224
Joyce, Patrick, 75, 118, 224

Kershaw, John, 125, 134, 144, 161
Kershaw, Nathaniel, 54–55
Kitson, Thomas, 169
Koditschek, Theodore, 9, 11, 16, 117, 191, 224, 229, 235

Lancashire, 15, 227–28
Land tax, 101–2, 163
Langford, Paul, 3, 165, 191, 199, 208
Lawyers, 93–94, 100, 183
Laycock, Jonathan, 133
Lea, John, 129–30, 133, 139, 154, 177
Lea, Joshua, 171–73
Lea, Susannah, 172–73
Leeds, 15, 52, 100, 137, 145, 158–59, 226–27
Lees, Samuel, 57, 66, 68, 71–73, 79, 91, 125–26, 134, 173
Lees, Susanna, 173–74
Legh, Dr. George, 144, 161
Levine, David, 103–4, 192
Linguistic turn, 5–8, 224–25

Index 239

Lister, John, 55, 91
Lister, Phoebe, 206
Lister, Samuel, 55, 85, 89, 91
Listers of Shipden Hall, 29
Liverpool, 145
Local government and administration, 19–20, 37, 127, 130, 134
  and poor relief, 103–6
Local history:
  advantages of, 14–17, 225
  interplay with national history, 15, 82–83, 85–87, 90–91, 99–100, 155, 165–66, 218, 226–36
Lodge, Jeffrey, 168, 170
London, 100, 228–29
Loyal Georgian society, 196
Luddites, 231
Manchester, 145
Masonic lodges, 182–83, 195
Material culture, 37–38, 82–84, 95–101
McKendrick, Neil, 165
Metcalf, Thomas, 173
Middle class:
  historiography on, 10–16, 117–18, 167–68
  political culture of, 121–24, 132–34, 142, 153–55, 158–63, 201–5
  and relation of culture to experience, 105–6, 110, 142, 218–21, 231–32
  social relations of, 104–6, 192–94, 219–20
  vs. working class, 47, 230–31
Middling sort, 206
  defined, 26–27
  political culture of, 28, 30–34
  and relation of culture to experience, 31–32, 36–38, 42–43, 45, 70–71, 107
  social relations of, 28–29, 35–40, 103–4, 167, 180
Midgley, 147, 154
Milner, Joseph, 62, 65
Mitchell, Abe, 33, 41, 194
Mixenden, 32
Money, John, 228
Morris, Robert, 11, 117, 133, 229
Mortgages, 87–92
Mother Shipton's prophecy, 162
Mui, Hoh-Cheung and Lorna, 13
Music Club, 183

Neale, R. S., 84
Nonconformists. *See* Dissent/Dissenters
Northgate End chapel, 134–36, 144, 195

Organ, 136, 148–49, 151, 182, 184, 208

Palladian style, 197
Parker, Robert, 156–57, 203–4, 206–7
Parrat, Francis, 206
Partnerships, 73, 91, 134
Piece Hall, 142–44, 146, 182, 185, 229
Pollard, William, 4, 125, 134
Poll books, 161
Pontefract, 100
Population, 19, 22, 52
Priestly, John, 3, 129–30, 133, 139, 152, 177
Priestly, Jonathan, 28, 34, 41–42, 75
Priestly, Samuel, 26–32, 41
Private sphere, 164–66, 174–81, 186–87, 191, 214, 223
Probate records, 37, 88
Public sphere, 123–24, 133–40, 150–56, 181–83, 191, 223
  vs. private sphere, 164–66
Puritanism, 26–27, 30–32, 34–36, 42

Queen Anne's bounty, 137

Ralph, Rev. John, 144
Reddy, William, 200
Riley, John, 139
Riley, Susanna, 172–74
Roydes, Jeremiah, 85, 97
Roydes, John, 144, 162, 178, 197
Roydes, Robert, 136

Sahlins, Marshall, 7
Saville, Sir George, 138–39, 156, 160, 162, 182, 218
Saville, Sir William, 31
Saville family, 29
Schoolmasters, 94, 100, 126, 183
Seed, John, 8, 229
Senior, John, 182–83
Settlement laws, 105
Seven Years' War, 158, 182
Sewell, William, 8, 16
Shackleton, Elizabeth, 218
Sharp, John, 175, 180, 210

Sheffield, 228
Shopkeepers, 95, 126, 183
Skircoat, 133
Smeaton, John, 138
Social structure, 20, 24, 36, 101–2
Southowram, 133
Sowerby, 32, 37, 87, 102
  bids for parochial status, 152–53
  in parish politics, 127–33, 136, 147–54, 182
Sowerby chapel, 129–33, 139, 148, 195, 197
Square Chapel, 134–35, 197
Stamp Act, 158, 231
Stanhope, John, 162
Stansfield, David, 3, 57, 79, 125, 140, 159, 178
Stansfield, George Jr., 3, 115–16, 125, 180, 211–14, 216, 218–19
  and Fieldhouse, 97, 107, 110, 177
  in local politics, 129–33, 139–40, 151–52, 154, 159, 161–62
  and textile business, 57, 60, 64, 68, 71, 79, 83
Stansfield, George Sr., 57, 61–63, 68, 72, 75–79, 113
Starkey, William, 139
Stead, Samuel, 210
Stead, Valentine, 154
Styles, John, 87
Sutcliffe, John, 57–58, 64–67, 75, 86, 125, 205–6, 218

Talbot inn, 137–38, 182, 184
Tea, 97–98, 178
Teachers. *See* Schoolmasters
Terling, Essex, 24
Textile manufacturers:
  competitiveness of, 74–76
  and control over production, 64–66
  described, 53
  emergence of, 53–56
  and innovation, 66–67
  as merchants, 57, 69–70
  profit orientation of, 72–74
  reasons for success of, 58–68
  and relations with workers, 71, 76–80
  responce of, to fashion, 64
Textile markets and merchants:
  in domestic system, 62
  in England, 61, 68
  foreign, 60–64, 67
  and trading on advance orders, 63, 68
  and trading on consignment, 62, 68
Textiles, artisanal production of:
  compared to manufacturing, 53–55, 76–77
  described, 22–23
  impact of manufacturing on, 54–56, 59
Textiles, types of:
  kersey, 22, 58
  worsted, 57–59
Theater, 184
Theory of practice, 7, 9, 46–47, 72, 84. *See also* Cultural theory
Thirsk, 208–10
Thomas, Richard, 130
Thompson, E. P., 8, 12, 47, 223, 230–31
Thornhill, Thomas, Esq., 29, 33–34, 41, 185
Tory party, 161–62
Trademarks, 65–66
Turner, Chomley, 161
Turnpikes, 137

Underage children, 168–71
Underdown, David, 27, 103–4, 192
Union Club, 138, 182

Vickery, Amanda, 199, 218, 227
Visiting, 175, 178, 183
Voluntary associations, 121, 126–46, 181–83, 186, 229

Wahrman, Dror, 117, 199
Wainhouse, John, 96
Wainhouse, Michael, 57
Wakefield, 15, 52, 100, 137
Wakefield, Manor of, 87
Walker, Caroline, 175, 184, 208–11, 219
Walker, Elizabeth, 208–10, 217–18
Walker, John, of Southowram and Halifax, 136, 208–10, 219–21
Walker, John, of Sowerby, 133
Walker, William, 69, 162, 209
Walterclough, 180, 209–10
Walton, Thomas, 57–58, 79
Warley, 147, 154
Waterhouse, John and Samuel, 4, 154, 161

Index 241

Waterhouse, Nathaniel, 148, 155
Waterhouse workhouse, 155–57, 162
Waterworks, 90, 157
Watson, John, 3, 125
Weatherill, Lorna, 13
Wells, Joseph, 130
Welsh, John, 152
West Country, 51, 232
Wetherherd, Christopher, 70
Wetherherd, James, 136
Whig party, 161–62
Wilberforce, William, 161

Wilde, Israel, 129–30, 133
Wilson, R. G., 226
Window tax, 129
Wolrich, Thomas, 58
Women, role of:
  in family economy, 83, 167–76
  social, 40, 98–99
Workhouse, 148–51
Working class, 12, 47, 230–31
Worsted Committee, 232
Wrightson, Keith, 103–4, 192
Wyvill, Christopher, 161